DUKE UNIVERSITY PUBLICATIONS

THE GAUCHO

THE GAUCHO

Cattle Hunter · *Cavalryman*
Ideal of Romance

by

MADALINE WALLIS NICHOLS

Gordian Press
New York
1968

Originally Published 1942
Reprinted 1968

Library of Congress Catalog Card Number: 68–58423

Copyright © 1942 by
Duke University Press

Published by Gordian Press, Inc.

By Arrangement

To

DR. PERCY A. MARTIN

Pioneer scholar in the field of Brazilian studies
and
Loyal friend of Latin America

Preface

This book tells how the highly disreputable gauchos emerged from the background of a pastoral society and how those gauchos came to win honor.

There have been many fragmentary studies of the gaucho. Since most of these works have, unfortunately, reflected purely personal impressions of what a gaucho ought to be, rather than what a gaucho was, almost as many types of gauchos as writers on the subject have appeared. Yet no properly documented history of the gaucho class has been printed. There has been scant analysis of the pastoral background from which the gaucho emerged or of the importance in that emergence of the general closing in of the Indian on La Plata frontiers. There has been no careful study of the trade in hides, and particularly the contraband trade, which was, possibly, the greatest single factor in gaucho origin. Little explanation has been given for the transformation of a most undesirable member of society into the figure of romance and the symbol of nationalism which the gaucho has become.

In view of the generally inspirational approach to the topic, it is hoped that the Essay on Authorities, which concludes this study, may prove to be one of the most valuable contributions of the work. The first part of this bibliography is a study of the real gaucho. It not only contains a great number of items giving contemporary accounts of gaucho society—accounts on which the picture is based—but it also assembles material on the pastoral society of the Plata lands and on those economic and social developments which led to the gaucho class.

The second part of the bibliography is a study of the gaucho of romance. Its length is indicative of the tremendous importance of this gaucho ideal in La Plata society. And this bibliography is far from complete; it includes only works actually read and so known to contain gauchos, or works with titles which definitely indicate that they refer to gauchos. The value of these works is largely numerical, rather than literary. They mark that noteworthy insistence on the gaucho motif, explanatory of the change in the concept of the gaucho and the growth of his symbolic value.

In conclusion, I have many friends to thank for aid received in the writing of this book: first of all, Mount Holyoke College and the members of its class of 1905, who gave the fellowship which made the study possible; Dr. Arturo Torres Ríoseco, of the University of California, who first introduced me to literary gauchos and convinced me that they were interesting characters well worth further attention; Dr. Charles E. Chapman, leading Hispanic American historian, who called my attention to the caudillos of La Plata history and to their picturesque gaucho bands; Dr. S. Griswold Morley, who procured for me a special library grant for the purchase of books on the gaucho; Dr. Lucia Burk Kinnaird, who read the original manuscript and made many valuable suggestions for its improvement; and, finally, Dr. Percy A. Martin, of Stanford University, that generous friend, no small part of whose life-work has been his aid to new students in the Hispanic American field where he has long been a pioneer.

M. W. N.

Contents

THE GAUCHO

Introduction To The 1968 Reprint

This book is the record of the growth, recognition, and transformation of a class of society. The recognition, and the new name that was its mark, came only in the late eithteenth century, but the gaucho had existed from the beginning. Like his peer, the Spanish vaquero, the first gaucho was a horseman skilled in the handling of cattle. Unlike the vaquero, he preferred, and managed to live, a vagrant life, unconfined by any steady employment on an estancia. From the vast herds of wild horses that ran the pampas, he could pick, catch, and break his own. Equally wild cows provided a constant supply of meat, as well as the hides that could be sold to supply other needs. In moments of economic distress—or, more probably, at rodeo time when he could display his superb skills in competition with the prosaic vaquero—he would hire on as an extra hand at some estancia, to be gone when the fun was over. He was a man best stirred to action by competition or combat.

A rebel against society, the gaucho was regarded by its more stable members with jealousy, suspicion, and aversion. Envy of his independence was coupled with wariness toward the stranger who so frequently was involved in the brawls at country horse races or in the little local stores that were the local saloons as well. Too, the gaucho was regarded as dangerous to women; he had the reputation of possessing a skill in making off with them which was fully equal to his skill in cutting out from a herd any horse or cow he might desire. Such a man, who took what he wanted, received scant approval from society. A vagabond, often in trouble with the law, he became a prime candidate for the draft and forced service against the Indians on the frontier, where he also became unwillingly useful as a settler at the military posts. There the raids grew in number and danger when both Indian and Spaniard competed for the cattle hides that had become the chief product which each offered in trade. Gauchos who succeeded in escaping the draft often joined the vaqueros of the estancias in the exciting cattle hunts out in Indian territory. Eventually, in order to fill the ever increasing orders for hides, cattle had to be raised on the estancias, where they needed increasing protection from ever bolder Indian raiders.

It was the mounting demand for hides and the opportunies to dispose of them in contraband trade that provided work for which the gaucho was supremely qualified and which he found enjoyable. It was dangerous and called for his courage. It involved display, and recognition, of his skills in riding and roping and survival in the desert. It was as exciting and entertaining as any horse race. Under such conditions gauchos flocked to the work and became finally recognized as a separate class in society, with their new name at last to mark their change in status. Only after the trading *asientos* (agreements) of the early eighteenth century had led to the increase in trade and contraband, did the gaucho gain his separate identity.

Even then he was at first variously known as *changador, gauderio, guaso* or *gaucho*: this latter term was the one to survive. The origin of all the terms is unknown.[1] But whatever his name, there was no doubt as to the kind of individual it represented. He rode a horse and chased a cow like his vaquero peer, but the gaucho differed from the vaquero in the usually temporary or illegal character of his work. His emergence from the pastoral society of the pampas was definitely related to the opportunity to lead a happy, outlaw life presented by contraband trade. This development was localized in the Banda Oriental that was to become modern Urguay, but on the western and southern frontiers there was a parallel development which has been unduly ignored because its contraband opportunities were not as spectacular as those to the northeast and because the element of foreign danger was lacking. In the south, the contrabandista was the little local storekeeper making up his personal order for hides or the Indian hunter who wanted hides to exchange for aguardiente. Contraband flowed to the sister Spanish provinces of Tucumán, Cuyo, and Chile. On the Eastern Shore the business involved a foreign danger to Spain's monopoly of colonial trade.

The gaucho class existed as a separate entity in society for only the approximately one hundred-year period from 1775 to 1875. The interesting transformation of gauchos, first regarded as the "scum of society," into the national heroes they were later to become was due to two factors: gaucho success in war and the success of the literature written about them. For as the gaucho became a more useful member of society—politically, economically, and socially—he became idealized. It is the gaucho of romance that lives on, and the modern hard-working cattleman is now proud to bear the once scorned gaucho name.

In view of the number and the value of his eventual contributions to La Plata society, the gaucho deserves the honor he has won. Politically, he was instrumental in the Spanish governmental reorganization of the Plata area, which achieved the distinction of its own viceroy only after gaucho successful co-operation in contraband trade had made political reorganization necessary, if Spain was to be protected from the economic, and political, penetration of her lands by her European enemies. It was the gaucho who later became largely responsible for the winning of independence and who drove the proud Spaniards back into Upper Peru[2] and the Portuguese from the Banda Oriental, as he had driven the Indian from the southern frontier. It was because of the scattered population of a pastoral society and the comparatively large proportion of gaucho followers of caudillo gaucho leaders, that civil war became the Argentine fate and Juan Manuel de Rosas became the biggest caudillo of them all. The regional character of the wars, the spirit of loyalty to a local leader, gaucho hos-

---

[1]It has been suggested that the term *changador* may date from the days of pirate Moreau and his French smugglers who begged Spanish natives to exchange (échanger) hides for the goods they were offering to sell. More logically, the term may have come from the custom of transporting goods across rivers on floats, *angadas* or *changadas*, especially as the modern term is applied to porters, who carry things. The meaning of the term *gauderio* also remains a mystery, despite one hopefully Latin derivative explanation, according to which a gauderio was one who enjoyed something, whether that something be a carefree and dangerous Uruguayan or Brazilian existence, or pleasant riding over Argentine plains. *Guaso* was apparently a Chilean importation. Later, the equally mysterious *gaucho*—also apparently an immigrant word from the west—replaced the others; it seems related to Indian words with the connotation of loner, wanderer, orphan.

[2]By diverting Spanish attention and Spanish armies to the Tucumán country, gauchos also gave time for the reorganization of the several independence moves of Hispanic America as a whole.

tility towards the stronger from another region—all these were behind the federalist character of La Plata governments.

Economically, the gaucho was largely responsible for much of the present Argentine stockraising industry, for it was only after the wild cattle had been killed off by over-hunting and by the long civil wars that modern stockraising on the estancias could prosper. In the new law-abiding society he had helped to create, there was no place for the gaucho's old self-sufficient vagrancy. Forced at last into the cattle-hand work on the estancia, which he had so long avoided, the gaucho became one with the vaquero, but it was the now proud gaucho name that was applied to both.

Socially, the gaucho role in the ethnic composition of the Argentine people has been over-emphasized. It is true that in colonial days there were too few Spanish women to go around, and in the racial mingling of Spaniard and Indian which followed, the gaucho in the army on the frontier had unusual opportunities. Probably more little mestizos resulted than would have occurred back in town. The term "gaucho," however, describes the kind of person he was and his way of life; it was not a reference to his ancestry.

Finally, some of the most interesting of Spanish American contributions to world culture have drawn their inspiration from the gaucho. True, much of the literature about the gaucho is trash. But from much that is bad, the poesy of the Santos Vega theme, the quaintness of gaucho folk song and dance, the dry humor or satire of riddle and proverb, and the realism of such descriptions of pastoral life as those in Ascasubi's *Santos Vega* or of the frontier life described in the poem of *Martín Fierro* are a literary heritage of which any nation might be proud. And while the gaucho theater is still without a masterpiece, the Juan Moreira theme—with the stage properties acquired in its circus days—is not without dramatic and scenic possibilities. More and more the gaucho is influencing works of art and music. Argentina has also accepted as her own such gaucho traits as an insistence upon independent self-sufficiency, stoic courage, and patriotism, and this has had a very real influence upon the assimilation of the new immigrants into the unity of the national pattern. While exaggerated in statement, Vicente Rossi's belief that "in the soul of every Creole, of every man born in the Plata lands, there sleeps a more or less authentic gaucho" is not without its factual basis. Gaucho ideals and La Plata ideas about them still live in the Plata lands.

Introduction

The Spanish horse and cow were pioneers in the Spanish colonization of the Plata region. They multiplied rapidly, and soon innumerable herds ran the vast, deserted pampas. Adapting himself to this peculiar state of affairs, man became equestrian. He caught and broke the wild horse which he rode to catch other wild horses and equally wild cattle. Upon them depended his food, clothing, shelter, many of the lesser conveniences of life, and the defense of that life itself. For centuries the Spanish horse and cow conditioned Spanish civilization.

Hides of horses and cows became the staple produce around which revolved the economic life of the Plata lands. They were the product which might be offered in exchange for the satisfaction of the needs of La Plata people. Consequently, hides acquired commercial value. As Spanish colonists fought against the trade restrictions of their mother country, contraband trade began to thrive. French, English, Dutch, and Portuguese traders hastened to profit thereby. A class of illegal hunters of hides grew up to fill these orders and to smuggle into the country the contraband goods offered in exchange. These hunters were the gauchos.

At first he was variously known as *changador, gauderio, guaso,* or *gaucho;* this latter term was the one to survive. The origin of all the terms is unknown.[1] But whatever his name, there was no doubt as to the kind of individual it represented. Although he rode a horse and chased a cow like his Spanish vaquero ancestor, the gaucho differed from the vaquero in the illegal character of his work. The vaquero worked on the estancias, or he aided in filling the legitimate orders for hides. The gaucho worked for his own amusement or for the attainment of occasional luxuries. He entered society only after contraband trade in hides began to prosper. It is because that trade did not attain distinguished proportions until after the *asientos* (treaties) of the early eighteenth century, that the gaucho was a late development in La Plata life. The emergence of the gauchos from the pastoral society of the pampas was definitely related to the opportunities to lead a happy, outlaw life pre-

[1] It has been suggested that the term *changador* might be due to the days of pirate Moreau and his French smugglers who begged Spanish natives to exchange *(échanger)* hides for the goods they were offering to sell. More logically, the term may have come from the custom of carrying goods across rivers on floats, *angadas* or *changadas,* especially as the modern term is applied to *porters,* who carry things. The meaning of the term *gauderio* also remains a mystery, despite one Latin derivative explanation, according to which a gauderio was one who enjoyed *(gaudere)* something, whether that something be a carefree and dangerous Uruguayan and Brazilian existence, or pleasant riding over Argentine plains. *Guaso* was apparently a Chilean importation. Later, the equally mysterious word *gaucho*—also apparently an immigrant Indian word from the south and west—replaced the others.

sented by contraband trade. This development was localized in the Banda Oriental, or modern Uruguay.

But on the western, and notably on the southern, frontiers there was a parallel development of a class of vagabond, outlaw cattle hunters —gauchos. This development has been unduly ignored because its contraband opportunities were not as spectacular as those to the north, and because the element of foreign danger was lacking. To the south, the contrabandista was the little local storekeeper making up his personal order for hides or the Indian hunter who wanted hides to exchange for aguardiente. Contraband flowed to the sister Spanish provinces of Tucumán, Cuyo, and Chile. Here, as to the north, the business of hide-hunting and the confusion incident to racial mixing across an unkept frontier line, resulted in gauchos.

The gaucho class existed as a separate entity in society only for approximately the one hundred-year period from 1775 to 1875. Individual gauchos had existed previously; as soon as an illegal hunter of hides ranged the pampas, we have a gaucho. But there was no recognized gaucho *class* until a relatively large and distinctive group of men were involved in their illegal work. Gauchos grew only with large shipments of hides. And gauchos were definitely regarded as "the scum of society."

The interesting transformation of such gauchos into the national heroes they have since become, was due to two factors: gaucho success in war and the success of gaucho literature. It is interesting to note that while the so-called gaucho literature does not portray the real gaucho, it has caused that real gaucho to be forgotten. Only the gaucho of romance lives on.

In view of the number and the value of his contributions to La Plata society, it is doubtless quite fitting that the gaucho should be remembered. Politically, economically, socially, he has been of the highest importance. In literature, art, and music, the works utilizing the gaucho as theme have proved to be one of Hispanic America's interesting contributions to world art.

Politically, the gaucho was largely responsible for the winning of independence, the success of caudillism with its civil wars and tyranny, and the emphasis on federalism in modern La Plata governments. The Plata region achieved the distinction of its own viceroy only after gaucho successful co-operation in contraband trade made imperative a political reorganization if Spain was to be protected from the economic—and political—penetration of her lands by her European enemies. In the Plata wars it was the gaucho soldier who drove the Portuguese from the Banda Oriental, the Spaniard from Upper Peru, and the Indian from the frontier.[2] It was because of the scattered population of a pastoral society and the comparatively large proportion of gaucho followers of caudillo gaucho leaders, that civil wars became the Argentine fate. Certainly the weighing of gaucho caudillo against gaucho caudillo was responsible for the long tyranny of the biggest caudillo of them all, Juan Manuel de Rosas. The regional character of the wars, the spirit of loyalty to a local leader, gaucho hostility towards the stranger from another region—these factors were behind the federalist character of La Plata governments.

Economically, though through no fault of his own, the gaucho is largely responsible for much of even the present Argentine economic pattern. For over two hundred years of history, it was the gaucho who collected the hides which were the main item of trade. After approximately a seventy-five-year interval of war, the gaucho was faced with the ironic necessity for withdrawal from the new society he had been helping to create or an adaptation to that society. Forced into a new, law-abiding life and into legitimate work, the gaucho turned to the familiar handling of livestock. He gave up his independent vagabond existence, became a hireling on some estancia. Though the gaucho name had become too well fixed in men's minds to be forgotten, the gaucho had really circled back to become again the Spanish vaquero, the cattle-hand, of the Plata lands. And, as vaquero, it became once more his duty to care for cattle rather than to hunt it and destroy it.

Socially, the gaucho has had an equally important role. He has been the settler of the wilderness, the soldier defender and the soldier settler on the frontier, the conqueror of the Indian. In his frequent mixing with Indian and Negro, he has altered even the national ethnic composition of the Argentine people.

When he has been utilized as a theme in literature, art, and music, some of the most interesting of Hispanic American contributions to world culture have resulted. True, much of gaucho literature is trash. But from much that is bad, the poesy of the Santos Vega theme, the quaintness of gaucho folk song and dance, the dry humor of riddle and proverb, the realism of such descriptions of pastoral life as those to be found in Ascasubi's *Santos Vega* or of the frontier life described in the poem of *Martín Fierro*—these things should be salvaged, and they well deserve to be cherished as a heritage of which any nation might be proud. And while the gaucho theater is still without a masterpiece, yet the Juan Moreira theme—with the stage properties acquired in its circus days—is not without dramatic and scenic possibilities.

[2] By diverting Spanish attention and Spanish armies to the Tucumán country, gauchos also gave time for the reorganization of the several independence moves of Hispanic America as a whole.

Finally, through gaucho life and literature, the Plata peoples have come to accept as their own certain ideals—ideals of independent self-sufficiency, stoic courage, pride in worthy national achievement. These ideals have become a very real force in the assimilation of the new immigrant into the unity of the national pattern. While exaggerated in statement, Vicente Rossi's belief that "In the soul of every Creole, of every man born in the Plata lands, there sleeps a more or less authentic gaucho" is not without its factual basis. Gaucho ideals and La Plata ideas about those ideals still live in the Plata lands.

☙ 1 ❧

Who Was the Gaucho?

The gaucho has been variously portrayed as dashing cavalryman, successful lover, singing minstrel of the plains, noble defender of the unfortunate. Connected with all these concepts is a vague, unromantic association of the gaucho with cows, coupled with a tacit recognition of his skill in their pursuit. In this composite concept there is, indeed, some truth; its fallacy derives from the fallacy of a basic assumption—the essential nobility of the gaucho character. It involves as well a fallacy of misplaced emphasis.

For the gaucho of history was by no means idyllic in character.[1] Fundamentally he was a colonial bootlegger whose business was contraband trade in cattle hides. His work was highly illegal; his character lamentably reprehensible; his social standing exceedingly low. Society's initial contempt, however, changed to fear of its despicable contrabanders as they increased in number and in power. Too indeterminate at first even to have a name—they were variously known as gauderios, changadores, or gauchos, though such terms were all usually accompanied by highly uncomplimentary adjectives—the gaucho class grew to a power which won fear, and even admiration, when gauchos became profitable rather than detrimental to society. But all admiration was a late development.

Early contemporary descriptions of the gaucho are uniformly uncomplimentary. Padre Tadeo Xavier Henis in 1754 tells of "Paulistas who have the property and custom of selling what is not theirs and who are called gauderios."[2] Calixto Bustamante Carlos, who wrote under the name of Concolorcorvo in 1773, tells of "many lazy creoles" who are most appropriately called gauderios.[3] His gauderios seem to be dif-

---

[1] To get a picture of the real gaucho, one must turn to contemporary records and piece together the fragments of evidence so found. This, incidentally, is not the usual procedure encountered in studies on the gaucho. Of all these records, those by observant travelers are doubtless the best, since a foreigner would be more apt to note the appearance and manners of a distinct class of society than one made unobservant by familiarity.

The eighteenth-century sources for the material in this first chapter are quoted as used. For materials of later date, those used in Chapters II and III, see Chapter II, n. 1.

[2] P. Tadeo Xavier Henis, "Diario histórico de la rebelión y guerra de los pueblos guaranis, situados en la costa oriental del río, Uruguay (1754)," Pedro de Angelis, *Colección de obras y documentos relativos a la historia antigua y moderna de las provincias del Río de la Plata* (5 vols., Buenos Aires, 1910), IV, 244.

[3] Calixto Bustamante Carlos ("Concolorcorvo"), *El lazarillo de ciegos caminantes desde Buenos Aires hasta Lima.* 1773 (Buenos Aires, Junta de historia y numismática americana, *Biblioteca*, IV), p. 27.

ferent from the general run, however, in that they pass their time in song rather than in crime. They have a guitar which they learn to play very badly; they sing out of tune; yet they pass whole weeks stretched at length on a hide, singing and playing. He defines gauderios as "young fellows born in Montevideo and neighboring districts," but the gauderios he describes at length are those in Tucumán. The verses, or *coplas,* which they sing are "very extravagant" and treat of love; again, they are "horrible." "These gauderios make no other provision save storing a large piece of meat under their ramada or often exposed to the inclemency of the weather; their whole regalement is based on this provision. Their furniture is limited to a bad bed, a worse covering, a pot, and a stick to serve as spit for roasting their meat, saddle, bridle, blankets; they have lassos and bolas in order to replace their horses and to pass their time simply in violent races or impertinent visits. These people . . . form the greater part of the inhabitants of Tucumán."[4] Dávila (1773 and 1774) mentions one mulatto who "leads the gauderio life" and another who is a "known gaucho and thief."[5] Felipe de Haedo, in 1778, mentions a class with "neither goods and chattels nor real estate to hold them in one place." They "are wandering from province to province, occupied in gambling and many other vices, committing robberies on the highways, stealing cattle, living in the woods. They cannot be subdued because of the general insecurity of the jails and because there is no prison to which they may be sent for safe keeping."[6] He does not actually name this class "gaucho" or "gauderio," but it is obvious that they are meant. In 1780 Viceroy Vértiz reported gauderios who were causing him trouble "on the other shore."[7] Juan Francisco Aguirre was in Uruguay in 1783, though his diary was published later. He mentions both gauchos and gauderios. In addition to the country people holding estancias of considerable size, there are many who have no property and who are known as gauchos. "Gauchos or gauderios . . . are people who, taking advantage of the solitude of this land, have, among other skills, that of slaughtering cattle for their hides. It is said that the number of men who are engaged in this business mounts into the thousands. Changadores . . . are gauderios who kill cattle without any government permit to do so."[8] Félix de Azara was in the country in the early 1780's. While his *Historia de los cuadrúpedos* was published posthumously, it dated from the same general period as the *Viajes* and the *Descripción e historia de La Plata y del Paraguay*—1784. In the

[4] *Ibid.,* pp. 29, 134, 135, 143.
[5] Quoted in Martiniano Leguizamón, *La cuna del gaucho* (Buenos Aires, 1935), p. 20.
[6] Felipe de Haedo, "Descripción de la Colonia del Sacramento y puertos del Río de la Plata al norte y sud de Buenos Aires (1778)," *Revista del Río de la Plata,* III, 462.
[7] Juan José de Vértiz, "Memoria (1784)," Buenos Aires, Archivo general, *Revista,* III, 462.
[8] Juan Francisco Aguirre, "Diario," Buenos Aires, Biblioteca nacional, *Anales,* IV, 138, 147.

last work, after describing the ordinary inhabitants of the country (the descendants of the Spanish vaqueros), Azara adds:

Besides the said people, there is in that land, and particularly around Montevideo and Maldonado, another class of people, most appropriately called gauchos or gauderios. Commonly all are criminals escaped from the jails of Spain and Brazil, or they belong to the number of those who, because of their atrocities, have had to flee to the wilderness. Their nakedness, their long beards, their ever uncombed hair, and the uncleanliness and brutishness of their appearance, make them horrible to see. For no motive or interest will they work for anyone, and besides being thieves, they also make off with women. These they take to the woods, and they live with them in huts, catching wild cattle for their food. When the gaucho has some necessity or caprice to satisfy, he steals a few horses or cows, takes them to Brazil where he sells them and where he gets whatever it is he needs.[9]

Azara also mentioned "the country workers who are called peons, horsemen, gauchos, camiluchos, and gauderios";[10] gauchos and changadores are "the dregs of the Río de la Plata and of Brazil."[11] Diego de Alvear's *Diario* (1784-1791) is in kindlier tone in that he defines gauchos and gauderios merely as "country-men."[12] In 1785 Gonzalo de Doblas mentions gauderios in Uruguay, though he limits his description to their work in contraband. "They go about . . . killing cattle so as to make use of their hides,"[13] which they forward to Montevideo or, with the aid of the Portuguese of the Viamont and the river Pardo, direct to Brazil. They also drive cattle to these northern allies. A report of Viceroy Arredondo in 1790 mentions "the destructive hands"[14] of gauderios and changadores. Pedro de Lerena in the same year tells of "vagabonds, otherwise known as gauchos, who live by stealing cattle from the estancias and selling the hides at less than their real value to the *pulperos* (shopkeepers) scattered over the countryside. So they provide daily for their desires;[15] neither the cattle owner nor the government can prevent it."[16] Miguel Lastarria, in 1805, gives a more complete picture of "our peaceful countrymen":

These men will not fail to astonish one who is not accustomed to see them. They are always dirty; their beards are always uncut; they go barefoot, and even trouserless under the cover-all of the poncho. By their manners, ways,

[9] Félix de Azara, *Descripción e historia del Paraguay y del Río de la Plata* (2 vols., Madrid, 1847), II, 310.
[10] "Apuntamientos para la historia natural de los cuadrúpedos del Paraguay y Río de la Plata," Argentine Republic, Ministerio de agricultura, *Anales* (Buenos Aires, 1900), p. 4.
[11] Azara, "Geografía física y esférica de las provincias del Paraguay y Misiones Guaranies (1790)," Montevideo, Museo nacional, *Anales del museo de Montevideo* (Montevideo, 1904), I, 116.
[12] Diego de Alvear, "Diario de la segunda partida demarcadora de límites en la América Meridional," Buenos Aires, Biblioteca nacional, *Anales*, I, 320-321.
[13] Gonzalo de Doblas, *Memoria . . . sobre la Provincia de Misiones de Indios Guaranís (1785)* (Buenos Aires, 1836), p. 55.
[14] Nicolás de Arredondo, "Informe (1795)," Buenos Aires, Biblioteca nacional, *Revista*, III, 325.
[15] In this connection the term *vicios* ("vices," "desires") implies such luxuries as yerba mate, tobacco, aguardiente, saddle equipment, or articles of clothing.
[16] Pedro de Lerena, "Informe," Buenos Aires, Universidad nacional, Facultad de filosofía y letras, *Documentos para la historia argentina* (14 vols., Buenos Aires, 1913-1921), VI, 455.

and clothing one knows their customs, without sensibility and almost without religion. They are called gauchos, camiluchos, or gauderios. As it is very easy for them to kill cattle for food, since none lack a horse, bolas, lasso, and knife with which to catch and kill a cow, or as anyone will give them food free, and since they are satisfied to have nothing but roast meat to eat, they work only to acquire the tobacco they smoke and the Paraguayan yerba mate which they drink, ordinarily without sugar and as many times a day as possible. Or they may work to obtain gifts for their sweethearts, who, not being quite so dirty—and on the contrary rather inclined to change and improve their clothing —will finally excite sensibility and self-esteem (in the men) so that they may become rivals for their preference by presenting a less shocking appearance. Such is . . . the lowest class of the peasantry.[17]

This was the real gaucho—not the figure of romance, the later fiction of history and of literature. He lived outside the law; in this respect he differed from his Spanish herdsman ancestor (the vaquero), even though both men often did the same kind of work. In early times the names "gauderio" and "gaucho" were synonyms for loafer or tramp or evildoer or thief or bandit. The gaucho was an example of a reversion to the primitive on the frontier. Generally (though not necessarily) mestizo, he always borrowed from both the Spanish and the Indian civilizations. Thus on the boundary line of two civilizations, on the line dividing estancia from pampa, there was formed a new type which, increasingly with every generation, betrayed the influence of the barbarity in which it had developed.[18]

[17] Miguel Lastarria, "Reorganización y plan de seguridad exterior de las muy interesantes colonias orientales del Río Paraguay de la Plata (1805)," Buenos Aires, Universidad nacional, Facultad de filosofía y letras, *Documentos* . . . , III, 201-202.
[18] Emilio Daireaux, "Las razas indias en la América del Sud," Buenos Aires, Sociedad científica argentina, *Anales,* IV, 223.

2

How a Gaucho Lived

Possibly the essential barbarity of the gaucho class may be best realized through a description of the gaucho way of life—his home, clothes, education, amusements—and through an analysis of predominant traits of gaucho character.[1] Certainly the gaucho home was not the

[1] The description of gaucho life given in this and in the following chapter is based almost exclusively upon the reports of nineteenth-century travelers. While by no means complete, the following list indicates which materials proved of most value for the purposes of this study.

For the period from 1800 to 1830, see such works as those by Anthony Zacariah Helms (*Travels from Buenos Aires, by Potosí, to Lima*, London, 1807); Pedro Andrés García ("Diario de un viaje a Salinas Grandes en los campos del sud de Buenos Aires (1810)," Angelis, *op. cit.*, III, 197-261); Henry Marie Brackenridge (*Voyage to Buenos Aires, in 1817 and 1818*, London, 1820, in Sir Richard Phillips, *New voyages and travels*, III); Jacques Étienne Victor Arago (*Promenade autour du monde, pendant les années 1817, 1818, 1819 et 1820, sur les corbettes du roi, l'Uranie et la Physicienne, commandées par M. Freycinet*, Paris, 1822); Robert Proctor (*Narrative of a journey across the Andes and of a residence in Lima and other parts of Peru in the years 1823 and 1824*, London, 1825); John Miers (*Travels in Chile and La Plata*, London, 1826); Captain Joseph Andrews (*Journey from Buenos Aires through the provinces of Córdova, Tucumán, and Salta, to Potosí*, London, 1827); Lieutenant Charles Brand (*Journal of a voyage to Peru; a passage across the Cordillera of the Andes, in the winter of 1827, performed on foot in the snow; and a journey across the pampas*, London, 1828); Captain Francis Bond Head (*Rough notes taken during some rapid journeys across the pampas and among Andes*, Boston, 1827); and John Miller (*Memorias del General Miller*, Madrid, 1829).

For the period from 1830 to 1840, see Charles Darwin (*Journal of researches into the natural history and geology of the countries visited during the voyage round the world of H.M.S. "Beagle,"* 2d ed., London, 1913); Samuel Haigh (*Sketches of Buenos Aires, Chile, and Peru*, London, 1831); Alcide Dessalines d'Orbigny (*Voyage pittoresque dans les deux Amériques*, Paris, 1836); and Peter Campbell Scarlett (*South America and the Pacific*, 2 vols., London, 1838).

For the period from 1840 to 1850, see John Parish and William Parish Robertson (*Letters on South America*, 3 vols., London, 1843); John Milton Niles (*South America and Mexico*, Hartford, 1844); Domingo Faustino Sarmiento (*Civilización y barbarie; vida de Juan Facundo Quiroga*, Madrid, 1924; 1st ed., 1845); and Colonel John Anthony King (*Twenty-four years in the Argentine Republic*, New York, 1846).

For the fifties, see Alfred de Brossard (*Considérations historiques et politiques sur les Républiques de la Plata dans leurs rapports avec la France et l'Angleterre*, Paris, 1850); Lieutenant Isaac G. Strain (*Cordillera and pampa, mountain and plain. Sketches of a journey in Chili and the Argentine provinces in 1849*, New York, 1853); Woodbine Parish (*Buenos Aires and the provinces of the Río de la Plata*, London, 1852); Friedrich Wilhelm Christian Gerstaecker (*Narrative of a journey round the world*, New York, 1853); Nathaniel Holmes Bishop (*A thousand miles' walk across South America*, Boston, 1881); Alejandro Magariños Cervantes (*Estudios históricos, politicos, y sociales sobre el Río de la Plata*, Paris, 1854); Thomas Jefferson Page (*La Plata, the Argentine Confederation, and Paraguay*, London, 1859).

For the sixties, see Hermann Burmeister (*Reise durch die La Plata-Staaten, mit besonderer Rücksicht auf die physische Beschaffenheit und den Culturzustand der Argentinischen Republik; Ausgeführt in den Jahren 1857, 1858, 1859, und 1860*, 2 vols., Halle, 1861); Wilfrid Latham (*The states of the River Plate*, 2d ed., London, 1868); Paolo Mantegazza (*Viajes por el Río de la Plata*, Buenos Aires, 1916; 1st ed., 1867); Major Francis Ignacio Rickart (*A mining journey across the great Andes, with explorations in the silver mining districts of the provinces of San Juan and Mendoza, and a journey across the pampas to Buenos Aires*, London, 1863); Thomas Joseph Hutchinson (*Buenos Aires and Argentine gleanings: with extracts from a diary of Salado exploration in 1862 and 1863*, London, 1865, and *The Paraná, with incidents of the Paraguayan war and South American recollections from 1861 to 1868*, London, 1868); Santiago Arcos (*La Plata*, Paris, 1865); and Albert Joseph Kennedy (*La Plata, Brazil, and Paraguay, during the present war*, London, 1869).

For the seventies, see Captain Richard Francis Burton (*Letters from the battlefields of Paraguay*, London, 1870); Lucio Victorio Mansilla (*Una excursión a los indios ranqueles*,

dwelling of any civilized member of society. It was a little hut, roofed with straw. The walls were of sticks driven vertically into the ground, and the chinks between were filled with clay. It was not whitewashed after the fashion of a proper Spanish home. It had neither doors nor windows. Furniture was primitive or nonexistent, though there might be a barrel for carrying water, a horn out of which to drink it, a wooden spit for the roast, and a pot in which to heat water for the *mate*. In a land lacking fuel, fires for cooking and for warmth were made from dung, bones, and fat. There were no chairs, no beds, no tables. One sat on a cattle skull. Usually one slept on a hide, stretched out on the floor, but occasionally beds were to be found made of a hide stretched on a frame and fastened to the four stakes which served as legs. Mattress, sheets, pillows were absent. Babies swung in hide cribs. Bullock tallow and mare's grease were used for light; bones, as candelabra. Since roast meat was the only food eaten, the only utensil required was a knife. One put the end of a piece of meat in his mouth and then sliced off a bite. At the end of the meal the knife became a toothpick; then it and one's fingers were carefully wiped clean upon one's boots. Any parts of the cow not eaten were thrown out, where their odor soon attracted carrion birds and infinite flies and beetles. Many dogs were also to be found in and around such a rancho; possibly, as one owner said, because they were good for collecting the fleas.

Buenos Aires, 1928; 1st ed., 1870); John Hale Murray (*Travels in Uruguay, South America*, London, 1871); and George Chaworth Musters ("At home with the Patagonians," La Plata, Universidad nacional, *Biblioteca centenaria*, I, 127-388; first published in English in London in 1873).

For the period of the eighties, see Julius Beerbohm (*Wanderings in Patagonia*, London, 1881); Xavier Marmier (*Lettres sur l'Amérique*, 2 vols., Paris, 1881); Mrs. Michel George Mulhall (*Between Amazon and Andes*, London, 1881); Sir Horace Rumbold (*The great silver river. Notes of a residence in Buenos Aires in 1880 and 1881*, London, 1887); A. F. de Fontpertius (*Les états latins et l'Amérique*, Paris, 1882); Estanislao Severo Zeballos (*Descripción amena de la República Argentina*, 3 vols., Buenos Aires, 1881, 1883, 1888); Bartolomé Mitre (*Historia de Belgrano y de la independencia argentina*, 2 vols., Buenos Aires, 1887; and *Historia de San Martín y de la emancipación*, 4 vols., Buenos Aires, 1890); and Emilio Daireaux (*Vida y costumbres en el Plata*, 2 vols., Buenos Aires, 1888).

For the nineties, see Ángel Scalabrini (*Sul Rio della Plata*, Como, 1894).

It would be possible to compile a much more complete list of the nineteenth-century commentators, but this list will serve as an illustration of the type of material which must be consulted. All of these items give fairly extensive treatment to the topic of the gaucho. It is interesting to note the gradual regeneration of the gaucho type in works of advancing date, as the influence of the gaucho's role in war and his romantic role in literature begins to be felt.

For modern studies on the gaucho, see Arturo Costa Álvarez (*El castellano en la Argentina*, La Plata, 1928) with his discussion of the region of the origin of the gaucho type; for an analysis of gaucho regional characteristics see the articles by Emilio Cono ("Contribución a la historia del gaucho," Buenos Aires, Universidad nacional, Instituto de investigaciones históricas, *Boletín*, XVIII, 48-79; "Los gauchos de Salta," *La Nación*, Aug. 9, 1936; "Los gauchos del Uruguay hasta la fundación de Montevideo," *La Nación*, Sept. 8, 1935). See also the articles by Madaline W. Nichols ("The gaucho," *The Pacific historical review*, March, 1936, pp. 61-70; "The gaucho," *The Hispanic American historical review*, Nov., 1937, pp. 532-536; "El gaucho argentino," *Revista iberoamericana*, I, no. 1, pp. 153-164; and "Pastoral society on the pampa," *The Hispanic American historical review*, Aug., 1939, pp. 367-371).

Gaucho clothes were equally unprepossessing.[2] Gauchos usually had neither shirts nor trousers, although they never lacked a poncho and the *chiripá*, which was a piece of coarse cloth coming down to their knees and tied at their waists by a broad sash, or *tirador*, adorned with its silver coins if our gaucho were wealthy. They also wore boots, *botas de potro*, coming halfway up their legs, and made of the skin stripped from the legs of horses or cows. Around their heads was a *vincha*, or headband, and on top of this, but pushed back, was a narrow-brimmed little hat, held in place by the *barbijo*, or strap, which went under the chin. Around their necks fluttered a handkerchief, preferably of silk, for the utilitarian purpose of serving as dust screen or as water filter. Clothing often seems to have been made of hide, possibly because, as Alvear once noted, the mosquitoes ate through everything else. One of the most essential parts of gaucho dress was the 14-inch knife, or *facón*, worn behind, stuck in a leather sheath.

Several of these items of gaucho dress were inheritances from the Indian—the poncho, the chiripá, the vincha, and the bota de potro. Of his three weapons, lance and bolas were used by Indians; the facón was Spanish. The facón was the most useful of all, for with it the gaucho protected himself, he killed and ate his meat supply, he made other tools by using it in the handling of hides, and he even shaved with it. Possibly this explains why our gaucho so seldom shaved.

Gaucho women, *chinas*, were described as "dirty." They went barefoot, and their only clothing was a shift like those worn by the Indian women. Their occupations were commonly making fire to roast meat and to heat the water for the *mate*. In contrast to their husbands, they seem to have been thoroughly colorless in personality.

In view of this general unprepossessing appearance of gauchos and their wives, it is good to come upon an occasional description of a gaucho dandy. Captain Joseph Andrews described one he met:

He was dressed in the pink of the mode in his own part of the world; he wore a handsome white figured *Poncho*, something in appearance like a fine Indian shawl. Beneath it hung the lower extremities of a pair of white trowsers [*sic*], with open lace work round the bottoms, in the way of trimming; a falling fringe, about two inches deep, fancifully knotted to answer that which depended from the poncho, encircled his ancles [*sic*]. His sandals, formed of colt's skin, prepared as we have mentioned before, and delicately white, enclosed the smallest foot I ever beheld belonging to a man of six feet high. On his heels were affixed a pair of ponderous

[2] Gaucho dress became a subject of romance even as the gaucho person. So a popular riddle reads:

> Con melena, con chambergo,
> Barba, poncho y cinturón,
> Con pañuelo, con guitarra,
> Con espuelas y facón,
> Con rebenque y chiripá,
> ¿Quién sera?

Obviously, a gaucho. But a gaucho of romance.

richly chased silver Peruvian spurs, which must have weighed a pound each. A scarlet worked scapular hung from his neck; which with [sic] his throat was bare, and supported the handsomest head I ever beheld, while upon its crown, was stuck a hat so small, it would hardly have fitted a child of three years of age. The hat had a brim an inch wide. A ribbon was destined to keep this hat in its place when riding, and to fasten under the chin, but on this shew-off and lounging occasion, it had slipped as it were by accident to the lower lip, giving a knowing turn to the expression of his face. His hair was cut short, excepting near the ears, where it hung in ringlets entangled with a pair of gold earrings. . . . It must be admitted that his manner was withal very cavalier-like.[3]

This romantic and relatively civilized gaucho was a traveling gambler by profession.

Gaucho education was limited to the acquiring of skills for work or play. A boy was hardly born before father or brother took him riding; when he cried, they hastily took him home to be nursed, and then he went riding again. That state of things lasted until he was old enough to be trusted alone on one of the older horses. In writing of these very young gauchos, Peter Campbell Scarlett says:

They will try to climb up a colt of three years old [sic] by the tail, when they are not older themselves, and are accustomed to the exercise of throwing the lasso from the time they can scramble out from the door of their hut—practising with a string and a noose, on a chicken or a puppy, until of strength to pursue, on horseback, the bull and the ostrich.[4]

A gaucho's skills had to do with riding, horsebreaking, cattle work, and self-defense. He must be able to ride any horse. Should it fall, he should be able to land afoot, to one side, and with reins in hand so the horse might not escape. A gaucho must be able to find his way over the pampa, to catch his food, to build his shelter. He must be apt at self-defense and the wielding of the knife with which his duels were fought; this meant not skill in murder, but skill in "marking" an adversary by slashing at nose or eyes. In later romance a gaucho was described as "Puro cuchillo grande en la cintura, y tocar la guitarra" (purely a big knife in a belt and [skill at] playing a guitar). But he was more than that. Fundamental was his skill in riding; no one could be a noteworthy gaucho were he not a clever rider as well. Gaucho and horse were almost one. Among other gaucho skills, Santiago Maciel lists ability in playing with knucklebones, at the *sortija* game,[5] in dancing all dances, playing the guitar, and, above all, not becoming dizzy with liquor.[6] But these were later accomplishments and involved amusement rather than work.

The *pulpería,* or country store, was the gaucho meeting place. There a game of cards might be had, or a horse race might be arranged. And in

---

[3] Andrews, *op. cit.,* I, 121-122.   [4] Scarlett, *op. cit.,* I, 271-272.
[5] This is a game in which one rides rapidly under a hanging little ring and tries to spear it in passing. Described in Hutchinson, *Buenos Aires,* p. 52.
[6] Santiago Maciel, *Los cuentos del viejo Quilques* (Buenos Aires, 1928), p. 149.

each pulpería was a guitar and someone eager to play for customers eager
to sing the usually monotonous and frequently ribald *coplas* or the ever
sad *yaravíes* and *tristes,* Peruvian songs which told of the ingratitude
of love.   While contemporary descriptions of gaucho character were
never complimentary, even more eloquent was the *reja,* or grating, considered necessary in every pulpería to protect the shopkeeper and his
wares from his gaucho customers.[7]   Gauchos might, indeed, be hospitable, willing to give food and lodging to any chance traveler, even
though they did not know who he was or where he was going or why.
They might indeed be personally courageous and stoic in the endurance
of hardship or pain.   But a hearty dislike for walking had led to a
lamentable inclination to steal horses, and the cruelty of their everyday
occupations had its general effect upon their characters.   Having busied
themselves from childhood in cutting the throats of cattle, they did not
hesitate to do the same with men, and this coldly and dispassionately.
They set little value on life, and still less did death disturb them.   No
one ever interfered in another's disputes or quarrels; neither were delin-
quents arrested.   Gauchos even considered it dishonorable to expose
their fellow criminals and not to hide and help them.[8]

A gaucho was reputedly indolent, but this indolence would usually
disappear at the sight of his horse which reminded him of the hunt,
his favorite occupation.[9]   Charles Darwin wrote:

> Robberies are a natural consequence of universal gambling, much drinking,
> and extreme indolence.   At Mercedes I asked two men why they did not work.
> One gravely said the days were too long; the other that he was too poor.   The
> number of horses and the profusion of food are the destruction of all industry.
> Moreover, there are so many feast days; and again, nothing can succeed without
> it be begun when the moon is on the increase; so that half the month is lost
> from these two causes.[10]

And the gaucho was highly independent.   He would work only when
he so chose; he would leave an employer whenever he saw fit.   His
interest was purely in an enjoyment of present fancy.   An exaggerated
feeling of mastery over destiny came from the simple act of riding on
horseback across the immensity of the plain.   General Páez, in far-off
Venezuela, had already noted this psychological influence of the horse
upon man when he remarked, "There is no sane man on a horse."   And
both gaucho dress and gaucho equipment guaranteed the sureness of
this gaucho liberty; it was possible to survive on the pampa without
work and with relative comfort.

[7] "La reja, al través de la cual se cambiaba la bebida y el dinero, habla del carácter del
gaucho más elocuentemente que todos los libros que de él se han escrito" (Emilio P. Corbière,
El gaucho.   Desde su origen hasta nuestros días, Buenos Aires, 1929, p. 182).
[8] Azara, *Descripción* . . . , p. 308.
[9] José Coroleu, *América.   Historia de su colonización, dominación e independencia* (Barcelona, 1895), p. 58.
[10] Darwin, *op. cit.,* pp. 165-166.

One of the essential characteristics of the gaucho was his wanderlust. Lucio Victorio Mansilla, who knew his gauchos, wrote:

> The real gaucho is the vagabond creole—here today, tomorrow there— gambling, quarrelsome, hostile to all discipline. He runs away from military service when drafted. If unlucky in some dagger thrust, he takes refuge from the law among the Indians or joins the montonera[11] if it appears. . . . He loves tradition, hates the foreigner. His pride is in his spurs, his silver saddle decorations, his tirador, his facón.[12]

It was highly fitting that the gaucho chose Saint Anthony, patron of travelers, as his patron saint.

Finally, and possibly most fundamental of all, the gaucho was combative. It was not enough for him to possess the special skills which his type of life made necessary. He must weigh them against those of others, with the idea of imposing his superiority and with the hope of maintaining it against all comers. It was this quality which made the gaucho so peculiarly apt in war. But it was evident in every phase of gaucho life.

> On the estancias, his work consisted in breaking wild horses and in cutting out groups of animals. These operations were never executed in isolation, but always before a public of his peers, who were prompt to criticize or mock. This audience nerved him, stimulated him, drove him to the maddest recklessness so as to conquer his rivals and to win unanimous acclaim. And, moreover, he must be respected to live; the safeguard of the gaucho was his recognized valor. His manner of a man fearing no thing and no other man, saved him from aggression. . . .
>
> The life with his fellows excited him . . . gave him the soul of a pretentious actor, inspired in him the theatrical poses and the grandiloquent phrases of the swaggerer. Applause, esteem became necessary to him. He set his pride on being the best man with lasso, bolas, knife; on possessing the finest equipment, the swiftest horse, the most beautiful woman, the best arms.
>
> Even in his amusements, his eyes were turned to those of others. He must be the best singer, and singing took the form of public joust, where each contestant improvised to the accompaniment of the guitar until the recognized defeat of his rival. Horse races became duels, as each man rode his own. The card games preferred were those where skill prevails, and where one attacks and defends himself man against man. And it was not enough to be the one most skillful or most lucky; by his cunning one must prevent the subtle trickery of his foes and by force one must resist the bad humor of the losers. Races, games, dances, singing usually ended in duels or in drinking bouts where each strove to keep pace with his adversaries and to yield only when floored by alcohol. . . .
>
> This habit of competition followed him even in his sexual affairs. He as firmly desired to be successful in love as to possess the reputation of being invincible as horse-breaker, poet, and duellist. Rivalry, competition inspired him. A woman attracted him when she must be disputed with someone else, or when she must be ravished. . . . She did not tempt him in herself. . . .
>
> This longing for superiority which obsessed him led the gaucho into the most unheard of acts of courage . . . gave him a sense of the ridiculous and hardened him to pain.[18]

[11] The *montonera* was the armed, outlaw band.
[12] Mansilla, *op. cit.,* p. 346.
[18] Roberto Levillier, *Les origines argentines* (Paris, 1912), pp. 141-145.

In this description of the gaucho, it must be remembered that despite the usual mixture of Indian or Negro blood in those of the lower strata of La Plata society, the gaucho was a class and not a race.[14] While it is true that many a contrary statement can be found in modern literature on the topic, the reason is that so many gauchos *were* mestizos. But that the ethnic element was not fundamental is shown by the fact that the same ethnic mixtures frequently did not turn out to be gauchos at all. This was certainly true in cities; it was equally true of the country-men (paisanos, vaqueros, and peons) who led respectable, law-abiding lives on the country estancias. The gaucho was distinguished by the lawless kind of life he led, not by any ancestry. And there could be no gaucho without a horse.

[14] Walter Larden (*Argentine plains and Andine glaciers*, New York and London, 1911), after making such a statement, goes on to say, "If a gaucho's son adopted other ways of life and other dress, he would cease to be a gaucho" (p. 64).

Costa Álvarez writes: "The thing which distinguished the gaucho, the thing which made it necessary to create a name for him, was not his physical constitution, but his peculiar manner of life, his personal social condition of vagabond outlaw. . . . A specific social condition is that which the word *gaucho* has meant during the entire existence of the type. There is nothing of race in this word; nothing ethnic" (*El castellano en la Argentina*, La Plata, 1928, p. 306).

Mark Jefferson (*Peopling the Argentine pampa*, New York, 1926, p. 43) notes: "The thing that was fundamental in the gaucho character was his familiar use of horses and cows. He might be poor or he might be rich; he might be white or he might have a considerable strain of Indian blood; he might be subservient to a patron or he might enforce homage as a land-owner or even as an outlaw."

And Ricardo Rojas (*Obras*, IX, 941): "That historic personage whom we call the gaucho was, not a race in the materialist sense of the word, but a spiritual type. . . . Not all gauchos were mestizos."

✍ 3 ✍

The Pastoral Society in Which a Gaucho Lived

Without a horse to ride and a cow to chase, there could have been
no gaucho.[1] Coming from a pastoral society, his emergence was gov-
erned by peculiar economic and social conditions. In the Banda Oriental,
hunters pursued cows, earned independence and a frequently illegal living by collecting hides for trade. To the south, it was only when
Spaniard and Indian rode in pursuit of the same cows that a Spanish
frontier army became necessary and that Spanish frontier settlements
grew. On both frontiers, horses and cows were of fundamental importance in the creation of the gaucho class; for this reason any study
of the gaucho may well turn first to a consideration of the pastoral
society from which his class emerged.

The extent of the dependence of this early La Plata society upon
the horse and cow is not generally realized.[2] Horses and cows furnished
food, clothing, shelter. Such furniture as the early settlers had, also
originated in either horse or cow. The equipment with which our settler
worked, was of hide—his saddle, bridle; the reins, traces, and lasso were
of twisted thongs. The bolas, most formidable weapons, were stones
wrapped in hide and connected by strips of hide. Ropes and cords were
of strips of hide; the bags in which things were carried or kept were
of hide, and they were sewn with strips of hide; grain was preserved
in cribs of hide swinging from stakes and protected by a hide shelter.
Boats, or *balsas,* were made of hide. Corrals were usually made of
stakes bound with thongs, though there are records of slightly more
artistic fences made of neat piles of the blanched skulls of cattle and
horses, with horns forming a decorative motif rhythmically repeated.
Thomas Woodbine Hinchliff tells of a dike protecting the land from the
encroachments of the Riachuelo River by a wall composed of thousands
of skulls of cattle patched with sod or turf.[3]

[1] For an account of the introduction of the horse and cow into the Plata region, see
Madaline W. Nichols, "The Spanish horse of the pampas," *The American anthropologist,*
XLI, 119-129.
[2] In general the sources for this chapter are to be found in the same kind of records as
those utilized in the preceding chapter. Collected from literally hundreds of books, the
items were widely scattered, constantly repeated. Again, general descriptive works by travelers
were those which proved most useful; unfortunately these descriptions were relatively late in
date, due to Spanish official inhospitality to visiting foreigners in the colonies.
[3] Thomas Woodbine Hinchliff, *South American sketches* (London, 1863), p. 67.

Hides were used to strengthen things. Carriages were strengthened by soaking hides and then cutting them into long strips. The poles, as well as almost all the woodwork of the carriage, were firmly bound with the wet hide, which, when dry, would shrink into a band almost as hard as iron. The spokes and the circumference of the wheels were similarly bound; so one actually traveled on the hide. Carriage springs were made of twisted hide. In the *carretas* for the transportation of produce, not a single nail was used in the whole construction. Where the parts of wood could not be joined by wedging, they were fastened with hide, and the covering for these carts was also of hide. Mendoza wine barrels were strengthened by pieces of raw hide drawn tightly over with thongs of hide. In fact, hide took the place of all kinds of materials— wood, iron, wicker, cloth—and since a knife was the only thing needed in order to handle it, it made life easy through a speedy provision of all things needed.[4]

Finally, hides were used in strengthening such intangible things as the control of the community. Offenders against society were sewn up in green hides and left in the sun to perish miserably when those hides tightened as they dried. Taxes on hide became the chief source of municipal income and the means of prosecuting the Indian wars. They paid the salaries of three companies of professional soldiers, *blandengues,* whose duty it became to hold the frontier against the oncoming Indian. And it was largely the income from the cattle industry which paved the streets of Buenos Aires and Montevideo, built their churches and jails, and all the other buildings proper to new municipalities.

While her hide was the most important part of a cow, a horse was more useful when alive. Horses were used to draw all kinds of objects. Even coffins were conveyed to the burying ground by being strapped transversely on a horse's back. Tell a peon to fetch anything a hundred yards off, and his first move would be to call for his horse. To get water from a well, a bucket was lassoed and a horse then pulled it up. Wood was brought on a hide drawn by a lasso. Horses were used even in such business as making butter. When milk had turned sufficiently sour, it was put into a bag made of hide; this bag, fastened to a long strip of hide rope, was attached at the other end to the leather girth which went round the horse's body; the horse was then mounted by a gaucho and ridden at a hard pace over the camp for a sufficient length of time to secure the making of the butter, by bumping the milk-bag against the ground.[5] Horses were used to thresh corn, to mix clay for bricks. They were used to measure distance, though here the

[4] Hernán Félix Gómez, *Historia de la provincia de Corrientes* (3 vols., Corrientes, 1928, 1929), I. 159.
[5] Hutchinson, *Buenos Ayres,* p. 48.

unit of measurement varied. Plump, lively horses made distance shorter;
while thin, tired horses added to its length. One fished on horseback,
casting his nets from its back; one bathed on horseback by riding into
a river and then swimming round the horse. Horse races, which, with
gambling, were society's main diversion, naturally depended upon the
horse. And the vertebrae of a horse's spine furnished the knucklebones
used for gambling.

Everyone rode—dentists, postmen, beggars. Hutchinson noted even
"a dentist operating on a poor fellow's grinders, the patient and his
physician being both mounted."[6] In town, one's daily journal was
brought by a cavalier, who handed it in without dismounting. Even
beggars would ride when soliciting their "limosna por el amor de Dios,"
and they had their licenses from the police in the shape of a piece of
branded wood suspended round their necks, to prove their worth. His
horse was no more indication of a beggar's being undeserving of aid
than the trousers of an ordinary man, for a horse came to be considered
not only a part of one's clothing but of his very body as well. Only
when sitting on his horse was a man reported to feel fully clothed, and
William Henry Hudson noted that the gauchos were accustomed to say
that a man without a horse was a man without legs.[7] A man afoot
became an oddity, inexplicable to the animal world. John Hale Murray
tells how birds and animals looked at him askance whenever he went
walking, how they came close to him to investigate what manner of
creature he might be: "Wild cattle . . . if they see you walking, . . .
will come round you—their heads up and ears extended—with signs of
the greatest astonishment. . . . Small lots of most beautiful and stately
mules have also come about me."[8] Man, however, did dismount to
sleep, and he dismounted to gamble. There are interesting descriptions
of the early settlers at their game, seated, in eastern fashion, upon their
heels, with bridle held under their feet, and generally with their knives
stuck in the ground beside them, for use upon any foul play, which
they were equally ready to practice and to suspect.

The horse was the means of the Spaniard's survival in his new
environment and of his adaptation to it. Not only was that horse the
principal defense against the Indian, but it was also the principal aid
in work, the link uniting the scattered population of the plains, and
the indispensable complement of the gaucho person. Without its aid,
cattle raising would have been impracticable on the vast, boundless
plain, and the care of the herds would have been impossible. Its gallop
shortened distances, brought men rapidly together either to realize com-

6 *Ibid.*, p. 49.
7 William Henry Hudson, *Far away and long ago* (New York, 1924), p. 23.
8 Murray, *op. cit.*, p. 68.

mon work, as at the rodeo, or for the equally social occasions of the pulpería reunions and the horse races. Its use conditioned society. Alberto Zum Felde believes that the cattle business was directly responsible for such fundamental elements of La Plata society as the estancia, the gaucho, the montonera, and the caudillo.[9] Ciro Bayo, concentrating his attention upon the basic human element in Argentine rural society, stated: "The gaucho . . . is what he is because of the horse. Without that helper, he would degenerate into a sedentary farmer, and instead of eating meat, he would eat beans or corn."[10] This statement, however, should be amplified to include the cow as well as the horse.

Finally, besides all their manifold uses in local society, horses and cows were the source of the only commodities which the Plata region had for export. Cattle, mules, and the various stock products—notably hides—were all that could be offered in exchange for any of the manufactured articles or luxuries desired from Spain. The horse and the cow, therefore, became of unique and fundamental importance in La Plata society; and in that society, the gaucho knew them best.

[9] Alberto Zum Felde, *Proceso histórico del Uruguay* (Montevideo, 1930), p. 18.
[10] Ciro Bayo, "Prólogo" to edition of José Hernández, *Martín Fierro* (Madrid, 1919), p. 159.

✎ 4 ✎

The Vaquería

"The first inhabitants of the land put . . . their mark upon those they could catch, and turned them into their enclosures, but they multiply'd so fast that they were forced to let them loose, and now they go and kill them according as they want them or have occasion to make up a quantity of hides for sale,"[1] wrote Acarete du Biscay. Such cow hunts were known as vaquerías.[2]

A vaquería became a colonial institution of the highest importance. It was the means whereby a man restocked his farm, the means of getting the land's sole product for export and trade, the source of governmental as well as private income, and the most important single element in exploration, extension of settlement and the creation of the frontier. Only when Spaniard clashed with Indian on the cow frontier, or met with foreign buyer on the contraband frontier, did Spanish defensive settlement become a necessity. The vaquería reached its height in the eighteenth century when the market for hides was most satisfactory; but it had existed from earlier times.

A typical vaquería of the eighteenth century involved the obtaining of an official permit,[3] the hiring of one of the many bands specializing in the vaquería business, and a lengthy expedition into the wilderness in pursuit of cows. Usually these expeditions had a military escort for protection against the rival Indian horse and cow hunters encountered on the pampas.

The troop of from thirty to fifty hunters was found by first finding a professional empresario. Only a real capitalist could supply the dozens

[1] Acarete du Biscay, *Account of a voyage up the River de la Plata and thence overland to Peru (1658)*, in Christopher d'Acugna, *Voyages and discoveries in South America* (London, 1698), p. 21.

[2] The most valuable source for the material in this chapter is to be found in the *Acuerdos* of the Cabildos of Buenos Aires and Montevideo, with their official records of licenses granted —where, when, and to whom—and of the Cabildo sorrows over the illegal vaquerías (Buenos Aires, Archivo nacional, *Acuerdos del extinguido cabildo, 1589-1820*, 45 vols., Buenos Aires, 1907-1934; and Montevideo, Archivo general, *Revista del archivo general administrativo*, 10 vols., Montevideo, 1885-1920). The description of the arrangements made for community vaquerías is also of use.

For descriptions of the actual working of a vaquería, see Azara, *Geografía física* . . . ; Miller, *op. cit.*; and the Robertsons, *op. cit.* For a study of their importance in the development of a new class of society, see Coni, "Contribución . . ."; Jefferson, *op. cit.*; and Manuel M. Cervera, *Historia de la ciudad y provincia de Santa Fe. 1573-1853* (Santa Fe, 1908).

[3] The vaquería license was one of the few sources of revenue of the poverty-stricken cabildo of Buenos Aires. While the tax on such permits varied, a third or a fifth of the hides collected was the amount usually paid.

of carts and the thousands of horses needed and could advance the funds
necessary for the provisioning of such an expedition and for the salaries
of the men. A vaquería often lasted for six months. It might be a
matter of from ten to thirty thousand pesos.

The vaquería band was generally composed of highly disreputable
men—criminals and outlaws. The difficulty in obtaining land—its purchase and ownership were practically forbidden by the laws of the Indies
—had produced in colonial society a large class of vagrants. Indians
and Negro slaves dislodged the proletariat from agricultural and indus-
trial occupations. To compete with them would have involved a loss
of caste, a stain upon Spanish honor. The cattle business, however,
was different. It was sport, not work. And in a land where every
Spaniard was a potential hidalgo, the cattle hunt furnished welcome
seasonal occupation for many a social outcast who at other times depended upon private initiative and skill in his own individual enterprise
of selling ill-gotten hides in contraband trade. The vaquería even served
as gaucho school, since the men practiced use of bolas and lasso, learned
the arts of hamstringing cattle, driving them, stripping off hides, pre-
paring them for shipment—and, even more important, heard of a ready
market for future disposal of illegal wares.

Armed with his permit, and having collected his band of hunters,
our capataz would then proceed to a land where cattle might be found.
Around Buenos Aires he took a large military guard along; they must
see him safely through annoying Pampas Indians and back to the shelter-
ing town. Similar escorts were needed by the expeditions proceeding
west from Santa Fe, for the Guaycurú from the Chaco land also proved
inhospitable. In Entre Ríos and the Banda Oriental, conditions were
somewhat easier, and many a hunter settled down to live in the country
after his work was done. The usual procedure, however, was for the
party to return to town after its sojourn in the country. Then it was dis-
banded, and each individual, having earned such luxuries as his supply
of tobacco and yerba mate, the silver decorations for the trappings of
his horse, or the gift of perfume which would win favor of his lady,
returned to his usual life of pleasurable idleness or of active, profitable
crime.

Though regarded as a gentleman's sport, the vaquería was a brutal
business. Azara has described a typical expedition. When the band of
hunters came upon the cattle, the men would line up in a half moon.
Those on the sides drove the cattle in toward the center, where there
was a worker who had a long pole tipped with a very sharp curved
blade and who hamstrung the animals until all were down or until they
had as many as they wished. Then he would ride back over the same

ground and stab the animals to death. The others dismounted to strip off the hides,[4] which were then staked and dried and collected for shipping. The meat, enough, so John Miller reported, to supply a whole army, was left for the jaguars, wild dogs, and carrion birds to devour. The director of such an expedition obtained thousands of hides, each of which, when dried, was worth four times the price of the whole animal. This was due to the cost of killing the cattle and of drying the hides.[5]

Not all vaquerías were for the collecting of hides. That was a comparatively late development. The earliest vaquerías were mere hunts for lost cattle. Then came hunts for cattle that had been allowed to run wild, but which were needed to restock haciendas. At first no permits were needed for such restocking provided that one wanted just a reasonable number of cows—say, not more than a few thousand. One simply gathered his personal band of friends together, and they collected his cattle merely for the trouble of cutting them out and driving them home. Men volunteered, with an eye to the cattle they would receive for their work. But for a greater number a permit was necessary, as, for example, if one wished to get thirty or forty thousand for export to Peru, or to stock Jesuit pueblo haciendas in Corrientes, or if a community wished to combine in a large drive for the restocking of its haciendas. The permit obtained, a royal official was assigned to see that all legal formalities were observed and proper taxes paid. Public announcement of the vaquería was made, with note of the day and of the assembling point for all who might wish to take part. As many as a hundred men might well appear for the hunt.

But these were relatively short expeditions, and it was only after hides began to be exported that long hide-hunting vaquerías became of importance. So from 1600 to 1625 the total number of hides exported by Buenos Aires was hardly over twenty-seven thousand.[6] Cattle were still relatively scarce; poor transportation facilities and trade restrictions closed the European market for hides; wild Indians were relatively near at hand. With time, however, cattle multiplied in the Indian land, since Indian interest had been in the horse rather than in the cow. Also the cattle introduced around the beginning of the seventeenth century into the Banda Oriental country multiplied fabulously. By 1650 wild cattle in respectable number were to be found on the pampas of Buenos Aires, in Entre Ríos, and in present Uruguay. Little use had yet been made of this cattle; vaquería permits had been few. In the second half of the seventeenth century, after a few ships from Spain had called at the port of Buenos Aires and returned laden with hides, the natives began to realize their value for trade, to covet them, and to go out to collect them.

[4] Azara, *Geografía física* . . . , p. 117.   [5] Miller, *op. cit.*, p. 160.
[6] Juan Álvarez, *Ensayo sobre la historia de Santa Fe* (Buenos Aires, 1910), p. 108.

Indians also came to realize that cattle hides could be exchanged for such luxuries as strong drink. The various French and English treaties of the early eighteenth century further enlarged this market for hides and proved a serious drain on the numbers of cattle to be found within a respectable distance of Buenos Aires town. Armed troops of men then rode out into the Indian lands of the Argentine pampas in quest for cattle hides. The Pampas Indians seriously rode to war around 1740, and balanced the Spanish search for cows with their own personal search for cows and for desirable Spanish women; the number of cattle to be found in the narrow corridor they had left along the Paraná was necessarily limited. The cattle of the old hunting grounds around Luján, Las Conchas, Magdalena, and Monte Grande presently had fallen victim to pursuing Indian or Spaniard or had run away to join their fellows in the quieter and less exciting region beyond the frontier, where they would be chased by only one enemy instead of by two. Spaniards wanting cattle must follow. The distance to be covered by vaquería bands continuously became greater, despite the discouragement applied by the Pampas Indian. Even by 1715 the stock around the city had been used up, and a Buenos Aires vaquería must go a long way into hostile Indian land in its search for cattle hides. As hides became ever more important for trade, Spaniards became possessed by a blind rage for killing all herds of oxen that they could lay hands on, and troops of horses were perpetually traversing those plains which most abounded in wild cattle. Such expeditions went over two hundred leagues.

In Uruguay and Entre Ríos, hunting was easier. Indians tolerated or even co-operated in Spanish cattle hunts, and from the Banda Oriental came the cattle used even for the meat supply of Buenos Aires and for the restocking of the badly depleted Buenos Aires estancias, raided by Spaniard and Indian alike. In their search for hides, hunting bands from Buenos Aires settled temporarily along the Uruguayan streams, and at the hunt's end many a member of the vaquería bands remained to live with a new Indian bride. Why not? His only possible dignified legitimate work was the hide hunt; it was to his advantage to live near his place of business. Moreover, only on the frontier was unoccupied land at his disposal; only there was life self-sustaining; and the Banda Oriental was the best base of operations for any personal venture into contraband trade. Our new hunter-settler must hold his land without any title, but he did not realize how quickly the city would overtake him. So squatters settled in Entre Ríos and on Uruguayan plains. Here, too, vaquería bands had explored, and now they were settling. And here the gaucho class of hide-hunting contraband traders grew and prospered.

5

Contraband Traders

The greatest single factor in the development of the gaucho class was the contraband trade which made it possible for a potential gaucho to lead, and enjoy, the outlaw life away from society.[1] Such contraband involved the gaucho specialty of skill on the cattle hunt.

La Plata colonial economic life was based on the cow, the horse, and the mule. These were offered in exchange for manufactured goods, for Peruvian silver, and for Negro slaves. Spain, however, adhered to the mercantilist policy. In common with other European nations, she held to one fundamental tenet: colonies were the property of their mother country, and it was fitting that they be exploited to her advantage. To accomplish this end, disturbing foreign goods and foreign people must be kept away from Spanish colonies; Peruvian silver must be jealously guarded and kept in Spanish hands; Spanish merchants, and incidentally the Spanish Crown, deserved all profit to be gained from American trade; such goods as might be allowed in exchange for Spanish products must be carried in Spanish ships and must pay taxes to the Spanish Crown. No competition could be permitted between Spanish and American industry. These principles formed the economic platform on which colonial trade had to stand.[2]

[1] An excellent source for any study on contraband is to be found in the collection of Royal Cedulas (Argentine Republic, Archivo general, *Archivo de la nación argentina, Época colonial Reales cédulas y provisiones, 1517-1662*, Buenos Aires, 1911) and in such collections of documents as that published by the Ministerio de relaciones exteriores (Argentine Republic, Ministerio de relaciones exteriores y culto, *Catálogo de documentos del Archivo de Indias en Sevilla referentes a la historia de la República Argentina, 1513-1810*, 2 vols., Buenos Aires, 1901, 1902). Such items are probably the surest index of the Spanish alarms. The records of the Cabildo of Montevideo *(op. cit.)* are also of use.

There is a good Spanish account of the Portuguese advance into Uruguay in Eduardo Acevedo, *Historia del Uruguay* (9 vols., Montevideo, 1916-1929), and Castilhos Goycochea (*A alma heroica das coxilhas*, Rio de Janeiro, 1935) presents the Brazilian version of the same story.

Good general accounts of the state of contraband, especially in the Banda Oriental, are those by Orestes Araújo (*Historia compendiada de la civilización uruguaya*, 2 vols., Montevideo, 1907), Bartolomé Mitre (*Historia de Belgrano . . .*), and Adolfo Saldías (*La evolución republicana durante la revolución argentina*, Madrid, 1919). John Campbell (*A concise history of the Spanish America*, London, 1741) describes just how contraband actually worked.

[2] Of all the sources for the materials on the Spanish legislation regulating La Plata trade, the study by Ricardo Levene, with its history of the development of Spanish economic policy, proved of the greatest value; see his "Introducción" in Buenos Aires, Universidad nacional, Facultad de filosofía y letras, *Documentos para la historia argentina*, IV, vii-cxvi. For the text of several of the Royal Cedulas on trade see the *Archivo de la nación argentina. Época colonial. Reales cédulas y provisiones. 1517-1662* (above). See, also, Carlos Bosque (*Compendio de historia americana y argentina*, Buenos Aires, n.d.), Bartolomé Mitre (*Historia*

Because colonial trade found such a platform unsatisfactory, contraband trade developed. The dates of Spain's prohibitory laws document the existence of the illegal trade; the dates of Spanish concessions punctuate the tale of contraband success.

Spain had established her fleet system in 1543. Unfortunately, however, the commerce of the little settlement in the Plata was not of sufficient value to warrant its fleet, with its badly needed guard of Spanish warships. Spain was busy with war[3] during the colonial period, and when the king had hardly a single fleet at his disposal, he necessarily used it in the protection of the northern route which, serving Mexico, the Antilles, and Peru, permitted the return of valuable New World metals. In the south, Buenos Aires might mark the speedier road to Bolivia and Potosí, but that route gave no outlet for the products of Mexico and Peru, and neither would its local commerce pay for its fleet. In the first years of her existence Buenos Aires had few products to offer in exchange for the badly needed goods from Spain. With increase in cattle, and a market for hides, the colony was permitted a limited amount of export, in 1618, by means of register ships.[4] In return for their products, colonists might receive the manufactured goods they so sorely needed; any possible competition with the merchants of Peru, however, was blocked by the establishment in 1622 of the royal customhouse at Córdoba, with its transit duties of 50 per cent. Even these register ships did not come regularly. Buenos Aires theoretically must obtain most of her goods by way of Peru. Her reply was to obtain her goods by contraband trade.

---

de Belgrano . . .), and Sigfrido A. Radaelli (*Capítulos de historia argentina,* Buenos Aires, 1931).

For a good general report upon colonial trade around the mid-eighteenth century, see John Campbell, *op. cit.;* Bernardo Frías, *Historia de Güemes y de la provincia de Salta* (3 vols., Salta, 1902, Buenos Aires, 1907, and Salta, 1911), also contains useful economic material.

[3] It was not enough that Spain and Portugal should divide the ocean between them and that the Pope should give his blessing to that division. There were other nations who had been omitted in the division and who demanded that their claims be heard. Charles V had his troubles with Francis I of France, a German Reformation, and westward-sailing Turks. Philip II's religious bias led to misunderstandings with The Netherlands, France, and England. The colonial expansion of the early seventeenth century brought its own clash of economic and political interests leading to the noteworthy wars of the late seventeenth century and of the eighteenth century and culminating in the establishment of the French Republic and in the freedom of British and Spanish colonies.

Outstanding among these wars were the War of the English Succession (1689-1697); War of the Spanish Succession (1702-1713); War of the Austrian Succession (1743-1748); Seven Years' War (1754-1763); the Napoleonic wars and the several revolutionary wars in France, the British and the Spanish colonies.

[4] "Se empezaron a conceder un año antes de reedificado Buenos Aires (1579) algunas permisiones de navíos de registro o sea buques sueltos, que con licencia expresa, pudieran ir hasta Cádiz o Sevilla a comerciar con la costa del Brasil, entonces dependencia de la corona de España bajo el cetro férreo de Felipe II. Por esta vía pudieron los colonos proveerse de fierro, acero, ropas y azúcar, que era lo que más necesitaban, introduciéndose a la vez algunos negros esclavos con licencia especial."

(The legal sanction of this traffic came in 1587.)

"Se reconoció la imposibilidad de que los habitantes del Río de la Plata acudieran al mercado de Potosí. . . . Se mantuvo hasta el comienzo del siglo XVII (1586-1602). . . . Muy poco aprovecharon de estas limitadas franquicias los pobres pobladores de Buenos Aires, quienes sin salida para sus frutos, carecían . . . de moneda."

See Mitre, *Historia de Belgrano,* I, 30, 31.

At first contraband trade was in manufactured goods imported by way of Brazil. Shortly after its founding Buenos Aires had become the port town for Potosí, despite all official regulations to the contrary. Presently Brazilian traders themselves learned the way to the silver capital, and though Spanish royal officials in the inland provinces loyally warned their king of the presence of these commercial travelers, the citizens of those provinces cheerfully bought their cheap goods and encouraged their crime. Passing through Buenos Aires, Córdoba, and Tucumán, this illegal trade even reached Lima, where it successfully undersold monopolist merchants and aroused their ire. Their protests, however, were as futile as the Spanish legislation was ineffectual. Spain had required the impossible. Trade went on despite all regulations,[5] regulations, which, in their recurring rhythm, serve as documentation of the fact that the rules were merrily being disobeyed.

Similarly there was contraband trade on the Chilean frontier, but it never attained the distinguished proportions encountered in Peru and in Uruguay. Without a Potosí, Chile's purchasing power was small, with a consequent ineffectiveness of her insistence upon a need for goods. And Pampas Indians rode in the way. In fact, those very Indians came to monopolize the business. Balancing their own ever-increasing desire for more and stronger Spanish liquor against the Chilean demand for greater numbers of Spanish cattle and hides, these Indians became active cattle hunters, and colonial records contain many an account of successful Indian cattle drives to a welcoming Chilean market.[6]

But the danger was greatest in the Banda Oriental country. This was the land most accessible to the eager foreign purchasers of the goods which the country had to offer. With attentive appreciation of the commercial profit incident to the opening up of a new market, coupled with glee at the discomfiture of Spain, merchantmen of hostile England, Holland, Portugal, and France carried to that Banda Oriental any such goods as might be appreciated by Spain's colonists. There they received a royal welcome.

[5] Slave importing concessions granted by the Spanish Crown to various foreign firms, offered an opportunity for the trade. See Mitre, *op. cit.*, I, 31. Mitre writes especially of the *asiento* of 1595-1596: "Aunque al asentista . . . le era prohibido comerciar ni aun con el sobrante de las ropas y víveres destinados a los negros . . . sin embargo, como tenían autorización para introducir hasta 600 negros en buques propios, bajo la protección del pabellón negrero pasaba el contrabando. Como además podían vender licencias sueltas, que se explotaban por segundas manos, con buques patentados por el asiento, el tráfico fué ensanchándose gradualmente."
And when busy at home, Spain allowed her allies to attend to the business of supplying her colonists. So in 1630 an exception had been made in favor of the English, who might enter the Río de la Plata, "en caso de arribo forzoso"; Acarete du Biscay reported Dutch ships at their trade in 1656; in 1660 trade was permitted with the French; finally, when Spain and England were busy at war from 1779 to 1783, Portuguese boats cared for the needs of Spanish colonists.
[6] See Félix de Azara, *Descripción e historia del Paraguay y del Río de la Plata* (2 vols., Madrid, 1847), p. 167; Francisco José Pascasio Moreno, "Viage a la Patagonia Setentrional," Buenos Aires, Sociedad científica argentina, *Anales*, I, 196; Robert Grant Watson, *Spanish and Portuguese South America during the colonial period* (London, 1884), p. 215.

Writing in 1741, John Campbell reported upon the actual procedure of Spaniards when about the business of contraband:

The Trade carried on between *Buenos Ayres* and *Europe* ought to be only by the Register-Ships from *Spain,* and the *Assiento* Ship, sent by the *South-Sea* Company from *England;* but besides these they are said to carry on a great contraband Commerce; in respect to which, as I have no authentick Memoirs, I do not think it proper for me to treat of it. When I say this, I would be understood only of the contraband Trade to *Spain* and *England;* for there is a third Sort of illicit Commerce of which I can very well speak. This is carried on with the Portugueze, who, as I observed before, possess the opposite Shore of the *Rio de la Plata.* Thence they take Occasion to send from time to time little Vessels laden not only with their own Commodities, but with such as they receive from *Europe;* and this in Spite of all the Care the *Spanish* Governor can or at least will take; for it is Interest governs every thing in the Indies. . . .

A Register-Ship is so called, from its being registered with all the Effects embarked in *Spain,* in the Books kept for that Purpose in the Chamber of *Seville.* . . . A Company of Merchants having, as they conceive, just Grounds to imagine that *European* Goods are greatly wanted at some particular Ports in the *West Indies,* they draw up a Memorial or Petition, containing these Reasons in the clearest and concisest Terms, and lay it before the Council of the *Indies.* The Prayer of this Petition is, That they may have Leave to send a Ship of three hundred Tons Burthen, or under, to the Port they mention. When Leave is obtained, they pay a certain Sum to the Crown, which is generally between thirty and fifty thousand Pieces of Eight, besides Presents, and those no small ones, to the King's Officers, from the greatest to the least. That this however may not induce any Suspicion of Fraud, they register their Ship and Cargo, that it may appear consistent with their Petition and Licence, and yet (such a Fatality there attends on all Custom-house Cautions) this Ship of under three hundred Tons generally carries upward of six hundred Ton of Goods, and affords Accommodation for Passengers besides. Copies from the Register are transmitted to the Governor and Royal Officers at the Port, to which the Register-Ship is bound; and such is their Diligence, such their Integrity, that when the Ship comes to an Anchor in the Port, they make a very narrow Enquiry, and yet there is seldom or never any Fraud discovered, but, on the contrary, this Ship of six or seven hundred Ton returns into *Europe* with an authentick Certificate from all the King of *Spain's* Officers, that she does not carry quite three hundred, together with a Bill of Lading in the same Strain of Computation. By these Register-Ships there is sometimes a Gain of two, or three hundred *per Cent.* which enables the Owners to pay so bountifully for cheating the King, having first got the Money by robbing his Subjects.

These Register-Ships go to *Buenos Ayres* . . . and other Places, to which neither the Galleons nor Flota come; yet, generally speaking, they return with those Fleets, as they sometimes go out with them, and so leave them in a certain Latitude. . . .

The *Portugueze* at *Rio Janeiro* entertain . . . a very beneficial Correspondence with their *Spanish* Neighbors. The Goods with which they supply them, are Sugars, Indigo, Tobacco, Wines, Brandies, and Rums, with some *European* Goods, and sometimes Slaves.

Ships frequently approach the *Spanish* Coasts under Pretence of wanting Water, Wood, Provisions, or more commonly, in order to stop a Leak. The first Thing that is done in such a Case, is to give Notice to the Governor of their great Distress, and, as a full Proof thereof, to send a very considerable Present. By this Means Leave is obtained to come on Shore, to erect a Warehouse, and to unlade the Ship; but then all this is performed under the Eye of the King's Officers, and the Goods are regularly enter'd in a Register as they are brought into the Warehouse, which when full is shut up, and the Doors sealed. All these Precautions taken, the Business is effectually carried on in the Night by a

Back-door, and the *European* Goods being taken out, Indigo, Cochineal, Vinellos, Tobacco, and above all Bars of Silver and Pieces of Eight are very exactly packed in the same Cases, and placed as they stood before. But then, that such as have bought may be able to sell publickly. . . . A Petition is presented to the Governor, setting forth the Stranger's Want of Money to pay for Provisions, building the Warehouse, Timber for repairing the Ship . . . ; in Consideration of all which, Leave is desired to dispose of some small Part of their Cargo, in order to discharge these Debts.[7]

Contraband had become a regular institution. It was furthered by the political complications of the European international wars. Whenever Spain was at war, her property became the legitimate prey of her enemies.[8] And Spanish wars were frequent during the colonial period. Of her many foreign enemies, the Portuguese were most troublesome. They were closest at hand in their neighboring colony of Brazil, and they were allies of the English—heretic manufacturers and ardent enemies of Spaniards. England, then, willingly supplied Brazilian colonists with those manufactured goods desired by colonists of Spain, and she bought the hides offered in exchange. The Portuguese of Brazil served as middlemen between the two complementary markets. When Spain was officially at war with Portugal or with England, this contraband trade was conducted brazenly, in the open. When the nations were at peace, it was conducted with a more decent privacy.

The status of the Portuguese contraband trade in the Banda Oriental land may be best illustrated by the history of their contraband outpost —La Colonia del Sacramento.[9] Founded in 1680, directly across the river from Buenos Aires, it was Portugal's monument to the success of her contraband trade. Local Spaniards realized its impertinent significance and promptly captured it, only to have it restored to their

---

[7] Campbell, *op. cit.*, pp. 278, 284-286, 316-318.

[8] Thus, around 1658, Acarete du Biscay reported that when he came before Buenos Aires he "found 22 Dutch ships, and among them two English, laden homewards with bulls-hides, plate, and Spanish wool, which they had received in exchange for their commodities. . . . The 22 Dutch ships that we found at Buenos Aires were each of them laden with 13, or 14,000 bulls-hides at least."
Spanish records of the early eighteenth century tell of the brave French corsair, Esteban Moreau, and of his nefarious work in the neighborhood of Rocha and Maldonado. When he was finally surprised and killed in 1720, his Spanish conquerors took possession of the eight thousand hides he had collected and of the stores which he had been offering in exchange. Around 1740 English contraband was reported as being highly annoying to his Spanish Majesty. And there were always meddlesome Portuguese about.

[9] Colonia was founded by the Portuguese and captured by the Spanish in 1680. It was returned to Portugal in 1681, and its possession was ratified in 1683 and again in 1701. Captured a second time in 1705, Colonia was again returned to the Portuguese by the treaty of 1716. Montevideo was built as a Portuguese lookout in 1726. Colonia was besieged in 1735, but when finally retaken, again diplomacy spoiled the Spanish work. By the treaty of 1750, it was exchanged for certain Guarani missions, an arrangement which brought trouble, and the unpopular treaty was canceled in 1761. In the war which presently followed, Spain captured Colonia as usual, only to lose it again to her rival by the provisions of the treaty of Paris of the next year (1763). In 1777 Viceroy Ceballos took Colonia. There he found the *corpus delicti*—"enorme cantidad de mercancias inglesas a la espera del contrabando que fuera internándolas." This merchandise was promptly confiscated, and the five hundred and twenty-three sinning Portuguese settlers of the place were exiled to far-off Spanish Cuyo, where they presently became responsible not only for many a new settler-family, but for the increased prosperity of the wine industry of the region as well. And, finally, by the 1777 treaty of Ildefonso, Spain at last succeeded in keeping her military conquests by the diplomatic way as well.

enemies in the juggling of European international peace treaties. When those treaties were broken and it was possible to return to the attack of their neighbors, no sooner were the Spanish colonists again in control than the official wars were over and peace again undid their work. In 1726 Montevideo was established, that Spanish settlers might at least be on hand to watch their untrustworthy neighbors, to gather data for protests to their king, and to have a base from which to operate whenever war should be proper.

Besides the confusion arising from a rapid succession of intervals of official peace and war, there were uncertainties arising over the delineation of the international boundary between Spanish and Portuguese possessions. As long as there should be doubt as to its exact location, the colonists of both nations might presume a balance in their favor. The slow survey of those boundaries was again followed by a succession of international treaties which prolonged the confusion for a period of approximately one hundred years.[10]

Certain facts, however, stand out very clearly in the colonial picture. The Portuguese and their English allies had goods to sell; the Spanish colonists needed those goods and had products to offer in exchange; it was to the mutual advantage of both that such exchange be made. That such trade must be illegal, could prove no effectual barrier in the presence of economic need. The trade prospered. Enterprising Portuguese commercial adventurers swarmed into the land, bringing European manufactures to trade for hides. A whole disreputable class of Spanish outlaws—the gauchos—grew up to catch the hides needed for the exchange. Indian allies came to the aid of both, thus furthering their own imports of such appreciated commodities as properly strong drink and their opportunities for the plunder of Spanish homes and the capture of Spanish women. The entire business was disreputable and prosperous. Hearty plunder, adventure, wealth, traveled together, and while the men who did the actual work might be recognized as without the law, and therefore as undesirable social acquaintances, the empresarios who hired them and directed that work were regarded with the respect which their success and their service to society deserved. One often comes upon the phrase "un alto y poderoso contrabandista," and many a modern Uruguayan geographical name bears witness to the social esteem in which these empresarios were held.[11]

---

[10] See such accounts as the *Diarios* of Juan Francisco Aguirre ("Diario," Buenos Aires, Biblioteca nacional, *Anales*, IV, 1-271, and VII, 1-490) and Diego de Alvear ("Diario de la segunda partida demarcadora de límites en la América Meridional," Buenos Aires, Biblioteca nacional, *Anales*, I, 267-384; II, 288-360; III, 373-464). See, also, Félix de Azara (*Geografía física y esférica de las provincias del Paraguay y Misiones Guaraníes (1790)*, Montevideo, Museo nacional, *Anales del museo de Montevideo*, I, 11-468) and Bartolomé Mitre (*Historia de Belgrano* . . . , II, 55).

[11] Ernesto Herrera, in his *El estanque* (Montevideo, 1911, p. 34), has described the typical attitude of society toward a contrabandista: "Los contrabandistas son guena gente. La mayoría

Spain had originally designed the Banda Oriental as a hunting preserve. She had stocked it with cattle; she had discouraged settlement there. For a long period, the only Spanish town in the region had been the little reduction of Santo Domingo de Soriano. The rest of the territory remained officially abandoned save for the Indian hunters. But here wild cattle ranged; here came the Spanish cattle hunter; and here found refuge many a Spanish outlaw. Here, also, came the Portuguese contrabandista. He came either in personal hunt of a supply of hides for export or to offer his smuggled manufactured goods in exchange for such hides as had been collected by his Indian or Spanish gaucho ally. Or he might drive live cattle and horses back to Brazil, where they were badly needed. Politically, his private enterprise served to stretch the Portuguese frontier.[12]

The cattle hunting ground of the Banda Oriental attracted Spanish as well as Portuguese hunters. Many of the Spaniards came legitimately, bearing their official permits from the Cabildo of Buenos Aires. They collected cattle with which to restock the Buenos Aires estancias; they came to fill contracts to furnish the meat supply for Buenos Aires; they came with permits to collect limited numbers of cattle hides for export. In return for these concessions, they paid taxes to the Cabildo, and thus furnished the main source of local governmental revenue. Unfortunately, many a Spaniard came without first obtaining his permit.

The Banda Oriental was the frontier where unpopular members of Spanish society could most easily live in comparative comfort. To the west, Spanish organization was strong. One might be caught by Spanish justice. To the south, Pampas Indians discouraged emigration. But to the north, the Minuanes and Charrúas were far more co-operative, and there was work which a man might do. The country was unsettled; troublesome Spanish authorities were pleasantly absent. If unaccountably pursued by a specially delegated police band, one could escape to safety across an indefinite international boundary line. In the Banda Oriental, then, grew up armed outlaw bands. The leaders of these bands and the men themselves were usually criminals—many of them refugees from Spanish or Brazilian jails. The leaders, with success, attained respectability. Their followers—called changadores, gauderios, or gauchos—were not so fortunate.

But no matter the name under which he rode; there was no doubt

son vecinos respetables, como dice el comisario. Eso sí, hay alguno que otro que no hace las cosas como es debido y a ocasiones lo ponen a uno en un apuro. De puro bestias que son, porque no les cuesta nada venir a decirme: 'Mire, che, sargento, esta noche vamo a pasar tantas carretas por el lao del paso,' un suponer. Ansi uno y sabe pa no aparecer por alli, pero no le dicen nada, y a lo mejor la polecia se ve obligada a cortar un alambrau pa no toparse con un contrabando. Porque siempre es gueno que nosotros estemos lejos . . . . Uste comprende. . . ."
12 Goycochea, *op. cit.*, p. 11.

as to the character of the type of man meant or as to the work he did. He collected Uruguayan livestock and drove it to purchasers on the Brazilian frontier; he hunted cattle for hides to be similarly sold; or, conversely, he smuggled European goods to their local market. His employer varied. He might work for some empresario from Santa Fe or Buenos Aires; or his employer might be a Brazilian of similar interests, or the captain of some passing French, English, or Dutch boat. His work, while illegal, received the social sanction of the Spanish community at large, save when it roused the ire of those individuals who personally lost their livestock.[13] The gaucho was the means whereby the community received the goods it needed, and at pleasantly advantageous prices. He might indeed be an undesirable social associate, but he was of value to local society. Because of that value, he himself prospered.

After the establishment of Montevideo, Spanish law moved into the land together with Spanish settlers. But Spanish Montevideo, as well as Portuguese Colonia, offered an enthusiastic market for European goods—and one near to the Brazilian illegal base of supply and to laborers expert in the work of smuggling. Little local shopkeepers, making up their orders of hides to exchange for European manufactures, bought without inquiring too closely as to the source. Spanish and Indian hunters ranged the land to supply this market for hides. When passing boats stopped at Montevideo, or some near-by and more con-

---

[13] Two depositions against thieves, taken in 1768 and presented before the Cabildo of Montevideo, illustrate gaucho procedure.

The first is by the capataz of an estancia: "A óras de la una de la noche poco más o menos llegaron a la dicha Estancia una de las quadrillas de Ladrones que se han reconosido infestar, y traer en inquietud con sus robos a esta Jurisdisión y que estando en ella el declarante con quatro hombres más, presenciándoseles en el Rancho la dicha quadrilla de mal hechores que se componía de onse hombres,—de ellos sólo uno castellano, que a oydo desir llamarse Juan Joseph Carrasco, Dragón desertor, que era el que hacía de Capitán de dichos mal hechores de los quales los más eran Portuguezes, todos armados con tres armas de fuego, pues sólo un Indio vieron que trahía por arma una Lanza—, éstos, montando las dichas armas de fuego, asegurando la puerta del Rancho hisieron poner al declarante y a los demás sus compañeros en ala, o fila, y echo esto, pasaron a desnudarlos hasta dejarlos sin cosa de ropa, la que dice se llevaron los mismos mal hechores, con los recados de andar a cavallo, y hasta veinte cavallos, que eran los que se havían ido juntando después del robo que en la misma Estancia hisieron estos Ladrones u otros de su clase, el día quatro del mes próximo pasado de Junio, en cuya ocasión se llevaron hasta cien cavallos: y que así mismo luego que desnudaron al declarante y a los demás sus compañeros, hiéndose los dichos Ladrones a poco tiempo, bolvieron al Rancho de donde alzaron y se llevaron en ancas del uno de ellos a Juan Joseph Berroeta, uno de los dichos compañeros del declarante, al que después se supo lo havían conduzido a la estancia de D. Juan Antonio Deaedo aquella misma noche, y que le havían preguntado y reconvenido les declarase donde avía más cavallos, y que sino les confesaba, y daba noticia de ellos, le avían de matar. . . ."

The second deposition reads: "Serca del Canto de los Gallos, llegaron a dicha estancia una Quadrilla de dichos Ladrones, los quales apeándose de sus cavallos a la Puerta del Rancho de la avitasión del expresado D. Juan Antonio, tirándoles éste un tiro, el que no salió por dar sólo fuego la Cazoleta, entendido esto por dichos Ladrones se venían dos de ellos para el Galpón donde estaba el declarante a pie, a los quales disparándoles el dicho Cuevas un tiro se pusieron en fuga, hiéndose a Espaldas de la Cosina, y montando a cavallo venían para el Rancho, a cuyo tiempo fingiendo el declarante que llamaba a un cavo de Esquadra, oyendo esto los dichos Ladrones, dixeron: Que Cavo de esquadra, ni que M. . . . ; pero al mismo tiempo dieron buelta desviándose de los Ranchos, y encaminándose para el Arroyo se pusieron a andar rodeando el Rancho sin ponerse a tiro de fusil tiempo de dos horas poco más o menos, después de lo qual, se fueron llevando de dicha Estancia como dies, o dose cavallos . . ." (Montevideo, Archivo general, *Revista del archivo general administrativo*, VII, 248-249, 249-250).

veniently deserted spot upon the Uruguayan coast, they were met by
eager traders offering hides for a return purchase of their European
wares. Those wares were then smuggled into Montevideo. Thus,
ironically enough, the establishment of that city fomented the success of
the very work it was founded to check. When it is reported that despite
the relatively limited population of this Banda Oriental country, there
were literally thousands of men hard at work and prospering at contraband,[14] its value as the leading local industry can be realized. The
whole eighteenth century was especially marked by Spanish contraband
scares.[15]

Well might Spain be alarmed. So extensive had the trade in hides
and the indiscriminate slaughter of cattle become, that their numbers
were frightfully diminished. The leading local source of wealth was
rapidly vanishing. While such statistics cannot be taken too literally,
the contraband trade with the Portuguese apparently attained distinguished proportions. From 1798 to 1804, it, alone, was reported as
keeping at work forty boats of from 200 to 250 tons, which imported
sugar, salt, and European wares in exchange for hides "bought or
stolen" in the country.[16] According to Spanish reports, the Portuguese
contraband trade was worth two million pesos annually, and the English
trade was said to be even more successful.[17]

Naturally Spain tried to meet this menace to her economic prosperity
and to her political prestige. She began by noting its existence in

[14] See Juan Francisco Aguirre, "Diario," p. 145; and Eduardo Acevedo, op. cit., I, 41.
[15] In 1716 men from Santa Fe were reported in the Banda Oriental, hard at their nefarious
work of providing hides for Brazilian purchasers. In 1721 the Portuguese themselves were
noted gathering hides there. From 1733 date several records of the Portuguese use of Colonia
as a smuggling base, and active Paulistas are locating on the Río Grande. In 1737, one,
José de Silva Paez, has taken possession of the fortress and sierra of San Miguel, 60 leagues
south of the Río Grande and only 75 leagues away from Montevideo. There are Portuguese
estancias and a little fort located on the Arroyo Chuy. Again, in 1744, the Portuguese are
reported on the Río Grande and in the Sierra of San Miguel. By 1748 legislation against
Uruguayan contraband increases to meet the corresponding increase in its persistent practice.
In 1750 the Portuguese attempt to settle Monte Grande and to advance to the Río Negro.
Another record of that year tells how the Portuguese, taking advantage of the new international boundary treaty, have possessed the land from Viamont toward the Río Pardo and
the Yacuy, and "very extensive lands toward Moxos." An Indian peace was arranged in the
year 1752. Ways and means were discussed of keeping the Portuguese from Monte Grande and
the Río Negro. In that very year the Portuguese were caught with one lot of 458 horses
which they were taking away to the Río Grande. By 1773 the Portuguese had estancias down
as far as the Río Icabacúa, and their incursions extended much farther to the south. In 1782
Spaniards fleeing from justice are reported as living in the woods of Entre Ríos, smuggling
contraband goods in from Brazil or stealing hides of Spanish cattle for export. Similar disreputable bands are in Corrientes, Misiones, and about Montevideo. Neither the establishment
of the viceroyalty, with its easing of Spanish trade restrictions and its treaty with Portugal
over the international boundary line, had availed. Contraband continued. In 1790 Spanish
outlaws are boldly stealing, not wild cattle, but that more conveniently at hand on the Spanish
estancias. They sell "without either the owners or the government being able to help it."
From 1792 date several laws against contraband. In 1795, "What most instantly calls for
remedy, is the guard of the cattle which are ceaselessly being taken from our fields on the
other shore, and in such large lots that their lack is being ever more constantly recognized."
[16] Orestes Araújo, Diccionario popular de historia de la República Oriental del Uruguay
(3 vols., Montevideo, 1901-1903), p. 131.
[17] Manuel M. Cervera, Historia de la ciudad y provincia de Santa Fe, 1573-1853 (Santa
Fe, 1908), p. 520. See, also, Thomas Jefferson Page, La Plata, the Argentine Confederation,
and Paraguay (London, 1859), p. 554.

thundering prohibitory laws. She ordered armed expeditions over into the land to drive off impertinent trespassers. When military success proved only temporary, she established Montevideo as a permanent base from which to operate. Permanently established mounted police forces replaced the early reliance on military expeditions, and they proceeded in earnest pursuit of the Portuguese and Spanish changadores, each of whom had already to his credit "as many crimes as Judas." The little country stores, or *pulperías,* were closed because their owners were found to have the execrable custom of either personally stealing hides for sale or of buying those previously stolen by the gauchos. Governor Zabala understood that only by establishing forts at strategic points along the coast could commerce be properly defended. Coast guard boats served in aid. Along the Portuguese frontier there grew a second line of little forts[18]—from Santa Tecla to the Guardia of San Martín— "in order to prevent in times of *peace* the introduction of contraband which might take place there and to hinder the extraction of hides and animals which Spanish and Portuguese gauderios and changadores effect in those lands."[19] Viceroy Vértiz stressed the possible efficacy of more settlements. Settlers had already been imported from Patagonia and from the Canaries, or were bribed to come over from Buenos Aires.[20] Soldier-settlers were drafted to live in the land and to back up the frontier line of forts. The viceroyalty was established; the barriers on legal trade were lowered; political and military organization was strengthened to oppose the Portuguese and English dangers, for the struggle for economic markets involved political control.

In the pleasant confusion of this picture, the gaucho class grew.

[18] Araújo, *Historia,* pp. 122-123.
[19] Gonzalo de Doblas, *Memoria . . . sobre la Provincia de Misiones de Indios Guaranís (1785)* (Buenos Aires, 1836), p. 105.
[20] Acevedo, *op. cit.,* I, 18.
Such typical bribes were offered as a lure to the settlers of Montevideo: "Declaración de hijodalgos y de noble linaje a favor de los pobladores y descendientes legítimos; pago de gastos de viaje; reparto de solares, chacras y estancias; regalo de 200 vacas y de cien ovejas a cada poblador; ayuda de brazos y de materiales para la edificación de viviendas; distribución de semillas; reparto gratis, durante un año, de carne, yerba y tabaco." Only aguardiente seems to have been forgotten.

❧ 6 ❧

Gaucho Frontiersmen

The Plata settlements had other frontiers besides that facing Brazil, and on these frontiers as well, there grew up an outlaw, gaucho, class. Again, the elements involved were the Spaniard and the Indian and their cattle hunts. Racial mixture and trade across the frontier went on. But to the south, the emphasis was on the racial mixture rather than on the trade, and the European international element of the north was absent. Because of its lack of foreign danger and the comparative weakness of the economic factor, this southern frontier has been unduly disregarded by historians. Yet this was the frontier where Spanish and Indian lines met most violently, and any study of the emergence of the gaucho class from the pastoral society of the Plata lands must involve a study of the Pampas frontier and of the Spanish-Indian relations there.[1]

The Indians on the southern frontier were known as the Pampas. Unfortunately, the exact meaning of the term is not always too clear. When European invaders came, they found the vast plains thinly peopled by nomad Indian tribes. After Spaniards invading Chile had made conditions there distinctly unsatisfactory for the Indian, and after that Indian had adopted the Spanish horse which made his travels easy, there began an Indian migration through the Andean mountain passes from Chile into the Patagonian plains. The history of this migration

---

[1] There is a great amount of excellent material available on the frontier Indian. For the Uruguayan and for the Pampas Indians, one of the most useful sources is to be found in the *Acuerdos* of the Cabildos of Montevideo and of Buenos Aires. See Montevideo, Archivo general, *Revista del archivo general administrativo* (10 vols., Montevideo, 1885-1920), and Buenos Aires, Archivo nacional, *Acuerdos del extinguido cabildo, 1589-1820* (45 vols., Buenos Aires, 1907-1934).

For the Pampas frontier, other valuable works are those by Padre Tomás Falkner ("Descripción de la Patagonia," La Plata, Universidad nacional, *Biblioteca centenaria*, I, 21-126), Félix de Azara ("Diario del reconocimiento de las guardias y fortines que guarnecen la línea de frontera de Buenos Aires, 1796," Angelis, *op. cit.*, V, 57-84), and Lucio Victorio Mansilla (*Una excursión a los indios ranqueles*, Buenos Aires, 1928).

Army conditions on that frontier are reported in the documents contained in the Archivo del general Mitre (Buenos Aires, Museo Mitre, *Documentos y correspondencia*, 28 vols., Buenos Aires, 1911).

For the material on the various tribes out of the Chaco, see such works as those by Nicolás del Techo (*The history of Paraguay, Tucumán, and the adjacent provinces in South America*, in Churchill, *A collection of voyages and travels*, VI, London, 1752), Martin Dobrizhoffer (*An account of the Abipones, an equestrian people of Paraguay*, London, 1822), and Manuel M. Cervera (*Historia de la ciudad y provincia de Santa Fe, 1573-1853*, Santa Fe, 1908).

Good general accounts of the Plata Indians are those by Alcide Dessalines d'Orbigny (*L'homme américain*, Paris, 1839, and *Voyage pittoresque dans les deux Amériques*, Paris, 1836) and Antonio Serrano (*Los primitivos habitantes del territorio argentino*, Buenos Aires, 1930).

is complicated by the indefiniteness of Indian nomenclature. Thus, the same name may refer to utterly different tribes, in that those tribal names are often matters of location. For example, the Picunches were "people of the north"; the Huilliches, "people of the south"; the Puelches, "people to the east." But such terms are relative and change as the Indians to whom they referred changed their place of abode. The term *Pampas Indian,* however, came to be applied loosely, but logically, in colonial records to the Indian *found* on the pampas, regardless of his origin or of his relative location with respect to that of other Indian tribes. If the fact that he was from the western mountain region was to be stressed, the term *Aucaes* or *Serranos* was used.[2]

Contrary to the general belief, the Pampas Indian was a comparatively peaceful Indian until annoyed into decidedly unpeaceful activity. He never was the villain that Spanish historians have delighted to portray. When Mendoza and his party first arrived, they were met by hospitable Indians who brought them food. But when Indian hosts noted in their guests an unreasonable disposition to rule and an apparent intention to remain—together with the increasing shortage in their own food supplies—the situation changed. The Indians diplomatically indicated this change by neglecting to bring the customary food. It was only when Spanish guests refused to take the hint that trouble started. In the battles that followed, the Indian held his own.

After the second founding of Buenos Aires, the Spaniard won. Juan de Garay and his half-breed settlers were men of a different stamp from the conquerors fresh from Spain. They had learned the ways of the frontier. Of even more importance: since they had not been hungry, they had not eaten up their Spanish horses and so had their aid in chasing Indian enemies away over the plain. Then it was that the Indian withdrew to the southwest, where he could not be so easily caught and put to unpleasant work. Having found the Pampas Indian to be a difficult individual to persuade against his will, the Spaniard tacitly accepted this situation, and though it was contrary to his usual practice, he did his own work or he purchased Negroes to aid him. The two civilizations progressed in parallel; the Spanish horse and cow multiplied on the intervening plains, where Spaniard and Indian alike pursued them. Since there were horses and cows enough for both,

[2] Strictly speaking, the Pampas Indians were Puelches, i.e., Indians who lived to the east of the mountains. In the eighteenth century they were generally to be found at home on the plains between the rivers Negro and Colorado (39 to 41 degrees south latitude), but their travels frequently found them at the Sierra de Ventana. Subdivisions of the Puelches were the mountain Pehuenches or Serranos (36 to 40 degrees) and the Aucas of the plains. The Ranqueles were a division of the Pehuenches and separated from that group in the years between 1770 and 1780.

The general consensus of belief is that these Indians were closely related to the Araucanians, and there are many notes of their migration from Chile. Ricardo Latcham believes in a still earlier migration westward from the plains. At least there is no question but that the coming of the Spaniard to the New World badly upset the nice balance of its American Indian tribes.

the general Spanish-Indian policy was one of mutual toleration.[3] For approximately one hundred and fifty years Spaniard and Indian lived in relative peace.[4] Only in the mid-eighteenth century did the two civilizations clash. And, as on the northern frontier, the motive of that clashing was economic. It involved the question of the possession of livestock.

The Indian had not been slow in recognizing the value of Spanish livestock. At first, Indian interest centered on the horse; it was only after the Pampas had been joined by other Indians from the west, Indians who had learned to like cows for food, and after they, themselves, had found a profitable Chilean market for cattle hides, that they turned their attention seriously to the cattle hunt. By this time the number of horses and cows had been badly depleted.[5] Cabildo records of advancing date show that Spaniards wanting to hunt cows must go

[3] Robert Grant Watson reports: "Until the latter part of the eighteenth century the inhabitants of the province of Buenos Aires, possessing ample lands safe from incursions of the Indian, had no particular object in extending their possessions farther south than the river Salado. The farther region was left to the Indian" (*Spanish and Portuguese South America during the colonial period*, London, 1884, p. 214).
The Indian attitude toward the Spaniard was a similar one. This does not mean, however, that individual bands did not cross the frontiers, and that small local conflicts did not result from such invasions. When Indian and Spaniard chased the same cow, there was trouble. The Pampas Indian was not patient at interference. A similarly difficult situation arose when an Indian was thwarted in an attempt to remove a few cows from a convenient Spanish frontier estancia. But such incidents were sporadic. They were purely personal matters; they involved no organized tribal aggression. The Indian was hungry or he was making up an order of hides to exchange for aguardiente. He regarded his business as legitimate, and to him the Spanish attitude seemed highly unreasonable.
[4] Thus in 1673 Don Gregorio Suárez Cordero, priest of Buenos Aires, reported that the Pampas had been subjugated. In 1682 the Governor of Tucumán in a report on the Pampas addressed to his Majesty recognized that "son domésticos, que se comunican los españoles con ellos, entrando y saliendo en sus poblaciones." Unfortunately, however, he finds the Pampas naturally uneasy and seditious and little addicted to work; they are desirous of liberty and run away and do not wish to live in reductions. In 1734 the Jesuits overcame Pampa dislike for reduction life, and further submissiveness was also recorded by the Cabildo of 1723: "Los yndios pampas . . . desde la fundazión de esta ciudad se hallan tan domesticados que de ellos se an compuesto las encomiendas de aqui." When the wars began in the 1740 period, the surprise at this strange new behavior of formerly peaceful Indians is well documented. In 1739 was mentioned the desirability of punishing warring Indians so that "this community may enjoy the tranquility of former times." In 1740 there was note of continued hostility of the "yndios ynfieles en las estancias . . . cosa nunca vista." In 1741 attention was called to the "enemigo ynfiel que de pocos años a esta parte ha dado en ostilisar los caminos de la Provincia de Cuyo y estancias de esta jurisdicción y en especial . . . el estrago nunca bista ni experimentado que dichos ynfieles executaron en el pago de la Magdalena." Again, in 1741, "De pocos años a esta parte se alla esta ciudad muy aquejada de los continuados ynsultos de los yndios." See the records of the Cabildo for many another similar report.
Further evidence of the reasonableness of the Pampas Indian can be gotten from the numerous colonial records of uneventful Spanish expeditions across the Pampas Indian territory, and from the Jesuit success in their reductions of the Pampas Indians.
[5] Azara, "Diario del reconocimiento . . . ," Angelis, *op. cit.*, V, 78-79:
"Los ganados vacunos vinieron con Garay y procrearon en las cercanías, hasta que por descuido o falta de aguas en los años de mucha sequía, se escaparon algunos al arroyo Salado, donde en libertad multiplicaron, extendiéndose hasta el Rio Negro, y más al Sur. . . . Los indios de la falda de la cordillera tuvieron noticia de estos ganados, y empezaron a llevar grandes manadas a Chile, cuyos presidentes tenían contratos de ganados con dichos indios. Éstos, que en su país no podían vivir sin algún trabajo, se fueron estableciendo en los campos de los ganados, y algunos se mezclaron con los pampas; de modo que hoy casi todos los indios son de la costa de la cordillera. Al mismo tiempo que los bárbaros destrozaban ganados en las pampas, no se descuidaban los españoles, llevándolos a Córdoba y Mendoza; y los de Buenos Aires hacian mucha corambre de toro y de vacas. . . . De ahí se siguió, que a mediados de este siglo estaba exhausto este precioso mineral de cueros, y no habiendo ya ganados alzados en las pampas, se vieron los bárbaros en una especie de precisión de robar el manzo o de rodeo en las estancias de esta capital.
"Ésta es la época y la causa de la guerra con los indios."

increasingly far from home. Gradually Spanish vaquería bands and Indian hunters found themselves using the same preserves. Then the Indian reversed the procedure by invading Spanish estancias to hunt. He had acquired a taste for luxuries—notably, strong Spanish aguardiente and charming Spanish wives;[6] he had learned that cattle hides would purchase the aguardiente and that Spanish women could be captured incidentally on the frontier. After noting these things, the Pampas Indian proceeded directly and intensely to the business of satisfying his wants. He raided the Spanish frontier estancias where Spanish stock could be collected in satisfying numbers and where, at the same time, Spanish women could be caught either to serve as wives or to be exchanged for ransom.[7] Then it was that Spanish active defense became imperative, and a line of little frontier forts sprang up to mark the passing of the Indian *malón,* or raid. Spanish and Indian frontiers had overlapped.

The first of these new Indian organized attacks occurred in 1737 at Arrecifes. From the Indian point of view it was a success, and it was repeated. When the Spaniards, in pursuance of their usual policy, committed an act of extraordinary cruelty to serve as an example to the sinning Indians, they found to their sorrow that the Pampas Indian was made of sterner stuff than they had imagined.[8] He retaliated firmly in kind, and the bitter Pampas Indian wars began. But they did not prove any inherent savagery in the Indian. He fought for food, for the luxuries he now found essential to his happiness, and for the revenge of unjust treatment accorded to his friends. "One cannot

---

[6] For the material on the frontier mixing of Spaniard and Indian, see nn. 31-35.

[7] Emilio Daireaux, "Las razas indias en la América del Sud," Buenos Aires, Sociedad científica, *Anales,* IV, 220.

"Las invasiones fueron por largo tiempo desconocidas, ninguno de los dos partidos tenía interés de emprender una guerra. El número de rebaños esparcidos por la campaña era tal y su explotación tan descuidada, que los indios pampas pudieron explotar esta mina fecunda sin tener que avanzar al país poblado y sin que nadie pensara litigarles el derecho de hacerlo. A la sombra de esta tolerancia, habían creado un comercio considerable con las tribus indias de Chile, quienes traficaban este botín con los Europeos establecidos en la Costa del Pacífico. Este goce apacible y este comercio rápidamente desarrollado, habían creado necesidades por otra parte; la destrucción de los rebaños fué tan rápida en las pampas durante el siglo 18, que a poco los indios tuvieron más dificultad en procurarse los animales necesarios para su consumo y comercio. Ésta fué la sola razón que motivó las incursiones en el país poblado y trajo conflictos. Los españoles les imputaron sin razón complicidad con las tribus sometidas y procedieron a una carnicería general de estas tribus, que vino a vengar la primer gran invasión armada de 1740. Nunca sin la idea deliberada de atemorizar los invasores por un gran ejemplo de crueldad, que siempre ha sido el sistema empleado por los españoles, las invasiones no hubiesen tomado el carácter odioso que tomaron después. . . .

"La invasión de 1740 fué seguida de una nueva carnicería. . . . Ésta carnicería trajo invasiones continuas que se han continuado."

[8] After the first wild Indian raids on the frontier, the Spaniards accused their Indian friends inside the borders of being accomplices of the others. There was a wholesale massacre in retaliation. The Indian chiefs, and notably Calelián, were shipped to Spain, and their women were sent over to the Uruguayan reduction of Santo Domingo de Soriano. It is noteworthy that even these "tame" Indian chiefs started their own little private war on board their ship sailing away to Spain and that when they saw that it was irrevocably lost they all jumped overboard and so honorably died. As for the women: within one month of their arrival at the mission, the worthy fathers were already presenting a bill for ten burials out of the number of their forty guests.

deduce from the deeds committed by a people fighting against extermination a barbarity anterior to this state of war."[9]

By 1740, three years after the beginning of the formal Indian invasions, the Spaniards were well defeated, and they eagerly purchased peace on terms so favorable to the Indian that he gained the highest sense of his own importance. A line was run at 35 degrees, and it was the Spanish understanding that the Indian had agreed to remain to the south of it. The noteworthy features of this initial period of the wars were the success of the Indian raids, the fierce antagonism aroused by Spanish defensive cruelty, and the Indian retaliation which culminated in Cacique Bravo's November, 1740, attack on Magdalena and a peace purchased by Spaniards.

It must be remembered, however, that despite any tribal treaties the private raids of relatively small Indian bands continued for well over a hundred years. They were especially troublesome in the years from 1751 to 1756, again around 1766, and during the period of the civil wars. These later raids were largely cattle forays. A Spaniard personally defending his cattle would be acting most unwisely, but the revengeful vindictiveness of the great early invasions seems to have been generally absent. But that did not make those smaller raids any less personally inconvenient and dangerous; they merely involved fewer people. Since no frontiersman could tell where they would strike, all were kept equally uneasy.

A typical Indian raid was a business adventure. Our Indian usually came from a goodly distance, and his horses were tired on arrival. The first essential for the success of his raid, then, was the capture of fresh horses to make possible a speedy attack and the necessarily even more speedy retreat. Frequently well advised as to the location of the local Spanish forces, the raid was well timed; the Indian rider had disappeared with his newly acquired Spanish livestock before their protective guard arrived. With no fresh horses left at hand, pursuit was relatively hopeless. Such raids usually occurred in October, November, or December after autumn and winter had destroyed the giant thistles on the plains and the naked bodies of Indian horse and rider were no longer exposed to the prickings of their formidable spines. Again, by October, Andean passes would be open, and the road was clear to the Chilean market for which the stock was being collected. For trade was an important element in these raids. The Aucas and the Araucanians were commercial nations, intent upon their business. They had learned to desire certain Spanish products; they must have hides or live cattle or Spanish women to offer in exchange. And so the raids went on.

[9] Emilio Daireaux, *op. cit.,* p. 220.

Spain met the menace of the Indian *malón* in various ways. One of the simplest was to avoid Indian trouble by avoiding Pampas Indians. There were cattle in Uruguay; hunting could be done there. This procedure was recommended in a Cabildo record of 1717. But there were difficulties in Uruguay as well. The Minuanes Indians might not be as dangerous as the Pampas, but they were thoroughly annoying. And they were allied to the Portuguese of Colonia, to the Jesuit Mission Indians, and to the Spanish deserters, all of whom were illegally chasing Buenos Aires' cattle in the land. Thus, in 1721, there was note of the many vagabond peons living in the Banda Oriental country. Since they had no known legal employment, it was to be feared that they were allied with the Portuguese of Colonia and that they were aiding them in their evil work. And more. Many of these Spaniards were said to be living with the Guenoas Indians married after their fashion, "and the rest can be deduced."[10]

One, Delgado, was sent with fifty soldiers to investigate. He reported that it was the policy of the Minuanes to annoy any legitimate cattle hunters sent over from Buenos Aires and to discourage their further visits. His report of May, 1721, tells of his suspicious distrust of these Indians and of their discourtesy:

There they were . . . under the orders of their two caciques, Sipe and Oloya, who received the said military detachment with evil grace and such actions as pulling the nose of a former ensign of the said detachment . . . slapping two soldiers of the said detachment, taking his hat away from a soldier named Batata, and using reins to whip away a settler named Polanco—one of those who went along with me. They also took from Corporal Quadra the cap he was wearing and they did other things just as though they were seeking a motive and an occasion to break the peace, so that they might succeed in accomplishing what they had plotted among themselves. And all to hinder the said detachment in its work because of their gratitude to the Portuguese, just as I told Your Excellency in my letters. For these Portuguese keep them well bribed with continual presents of coarse woolen cloth, hats, swords, caps, tobacco, and aguardiente, which they are constantly giving them so that they will serve as an advance guard in preventing the reconnoitering of our detachments and so they may be able to work unhindered. . . . These Indians are not the ones who get the hides for the Portuguese, because they are a highly lazy, vagabond people according to my observations and what I have been told about them. Neither do the Portuguese get these hides themselves, because they are people *who are not skilled in this work.*[11] They only get them through the work of the natives of these provinces, who, because of the greater earnings to be gotten there, hire themselves out to the Portuguese of Colonia.

Delgado goes on to recommend the removal of the Minuanes Indians to some other region, because they are protecting these Spanish criminals: "From all these provinces many Christian persons, who wish to live without God, King, or Law, come to live with the Minuanes; their

[10] Buenos Aires, Archivo national, *Acuerdos,* IV, Jan., 1721.

[11] Such a report would seem to indicate that the gaucho type probably did not originate among the Portuguese.

land has become a very den of wickedness." Things, however, were at such a pass that the Indians judged themselves to have such sovereign rights over the cattle that only by paying them might a Spaniard go about his work.[12]

Enclosed with Delgado's report was a *Memorial* on cattle-hunting conditions by one Escovar y Chiclana. He told how the Guinoas joined his party when they were at their work and made that work impossible. So many were their extortions and so heavy was the tribute they collected that the Spaniards were forced to retire:

> There are no funds to support the continual contribution of yerba and tobacco, to say nothing of the theft of the horses and the vexations to which we are submitted. When they had no respect for fifty armed men (here Escovar y Chiclana refers to Delgado's expedition), just consider, Your Excellency, what they will probably do to unarmed working men and with how much more reason we are forced to strip ourselves of all our possessions so they will allow us to go on working. Such is their persistence in begging that when there is nothing to give them, they drive as many horses aside as they wish and take them away without our daring to say a word in their defense.[13]

When potential Spanish conquistadores admittedly submitted to such Indian treatment, it is obvious that cattle hunting had its difficulties even in Uruguay.

The Minuanes seem to have been not only brazen in their disregard of Spaniards and of Spanish hunting licenses, but they were succinctly explicit in their replies[14] when anyone attempted to persuade them to guard their fields for His Catholic Majesty and to give no cattle to his enemies. They replied "that rather they *would* give them away, because it was thanks to the Portuguese and French that they had clothes to wear and it was thanks to the Tapes Indians that they had yerba and tobacco, and so they would never keep them from those fields nor from their cattle."[15]

But despite all such annoyances, the Banda Oriental offered a relatively safe hunting ground and made possible a temporary Spanish obliviousness to the Pampas Indians on the southern frontier. When those Indians turned from attacks on Spanish wild cattle to attacks on the tame cattle on frontier estancias—and to incidental capture of Spanish women and children—a Spanish dignified withdrawal to the Banda Oriental was no longer possible. Active defense was necessary. A line of frontier forts was built; companies of soldiers were raised to man

---

[12] Buenos Aires, Archivo nacional, *Acuerdos*, IV, May 23, 1721.
[13] *Ibid.*
[14] These Minuanes seem to have been as forthright as that little old woman witch doctor among the Abipones. An unregenerate sinner during a long life, the worthy church fathers urged confession and repentance before death so that the Devil might not carry her away forever. She is reputed to have answered dryly, and scandalously, that she had no fear of the Devil, "having been long acquainted with him!"
[15] Buenos Aires, Archivo general, *Acuerdos,* IV, March, 1722.

them; little frontier settlements sprang up. A definite frontier line was drawn against the Indian.

But that frontier line never did separate Spaniard from Indian. It served to mark where retreat was safe, rather than to denote where advance was inadvisable. Cattle hunters, visiting Indians, discontented Spaniards, crossed almost at will. And, as in the north, the mixing of races on the frontier, the cattle hunt, and the opportunity to dispose of hides in trade led to the rise of an independent, outlaw, gaucho class. Because of the wars which made this frontier, and because of the relative importance of the ethnic factor there, a summary of Spanish-Indian relations may well be in order.

The first Spanish defensive move against the oncoming Indian was to raise funds for the protection of frontier settlers. Funds were needed for soldiers and for the building of forts and defensive settlements. Early voluntary gifts did not suffice. Since there were no available royal funds upon which to draw and since the Buenos Aires municipality was too poor to have available funds of its own, in 1745 it was decided to levy a tax of one real on all transport carts entering Buenos Aires— or four reales, if their owners were not of the community. Ten mules were rated as the equivalent of one of these carretas and taxed accordingly. In 1746 a tax was levied on salt. In 1752 came still new taxes —one real on every hide shipped to Spain and one peso on each hundred weight of iron, or similar heavy goods, leaving Buenos Aires for the interior provinces. Later in the same year, twelve reales were levied on each jug or skin of wine or aguardiente entering the city, provided that they were "in good condition" upon their arrival. From these taxes an annual revenue of thirty-two thousand pesos was anticipated.

Now with funds in hand, local Spanish officials proceeded to the business of defense. The first essential was to put soldiers on the frontier. In 1751 the Cabildo agreed to the establishment of two or three companies to serve as a frontier guard. One such company of fifty men was put to work, but funds were still insufficient to provide for any more. The new taxes of 1752 made possible the other two companies of these professional soldiers, *blandengues*. Their duties were to garrison the frontiers, to reconnoitre the countryside, to act as convoy to those trade caravans passing through to the Upper Provinces. Three forts were established at Sanjón, El Salto, and Luxán. In 1779 the number of forts was increased to five, and two more companies of blandengues were added to man them. In the intervals between the forts were built little forts, *fortines*.[16] Twelve men of the country

---

[16] The forts were located at Chascomus, San Miguel del Monte, Luxán, Salto, and Roxas; the posts, at Las Lagunas de los Ranchos, Lobos, Nabarro, and Areco.

militia served as the guard of each little post; they served without pay "save for the usual rations." Generally these twelve men were highly unhappy in their work and frequently they ran off to join their Indian enemies, thus bettering their lot.

As Buenos Aires grew and more land was needed for its people and livestock, the frontier bulged to meet that need. By the time of Viceroy Vértiz it measured 155 leagues in length and was run from Chascomus to Esquina, where Córdoba's jurisdiction began.[17]

In view of their limited numbers and the amount of territory they were supposed to cover, the work of the frontier soldiers was remarkably well done, though there were occasional damaging records, such as that of 1754 when an Indian band slyly stole the horses of the military guard of El Salto fort. Occasional failure of the frontier guard may be explained by such frontier conditions as those reflected in a letter by one Mariano Billinghurst, written to General Mitre in 1863. That these conditions were true of early times as well as of the midnineteenth century period may be gathered from many an individual soldier's complaint when he found himself drafted to this slave labor of the frontier. Billinghurst queried:

> What is . . . the reason why our countryside is abandoned? My dear general . . . it is because they are deceiving you; because they review such and such a number of men who exist only on their musters and whose salary passes into the pockets of the officers in charge of the land's defense. It is because everything is thought of, save fighting the Indian or securing the frontier. Instead, (they think) of the estancias of those same commanders, who grow rich upon the money and the labor won from the public treasury and who heed neither the lament of their fellow citizens who are robbed, nor the prestige and honor of the government which pays them.[18]

And if the lot of the blandengue was hard, that of the wretched frontier militiaman was worse. Drafted against his will, unpaid, kept in the army beyond all legal expectancy—it was no wonder that he frequently ran away to kindlier Indian lands.

Along the interprovincial highways, posthouses were established, where travelers might stay the night and fresh horses could be hired for one's journey. They, too, were necessarily fortified against the Indian. Samuel Haigh tells of such a typical post in 1831. Prickly pears, which grow to the height of from twenty-five to thirty feet, were planted close together, and within this enclosure the inhabitants of the hamlet sheltered themselves. Since Indian horses were not taught to jump, a ditch was frequently dug around these defenses to serve as added protection; it had its medieval drawbridge. Usually armed only with bows and arrows and with their eighteen-foot lances, a small group

[17] Buenos Aires, Archivo general, *Revista,* III, 412.
[18] *Archivo del General Mitre,* XXIII, 30.

of naked Indians would have difficulty in making any impression upon these prickly "vegetable forts"; it was impossible for either horse or man to break through them. The corrals, however, were outside, and the livestock was easily captured.[19]

Besides its military guard and the line of forts, a third weapon of frontier defense was the frontier settlement. Isolated estancias proved dangerous once the Indian raids were on, and settlers either retreated back to town, abandoning the countryside, or they moved to the vicinity of the three forts established in 1752 with the blandengues as their settlers. The Cabildo record of May, 1752, had noted that it would be unreasonable to expect the new soldiers to remain always at the mercy of the inclemency of the weather and with no base of supplies where they might easily obtain "the provisions for human life." The new resultant frontier fort settlements were to serve for the protection of all the estancias of the jurisdiction, as soldier patrols went from fort to fort. At each settlement housing provision must be made, for frontier soldiers took their women along to look after them. Also there must be a chapel and a dwelling near by for a religious. So a frontier fort gradually became a town.

Besides Spanish defensive cruelty and the active Spanish defense of soldier, fort, and town, there were still other means of combating Indian aggression. Warnings from the Spanish authorities of Chile, telling of impending invasion, were one means of protection.[20] Indian raids were often directly related to Spanish attacks in Chile upon Indians who hastily took refuge elsewhere. So in 1723 a Cabildo record reads: "Some misfortune can now be reasonably anticipated, because, since the Señor President of Chile has undertaken a chastisement of the Auca Indians of that realm, their only recourse is to turn to our land and the slopes of the cordillera."[21]

Another defense measure lay in the peace treaties made with the Indians. These might also be classified under Indian trade. In return for hides and women, Indians got aguardiente; similarly were they so rewarded when they agreed to stay away from Spanish estancias and Spanish livestock. They might also be asked to return previously stolen property as was the case in 1732 in Uruguay. When the return of certain Spanish horses was suggested, the Indians demurred. They needed the horses; they had won them "en buena guerra." Persuasion prevailed, however: "All were given yerba, tobacco, beads, knives, and bridles, and the caciques received hats and canes and woolen cloth, so

[19] Samuel Haigh. *Sketches of Buenos Aires, Chile and Peru* (London, 1831), p. 60.
[20] There are Cabildo records of such warnings in February, 1754, July, 1758, and May, 1773.
[21] Buenos Aires, Archivo general, *Acuerdos,* Sept., 1723.

that all were well content and satisfied."[22]   In Buenos Aires an Indian peace was purchased in 1742.   Again, in 1788, there is an optimistic Cabildo note of an "inalterable peace" with the Indians.   It is to keep them from invading as they were wont to do in former years.   By 1861 Indian peace seems to have become legitimate Indian business.   One such successful businessman was Chingoleo.   The Spanish version of his success reads: "The present treaty with Chingoleo is the most shocking thing.   The government gives rations, clothing, and pay for some eighty Indians, and never are more than thirty to be seen, including the women and children.   But Chingoleo gets drunk, gambles at *monte,* and runs horseraces, in all of which he loses considerable sums."[23]

A final Spanish method of dealing with the Indians involved their use as allies.   Thus individual Indians won Spanish favor—and Spanish presents—by warning of the approach of their fellows.   Tribe was balanced against tribe, thereby weakening the strength of both.[24]   One amusing method of gaining Indian allies was the Cabildo's solemn adoption of an Indian son, who was to be educated to become a more proper cacique than his peers.   This was a comparatively late development.[25]

That Indian allies reversed matters and frequently used Spaniards for their own private ends, is also evident from the records.   Indian offers to aid their friends, the Spaniards, against invading British soldiers may not have been as ingenuous as they seemed to startled Spaniards.   Indians who guarded Spanish expeditions to the salt lakes, or who aided in the advance of the frontier forts, were not acting purely

[22] *Ibid.,* March, 1732.   [23] *Archivo del General Mitre,* XXII, 80.
[24] Similarly, in the midnineteenth century, General Rosas, remembering that present Indian allies might be future enemies, placed Indian friends in the front ranks of his armies, where their deaths would serve as guarantee of greater future safety, even as their lives served his present need.
[25] The Cabildo record of December, 1808, reveals how the commander of an expedition into the Indian land was to ask the several caciques for some children.   The plan was to bring them to Buenos Aires, where they were to be converted, baptized, and educated.   These, presently civilized, youths would then be returned to their tribes where their example would serve to banish barbarity and ignorance forever.
The plan was not successful.   Available Indian children were lamentably hard to find. The caciques made the general reply that separation from their children was very painful. However, the Chilean Indian, Juan Pedro, consented to surrender a little son of his, a boy of some ten to eleven years of age.   The Cabildo record of his reception reads:
"Deseosos de realizar las miras que siempre se han propuesto de atraer a sociedad y religión los referidos indios, y con especialidad los caciques . . . creyendo que la adopción de sus pequeños hijos es el medio más oportuno para que se realice así, acordaron: adopar [*sic*] como adoptan por hijo de este Excelentisimo Cavildo al joven Casique.   Y mandaron que por el tesorero de propios se le hagan dos vestuarios completos, uno pequeño y otro grande de Cadete de Artilleros de la Unión. . . .   Para evitar que por contagio de viruelas se exponga este joven, determinaron igualmente que se le bacune, y aun que se cure del achaque de la vista de que al presente adolece."
His name was to be Juan Ignacio de Buenos Aires.
Later in that month of December, 1808, the Cabildo received its first bill for Juan Ignacio —202 pesos 4¾ reales, for his uniforms, shoes, and the other things made for him.   In October, 1809, another bill was presented for 17 pesos 7 reales, "for the amount spent in clothes, shoes and laundry of the little Indian, Juan Ignacio de Buenos Aires."
And then Juan Ignacio vanishes from the records.   One cannot help but wonder as to his fate.

from friendship and generosity.   The Pampas Indians were traders; they expected a fair return for their favors.[26]

A final Spanish measure of defense against Indian attack was the direct measure of supplying the Indians with the aguardiente they desired.   It had been at the root of much of the whole trouble.   Spanish cattle and Spanish women had been captured largely to be offered in exchange.   Interprovincial trade had been sadly hampered.   San Juan mules, with their loads, ran especial risks; they frequently and mysteriously disappeared.[27]

[26] Cabildo records of Indian offers of aid against the British make amusing reading.   They begin in August, 1806, when the Pampa Indian Felipe called personally upon the Cabildo.

"Venía a nombre de diez y seis Casiques de los Pampas y Cheguelches a hacer presente que estaban prontos a franquear gente, cavallos y quantos auxilios dependiesen de su arbitrio, para que este I. C. hechase mano de ellos contra los Colorados, cuio nombre dió a los Ingleses; que hacían aquella ingenua oferta en obsequio a los cristianos, y por que veían los apuros en que estarían; que también franquearían gente para conducir a los ingleses tierra adentro si se necesitaba; y que tendrían mucho gusto en que se les ocupase contra unos hombres tan malos como los Colorados."

Their Excellencies, the members of the Cabildo, expressed their thanks for this offer, begged that Felipe express their satisfaction to his fellow caciques, said that they would take advantage of their kindness should the need arise.   Then they ordered that Felipe be given *3 barrels of aguardiente and a tercio of yerba.*   It had worked.

One month later Felipe was back again, with his friend, the Pampa Cacique Catemilla.   Catemilla expressed "el sentimiento que él y sus gentes havian tenido por la perdida de la ciudad y el contento por la reconquista de que daba la enorabuena; ratificó la oferta de gente y cavallos que a nombre de diez y seis casiques havía hecho el indio Felipe; y expuso que sólo con objeto de proteger a los cristianos contra los colorados, con alución a los ingleses, havían hecho paces con los ranqueles, con quienes estaban en dura guerra, bajo la obligación éstos de guardar los terrenos desde las salinas hasta Mendoza, e impedir por aquella parte qualquier insulto a los cristianos; haviéndose obligado el exponente con los demás Pampas a hacer lo propio en toda la costa del sur hasta Patagones."

When the members of the Cabildo had heard this so admirable offer and had taken note of a procedure so worthy of the greatest appreciation, they gave Catemilla a present of yerba and aguardiente.

Two months later came ten Pampas caciques.   They entered, were seated, and their interpreter spoke as follows:

"A los hijos del Sol; a los que tan largas noticias tenemos de lo que han executado en mantener estos reinos; a los que gloriosamente havéis hechado a esos colorados de vuestra casa, que lograron tomar por una desgracia; a vosotros que sois los Padres de la Patria, venimos personalmente a manifestaros nuestra gratitud, no obstante que por nuestros diferentes embiados os tenemos ofrecido quantos auxilios y recursos nos acompañan: Hemos querido conoceros por nuestros ojos, y llevamos el gusto de haverlo conseguido; y pues reunidos en esta grande habitación donde igualmente vemos a nuestros reies, en su presencia y no satisfechos de las embajadas que os tenemos hechas, os ofrecemos nuevamente reunidos todos los grandes casiques que veis, hasta el número de veinte mil de nuestros súbditos, todos gente de guerra y cada qual con cinco cavallos; queremos sean los primeros a embestir a esos colorados que parece aun os quieren incomodar.   Nada os pedimos por todo esto y más que haremos en vuestro obsequio; todo os es debido, pues que nos havéis libertado, que tras de vosotros siguieran en nuestra busca; tendremos mucha vigilancia rechazarlos por nuestras costas donde contamos con maior número de gente que el que os llevamos ofrecido: nuestro reconocimiento en la buena acogida que dais a nuestros frutos, y permiso libre con que sacamos lo que necesitamos es lo bastante a recompensarnos con este pequeño servicio; mandad sin recelo, ocupad la sinceridad de nuestros corazones, y ésta será la maior prueba y consuelo que tendremos; así lo esperamos executaréis, y será perpetuo vuestro nombre en lo más remoto de nuestros súbditos, que a una voz claman por vuestra felicidad, que deseamos sea perpetua en la unión que os juramos."

Their Excellencies, the members of the Cabildo, proceeded to embrace the ten caciques, "que manifestaron mucho contento en ello."   And the ten caciques received their presents.

In that same month there came three more caciques.   But they were less eloquent and more naïve.   They told how they had been "instruídos . . . del mucho agazajo" of the Cabildo to their friends.   Despite this confession, they received presents in turn.   Then follow many Cabildo records of bills for Indian presents and accounts of Indians who protest because their presents have not been delivered or paid in full.   Other gifts are added to the list, especially, and appropriately, nice red English coats.   Finally, by December, 1808, came Cacique Uchimán.

"And since the object of this attention was none other than to claim some present, their Excellencies ordered that he be given 34 pesos fuertos."

The Cabildo had finally "caught on."

[27] In the Cabildo record of December, 1744.   "Estos mismos indios en el camino de Las

Realizing its baneful influence, in 1747 certain priests had threat-
ened with excommunication those who sold aguardiente to Indians. But
this was most unwise. The error was stressed in a letter to the Cabildo
from the *maestro de campo,* who was apparently a realist, and one
acquainted with Indians: "The said prohibition is entirely displeasing
to the said Indians, and for this reason they may well break the peace
which we enjoy at present."[28] He then begs that the said excommunication in this matter of aguardiente be abandoned. He notes that
in Chile and the other provinces, selling liquor to Indians or permitting
it to be sold is current practice, for by that means may friendship and
quiet be obtained. The same system has been employed in the province
of Buenos Aires, and it has led to Spanish advance information of
hostile movements inland. And he again mentions as highly probable
the end of the peace which has meant serenity to the frontier settlers.
A month later this warning was repeated by the *alcalde de primer voto,*
with a list of the dire consequences which would result were the Indians
denied their aguardiente.[29] Apparently the warning was heeded, for
there is no further mention of excommunication.

On the contrary, the Cabildo itself gives gifts of aguardiente to its
favored Indians. This was a common practice in the English invasion
time and still later, when the frontier was being advanced and Indian
aid was sought. But it was done early as well. Less than twenty
years after the excommunication scare, there is a record of such a gift.
Cacique Lepin has proposed to the Cabildo that he collect his family,
friends, and allies—as many as seven hundred Indians, he says—and
fight the Tehuelches. May his Indians please leave their families at the
Laguna Salada while they are about this business, and will the Cabildo
give him a little yerba and tobacco and some aguardiente to be used
for purposes of the war council? The Cabildo remembered that the

Pulgas mataron a algunos pasageros que benian de la ciudad de San Juan con tropa de mulas
cargadas de aguardiente y . . . en esta jurisdicción se han bendido algunas mulas de dicha
tropa por dichos indios. . . . Algunos de dichos peones no paresen."
    The aguardiente, as well, had disappeared.
    [28] Buenos Aires, Archivo general, *Acuerdos,* July, 1747.
    [29] "El negárseles a los indios la bebida ceda [*sic*] en perjuicio del Reyno, pues por lo
acostumbrado que están a ella, no pudiéndola de otra suerte conseguir, sucitarán la guerra y
atajarán en los caminos de Mendoza y San Juan las carretas que conduzen estas bebidas para
el abasto de esta ciudad, con notable perjuicio y agravio del vecindario. . . .
    "A esto se agregó, que en el tratado de pazes que se celebró con los indios se extipuló
el que pudiesen comerciar libremente, trayendo perdizes, plumeros, lomillos, riendas, y lazos,
rayzes de teñir, y sobre camas, piedras bezales, cavallos mansos, y todos diversos efectos, que
continuamente entran en esta ciudad, y pudiesen sacar de ella los que nescesitasen para su
manutención y fuera tásitamente faltarles a lo extipulado si se les negase oy la bebida, objeto
principal de sus continuas venidas. . . .
    "Finalmente con no negarse a los indios las bebidas se consigue la mayor frequencia de
ellos con los christianos, y de ésta la mayor sociabilidad y poderse mejor reducir a la fee, y
de lo contrario se experimentarán infaliblemente no sólo los daños de guerra que se han
ponderado, y a que se halla esta ciudad expuesta, si no también que faltando el comercio de
los españoles con los indios se prive este vecindario del abasto de efectos que continuamente
introducen, y de las noticias de los otros indios bravos y de tierra adentro para las prevenciones
de armas en caso de alguna sublebación."
    Buenos Aires, Archivo general, *Acuerdos,* Aug., 1747.

Tehuelches, from the Patagonian land south of the Río Negro, were those making the last attack on the province of Buenos Aires, that it was eminently fitting that they receive punishment for this past sinning as well as a warning for the future. Cacique Lepin received his requested supplies.[30]

The important element in the whole active Spanish-Indian frontier relationship was the resultant foundation of a new class of society. This class originated in the Spaniards—and especially the Spanish women—captured by the Indians, the dissatisfied soldier-settlers of the frontier, the outlaws of Spanish society seeking escape from Spanish justice. In view of the relatively small number of the Pampas Indians, the gauchos resulting from the new outlaw mestizo race were of great importance. To be sure, a parallel development of such a class took place wherever were found the essential elements of a Spanish-Indian race mixing, the cattle hunt, and a possible outlaw living to be earned through trade in hides. Conditions had been found most favorable on the Banda Oriental, where Spanish justice had been absent, where friendly Indians favored rapid racial intermarriage, where international contraband provided an ideal background for illegal trade, and where cows were even more plentiful than on the Buenos Aires plains. But gauchos developed in Buenos Aires province as well. A similar class was also to be found on the western frontier, notably at Santa Fe. Its comparative unimportance there, as compared with the frontiers of the south and north, was due to the relative lack of cattle on the land to the west and northwest and to the relative lack of opportunity to dispose of the hides commercially. Santa Fe, because of its cattle hunts in Entre Ríos, proved an exception, and our new class is to be found there as well. Because it *was* new—in its usual Indian racial mixture, in its emphasis on the cattle hunt rather than on cattle care, in the illegality of its work—it received a new name which differentiated it from the kindred class of Spanish vaqueros.

The importance of the Pampas frontier in the creation of the gaucho has generally been understressed. The development in Uruguay was on a grander scale, a more spectacular scene. The presence of foreign danger fastened Spanish attention upon the Banda Oriental, even as foreign attention was attracted by the commercial and political opportunities presented by the region. More travelers came to investigate opportunities in Uruguay, wrote their impressions of the country; the mere relative weight of records has favored the northern region. In their study of the gaucho class, historians have been too prone to neglect the parallel developments on the southern and western frontiers. Particularly on the Pampas frontier racial intermixture was much greater

[30] *Ibid.*, Oct., 1766.

than is generally believed. It is true that the Pampas Indian did not settle down in friendly communion with the Spaniards. But in comparison with the few Pampas Indians, the number of captive Spanish women and the number of soldier-deserters were relatively large. Cow hunters, illegally at their work, continuously crossed frontier lines as well.

The Indians of Argentina probably never numbered over 250,000.[31] If one subtracts from this number the Indians of the northwest provinces and the Tierra del Fuego tribes and makes allowance for the havoc wrought by Spanish disease, the number of Pampas Indians on the frontier by 1737 must have been relatively small. Azara believed that they had at most 400 warriors,[32] though this may be an exaggeration in the other direction. Dr. Martin de Moussy, in 1860, estimated their number at 3,000.[33] Mansilla, in 1870, believed that the Ranqueles numbered from 8,000 to 10,000, but this figure included the women and children and from 600 to 800 captives.[34] In the 1860's General Antonio Taboada offered as his guess 6,000 fighting men, counting Araucanos, Ranqueles, Peguenches, Tehuelches, and a few others.[35] Since the Indians were everywhere on the decrease, the General's figure would seem to indicate a considerable gaucho sprinkling among the Indians by that period.

While all these figures involve uncertain estimates, it appears certain that the Pampas Indians were relatively few in number when they began their raids on the Spanish frontiers. Those numbers doubtless appeared greater to the Spaniard than they really were. Pampas Indians moved around; they could be counted in many a locality during the course of a year; their whole war technique consisted in raiding and returning to raid again. And the Pampas Indians did no inconsiderable amount of damage.

On the other hand, the number of Spaniards captured by the Indians was relatively large. Adequate figures are lacking, but the big November, 1740, raid on Magdalena netted the Indians over 100 captives[36] according to the most conservative estimate, and the Cabildo records year after year keep noting raids with their new captives. The religious of the Mercedarian order made it their business to collect alms for the pious purpose of redeeming captives, and whenever the funds of the War Department were not needed for war, they, also, were used in the ransom of captives. Peace treaties with the Indians always

[31] J. Fred Rippy, in A. Curtis Wilgus (ed.), *Argentina, Brazil and Chile since Independence* (Washington, D. C., 1935), p. 43.
[32] Quoted in Alexander Caldcleugh, *Travels in South America during the years 1819-1820-1821* (London, 1825), II, 362.
[33] Thomas Joseph Hutchinson, *The Paraná* . . . , p. 216 n.
[34] Mansilla, *op. cit.*, p. 458.   [35] Hutchinson, *op. cit.*, p. 216.
[36] This was the earliest estimate. By July, 1741, the number has reputedly doubled.

included a provision for the return of captives. Yet as late as 1861, many captive Spanish women are still reported in the power of the Indians and from 1860 dates a list of ten, all named, in the power of one Indian chieftain, Calfucura. Even the Indians met on their return from the invasion in the 1870's, spoke contentedly of the many women they had captured.[37] And Mansilla's proportion of 600 to 800 captives in the number of the 8,000 to 10,000 Ranqueles indicates no inconsiderable race mixture, since the Indian took only women and children as captives.

Neither should the number of deserters from the Spanish frontier posts be treated with casual disregard. Frontier troubles of 1766 were largely due to the fact that the frontier guard had deserted *en masse*. So unpopular was the frontier line that a law was passed to the effect that any vagrant might be sentenced to join the army, and only in this way could that army be filled.[38] Once in the army, it was almost impossible to get out. The legal length of service was forgotten or disregarded. The frontier militiamen, whether drafted men or sentenced vagrants, were unpaid save for the food they supposedly received. Instead of doing the military duty for which they came, they were put to what amounted to slave labor on the frontier estancias of the commanders. To supply the food they did not receive, regulations to the contrary, they left their forts and went hunting in the Indian land. To earn such essentials as clothing, they collected cattle hides or ostrich feathers, the two frontier commodities which could be offered for sale. Desertion was the only real salvation. And deserters were plentiful. Thus the Cabildo record of November, 1815, reports that the priest of Los Lobos has written requesting a supply of guns "in order to capture the deserters."[39] He has added that these guns are badly needed.

Besides the Spanish captive woman and the Spanish deserter soldier, there was a third class of Spaniards to be found living with the Indian. This class was formed of outlaws, many of whom, of course, might belong in the second class as well. They earned their living by illegal cattle hunts; they lived with the Indian and aided him in his raids in return for his protection; or they might continue to live among their Spanish fellows and just go calling upon Indian friends when occasion arose. In fact, it was largely due to this intercourse across the frontier line that Indian raids were successful. Indians learned where Spanish guards might be found absent, and when Spanish re-

---

[37] Buenos Aires, Sociedad científica argentina, *Anales*, I, 196.
[38] Real Ordenanza, April, 1745. Its provisions became constantly more severe. See the *Auto de buen gobierno* of Cisneros in 1809 (quoted in *Colección de papeles públicos*, X) and the laws of August, 1815, and July, 1823 (Álvarez, *Estudio*, pp. 99, 102). For the general attitude behind this legislation, see, in *Colección de papeles públicos*, VI, such articles as those of August 4, 11, and 18, 1810.
[39] Buenos Aires, Archivo general, *Acuerdos*, Nov., 1815.

taliatory expeditions were scheduled for an Indian raid. So serious did the matter become that it was suggested that a life penalty be exacted of anyone caught communicating or trading with infidel Indians.[40]

Such traders and hide hunters were far more dangerous to Spanish interests than the Indian himself. In the Cabildo record of 1812, when the Indians were reported to have offered to turn over the deserters who were living in their *tolderías,* the record adds: ". . . and they are the authors of the largest part of the thefts and the damage done on our haciendas."[41] Again in 1816 there is mention of "the continual and considerable thefts of cattle and horses committed by those who, under the pretext of Indian trade, enter those fields for their clandestine cattle slaughters and the collection of hides, tallow, and fat."[42] These changadores are mentioned in the Cabildo records as early as 1748 and 1751. Presently they were to become known as gauchos.

The most complete pictures of the southern frontier are to be found in José Hernández' *Martín Fierro* and in Lucio Victorio Mansilla's report of his visit with the Ranqueles. The frontier line portrayed in these works was far from rigid. Spaniard and Indian crossed it at will; renegade Spaniard led Indian raid. Many a Spanish woman was found married to an Indian lord and many a Spaniard to an Indian mistress. From this kind of society came that usually mestizo, vagabond, cow hunter—known as the gaucho.

[40] Vértiz, "Memoria." See Buenos Aires, Archivo general, *Revista del Archivo general,* III, 421.
[41] Buenos Aires, Archivo general, *Acuerdos,* Jan., 1812.
[42] *Ibid.,* Feb., 1816.

☙ 7 ❧

The Gaucho in War

Such economic advantage as society might have derived from the cheap prices of contraband trade, was nullified when, in 1809, Viceroy Cisneros passed a decree[1] making possible direct and open trade with Europe. Contraband was transformed into legitimate work. Not only was many a gaucho left without any adequate opportunity to earn his dishonest living, but his usefulness to society seemed as definitely terminated. But at the precise historical moment when, with the loss of its economic usefulness, the gaucho class seemed doomed, there arose a new demand for service. The need was so urgent, and the gaucho so efficient in its satisfaction, that society's disreputable outlaws at once became its defenders. The first half of the nineteenth century was a period of war in the Plata lands; the gaucho proved to be spectacularly useful as a cavalryman.[2]

The gaucho enjoyed war. To him it was a pleasantly exhilarating experience, one with promise of booty to be easily won. It was a social

[1] Juan Álvarez, *Estudio sobre las guerras civiles argentinas* (Buenos Aires, 1914), pp. 96, 97.

[2] Much has already been written on the gaucho role in war, but there has been little consideration of its importance in the social redemption of a previously scorned class of society.

For general documentary material, see the *Partes oficiales y documentos relativos a la guerra de la independencia argentina*, edited by the Archivo general of the Argentine Republic (2d ed., 4 vols., Buenos Aires, 1900-1903); the *Documentos y correspondencia* of the Museo Mitre of Buenos Aires (28 vols., Buenos Aires, 1911); and William Ray Manning (ed.), *Diplomatic correspondence of the United States. Inter-American affairs*, I (Washington, 1932).

For a consideration of gaucho war technique, see Leopoldo Lugones, *La guerra gaucha* (2d ed., Buenos Aires, 1926), Clemente L. Fregeiro, "San Martín, Guido y la espedición a Chile y el Perú" (*Nueva revista de Buenos Aires*, IV, 291-315). For the gaucho role in the caudillo period, see Lucas Ayarragaray, *La anarquía argentina y el caudillismo* (2d ed., Buenos Aires, 1925), and José Manuel Estrada, *Fragmentos históricos* (Buenos Aires, 1901) and *Lecciones sobre la historia de la República Argentina* (Buenos Aires, 1898). Excellent general studies of the gaucho role in war are those by Bartolomé Mitre, *Historia de Belgrano y de la independencia argentina* (3 vols., Buenos Aires, 1887) and *Historia de San Martín y de la emancipación* (4 vols., Buenos Aires, 1890), and by John Miller, *Memorias del General Miller* (Madrid, 1829).

For the several regions of the Plata, see such works as those by Eduardo Acevedo Díaz, *El mito del Plata* (Buenos Aires, 1917), and by Víctor Arreguine, *Estudios históricos* (Montevideo, 1913) and *Los orientales. Tierra salvaje* (Buenos Aires, 1924) for material on Uruguay; on Corrientes, see Captain Richard Francis Burton, *Letters from the battlefields of Paraguay* (London, 1870); on the southern Brazilian frontier, see Castilhos Goycochea, *A alma heroica das coxilhas* (Rio de Janeiro, 1935). For accounts of gaucho warfare in Upper Tucumán, and especially of the gauchos of Güemes, see José Coroleu, *América. Historia de su colonización, dominación e independencia* (Barcelona, 1895), Bernardo Frías, *Historia de Güemes y de la provincia de Salta* (3 vols., Salta, 1902; Buenos Aires, 1907; Salta, 1911), Andrés García Camba, *Memorias del General García Camba para la historia de las armas españolas en el Perú, 1809-1821* (Madrid, 1916), and General José María Paz, *Memorias póstumas* (2d ed., Buenos Aires, 1917).

occasion as well—like a game.   To invite gauchos to a war was like calling to the Tartars.

And well might the gaucho succeed in war.   Psychologically and physically, he was qualified.   Indifferent to death, a fatalist, brave to absurdity, combative—no career could be better adapted to his nature. In his new social role of soldier, he eagerly experienced those emotions he loved.   He rode, fought, killed, plundered.   Moreover, in war he had a cause to invoke as he destroyed.   This was especially true in the wars of independence, where the gaucho's enemy was the hated stranger, ever despicable through ignorance of such fine arts as throwing a lasso, of breaking a horse, of throwing a bull, or of skillful knife play.

The gaucho manner of life served him well in his new career.   He had always lived on the pampas, and he was the master of his environment.   He needed no guide to find his way in the wilderness.   He knew where water could be found.   If he felt the need of shelter, he knew how to build it on the plains.   When the gaucho became a soldier, he did not have to alter his life greatly; he merely changed from a hunter of cows to a hunter of worthier game—his fellow man.   Two great elements for war were everywhere at hand—the cow for food, the horse for mobility.   With the sun for a guide, the ordinary tools of its work for arms, saddle cloths for a bed, a gaucho army became as independent as any in the world.   Army supply lists usually involved only luxuries— yerba mate, tobacco, and possibly aguardiente.   The gaucho cared for his own necessities.

So the gaucho fought the Plata wars.   He fought for independence from Spain in the Banda Oriental and in Salta; he accompanied San Martín to Chile and Peru.   He fought with Artigas for Uruguayan independence from Spain, from autocratic Buenos Aires, and from Brazil.   He fought the war in Paraguay.   Gauchos followed their caudillo gaucho leaders in all the little local wars of the long first half of the nineteenth century, until gaucho Urquiza had vanquished gaucho Rosas, and government might be constitutionally organized at last. Finally, it was the gaucho who fought the Indian.

Of all these wars, possibly the one of greatest importance was the war of independence fought in the upper provinces of Tucumán, and notably, in Salta.   Here it was, according to Generals Paz and San Martín, that the gaucho first won the honor of society, and the name of gaucho finally changed from insult to compliment.   Well might this be true.   The fact that Spain had defeated the moves for independence everywhere in all South America save in Upper Peru, fixed the attention of Hispanic America upon that battlefield.   On such a stage, the gauchos of Salta under their gaucho leader, Güemes, successfully harassed the invading royalists and forced their retreat.   One specific gaucho cavalry charge won the important battle of Tucumán, when royalist horses turned tail and, fleeing before horridly flapping guardamontes,[3] carried their royalist riders with them right out of the battle.   But more important than any individual battle was the lengthy and unsuccessful occupation of the royalist troops in the Tucumán region, with their consequent absence elsewhere.   Not only were these royalists kept from advancing down into the Argentine plains, but royalist concentration in Upper Peru gave time for Hispanic American organization for a renewal of the struggle in other regions.[4]

The success of the gaucho forces in Salta was highly dramatic. Spanish generals began with statements of scorn of the uncouth hordes they found opposing them—a scorn, incidentally, which was shared by the more orthodox Hispanic American generals themselves.   Gauchos were still regarded as the "scum of society" in Hispanic America, even in Hispanic American armies.   They were notoriously hard to discipline. If they found conditions in an army unsatisfactory, they had the execrable habit of riding "like the wind away."   General Belgrano noted despondently in his *Memoirs* that one should never make use of gauchos in war, unless finding himself in a position as difficult as that in which he had unhappily been placed.   But Belgrano never did learn how to handle gauchos.   Güemes did.

Royalist General La Serna expressed the general view—both Spanish and native—of a gaucho army, when he wrote to Güemes: "Do you, by any chance, believe that a handful of men . . . maintained by robbery, with no more order, discipline, or training than that of bandits, can successfully oppose troops trained to war and accustomed to conquer the best in Europe, and which would be insulted at being compared with these so-called gauchos?"[5]   Unfortunately for La Serna, Güemes replied in the affirmative.

The appearance of a gaucho army was uncouth.   For arms it carried lances improvised by fastening knives to the end of poles.   Many a gaucho had only his dagger, his lasso, and the bolas.   There was no army uniform; this gave a strange appearance to the army, because of the variety of colors as ponchos floated behind, flapping in the wind of a cavalry charge.   Finally, the appearance of the riders themselves was savage.   A gaucho army still resembled the outlaw horde.

Gaucho methods of warfare were highly unorthodox.   Captain Burton noted merely "gaucho soldiers . . . galloping about, banging guns

---

[3] The *guardamonte* was the South American equivalent of the North American "chaps." It was a hide guard, used to protect a rider in wooded or scrub country.
[4] For example, San Martín's preparations for his invasion of Chile and Perú were made possible by the delay won by the gauchos of Salta.
[5] See Mitre, *Belgrano*, II, 495.

and pistols in the air, shouting the Redskin 'slogan,' and foully abusing
one another's feminine relatives . . . and cutting the throats of all
prisoners after the battle."[6]   But Burton was describing a later and
more extreme development of gaucho technique than that found in the
wars of independence, even though much of his description might well
be applicable.   For example, gaucho attacks customarily began with an
"infernal shouting."   Then came the charge upon the horrified horses
of the foe, as each gaucho vigorously grasped his lance or whirled lasso
or bolas through the air at enemy bodies or at the feet of enemy horses,
and the whole troop struck its guardamontes with the whip to produce
those sharp sounds similar to shots with which they were wont to drive
their cattle.[7]   No wonder enemy horses ran a hasty retreat.   The first
official name chosen for their force by the gauchos of Güemes was
Dragones Infernales.   By the Spanish royalists, it was regarded as a
singularly appropriate selection.

But there was much more to the gaucho technique in war than mere
noise.   The thing which gave it originality was that its peculiar tactics
were identified with each combatant; they did not hinder the spontaneity
of his individual initiative even while he obeyed the design of a superior
will.   There was systematized movement in the midst of apparent dis-
order.   One plan was in the mind of all; its execution then became an
individual problem.[8]   When the numbers of a gaucho band were inferior
to those of its enemy, direct combat was avoided.   Thus the Spanish
royalists of Peru often found themselves fighting an invisible foe.   Fires
swept down upon them across the plains; wild cattle stampeded their
camps; horses mysteriously sickened and died; provisions were stolen;
lassos whisked guarding sentries away; and gaucho armies were hardly
seen before they vanished as they broke and scurried away in all direc-
tions over the plain.

The royalist General Pezuela described to the Viceroy of Peru just
how it felt to be opposed to a gaucho army:

Although considerably reinforced from Buenos Aires and the towns of
Tucumán and its vicinity, I find that the enemy does not have a sufficient force
to undertake a formal attack.   They have only from three to four thousand
gauchos, or country people, armed with steel.   I discover that their plan is not
to engage in any decisive battle anywhere, but to worry us in our positions
and movements.   In conformity with this strategy I observe that these inter-
minable woods are overrun with bands of gauchos, all of which are supported
by three hundred musketeers assigned in proportion to their number; that
under the cover of the continuous and impenetrable thickets and by dint of
being very much at home in the region, and also because they are well mounted,
they frequently dare come to the very outskirts of Salta and to exchange shots
with our divisions of no matter how respectable a size they may be; that they
unexpectedly snatch away any individual of our forces who has the imprudence
of going a block away from the plaza or the encampment . . . ; and that they

[6] Burton, *op. cit.*, p. 466.   [7] Frías, *op. cit.*, II, 543-544.   [8] Mitre, *Belgrano*, II, 514.

are endangering my communications with Salta despite the two squadrons which I keep posted in between. In one word, I find that almost with impunity to themselves, they are waging upon us a slow but troublesome and prejudicial war. The way to repress and punish these insults would be to oppose gauchos to gauchos, with the re-inforcement of a good corps of musketeers. But there is no way to do this, because even if the necessary men could be obtained, we would stumble upon the difficulty of not having any horses upon which to mount them, because almost all the horses of this region have been taken off to Tucumán, and because, in addition, they are of so little spirit and endurance that every rider needs at least three in order to be always prepared on a campaign. To all these advantages which the enemy has over us, is added another no less prejudicial; it is that of being warned, hours ahead, of our movements and plans, by means of the inhabitants of these estancias and principally by the women who are related to the people here. . . .

Pezuela goes on to emphasize the necessity of suppressing these small gaucho bands, if the places already captured are to be maintained and if the meat and bread which his troops are beginning to need, are to be procured. He also notes the ingratitude of citizens of his captured towns; they are reported to be keeping their livestock safely hidden in inaccessible thickets and ravines, away from Spaniards, so as to deprive the King's army of it, despite the willingness of that army to pay for all provisions.[9]

After this war the name of gaucho was pronounced with respect, even by his enemies. Gaucho armies might be barbaric—and they certainly were during the civil wars—but when led by a leader who knew how to handle his men, they could be highly effective. Unfortunately for the gaucho, once all the wars were fought, there was nothing left for him to do. His opportunity to achieve honor in real life was over. As an historical character, he had served eighteenth-century society through an illegal supply of society's needs. He had manned the frontier. In the nineteenth century he had played an outstanding role with Güemes in the independence period, and he had won the admiring respect of society. With Quiroga and many another caudillo in the civil wars and with Rosas in the period of the Tyranny, he had won the fearful respect of society. With Roca, he had conquered the Indian of the desert. His military role in real life was of vital importance in Argentine national history. It was equally important in Uruguayan history. But when the wars were done, when law and order were established, gaucho usefulness and gaucho opportunity were over.

[9] Argentine Republic, Archivo general, *Partes*, II, 96-98.

❧ 8 ❧

The Gaucho of Romance

Only personal disaster followed upon gaucho success in the wars, but in 'direct contrast to this reality was the romantic use of the gaucho as a literary and artistic theme.[1] The gaucho became a symbol of the national spirit and of the national achievement. The picturesqueness of his character furthered this literary success, and when the works in which he served as protagonist became known and were welcomed abroad, the real gaucho was replaced in men's minds by the new idealized gaucho who had been so successfully advertised, first in war and then in letters. In general it may be said that this gaucho literature turns around three main characters: Santos Vega, Martín Fierro, and Juan Moreira.

[1] The story of the gaucho role in literature, music, and art is still to be written. The only phase of the whole topic which seems almost completely covered, is the study of the Santos Vega theme. (See Robert Lehmann-Nitsche, "Santos Vega," Academia nacional de ciencias, Córdoba, *Boletín*, XXII, 1-434.) But this does not mean that much significant work has not been done on the question of the gaucho role in literature.

For bibliographical studies of gaucho literature, see Domingo Caillava, *La literatura gauchesca en el Uruguay* (Montevideo, 1921), and Madaline Wallis Nichols, "Der Gaucho als literarische Figur: Eine bibliographische Studie," *Ibero-Amerikanisches Archiv*, XIII, 22-43.

General histories of literature which contain much material on the gaucho, are those by Ricardo Rojas (*La literatura argentina*, 8 vols., Buenos Aires, 1924-1925), Carlos Roxlo (*Historia crítica de la literatura uruguaya*, 7 vols., Montevideo, 1912-1916), and Alberto Zum Felde (*Crítica de la literatura uruguaya*, Montevideo, 1921). For a brief, general summary of gaucho literature, see Madaline Wallis Nichols, "The gaucho in literature," *The Moraga quarterly*, VII, 73-82.

For gaucho folklore, see such works as those by Ricardo Rojas (*op. cit.*), Robert Lehmann-Nitsche (*Santos Vega*, see above, and "Adivinanzas rioplatenses," La Plata, Universidad nacional, *Biblioteca centenaria*, VII, 9-493), and Jorge M. Furt (*Arte gauchesco. Motivos de poesía*, Buenos Aires, 1924).

For study of the "social reincarnation" of the gaucho, see Lehmann-Nitsche's accounts of gaucho clubs and periodicals in his *Santos Vega*, and see Ernesto Quesada's note of gaucho clubs and of the influence of the Italian immigrant to Argentina (*El "criollismo" en la literatura argentina*, Buenos Aires, 1902).

Short accounts of the gaucho in prose fiction are to be found in Roberto Fernando Giusti ("La novela y el cuento argentinos," *Nosotros*, LVII, 78-99) and in Emilio Suárez Calimano ("Directrices de la novela y el cuento argentinos, 1920-1932," *Nosotros*, LXXX, 337-370). For the theater, see Alfredo Antonio Bianchi ("Veinte y cinco años de teatro nacional," *Nosotros*, LVIII, 145-167), Edward Hale Bierstadt ("The drama of the Argentine," *Three plays of the Argentine*, New York, 1920, pp. xi-xliii), Roberto Fernando Giusti ("Orígenes del teatro rioplatense," *Nosotros*, XXVIII, 67-77), and José J. Podestá (*Medio siglo de farándula*, Río de la Plata, 1930). For verse, and notably for the *Martín Fierro*, see Henry Alfred Holmes (*Martín Fierro. An epic of the Argentine*, New York, 1923) and José María Salaverría (*Vida de Martín Fierro, el gaucho ejemplar*, Madrid, 1934). The best editions of the *Martín Fierro* are those by Eleuterio F. Tiscornia (*Martín Fierro, comentado y anotado*, Buenos Aires, 1925, and the edition published with the *Estudio, notas y vocabulario* by Tiscornia in the Colección de textos literarios, 2d ed., Buenos Aires, 1941) in Spanish and the English translation of the poem by Walter Owen (*The gaucho Martín Fierro*, Oxford, 1935).

An excellent general study of the gaucho is to be found in Leopoldo Lugones' *El payador* (Buenos Aires, 1916).

There has been no noteworthy study of the utilization of the gaucho as a musical or artistic theme.

Santos Vega typifies romance. He was the Argentine troubadour and the Argentine Don Juan. In life no woman could resist him in love; no man could defeat him in song. But one day Santos Vega unwisely dared a contest with a strange unknown man, who won in the poetic joust and then peculiarly vanished in flashing flame and a suspicious odor of sulphur. Santos Vega died of the shame of his defeat, but on moonlight nights his shade returns to ride the pampas and the breezes carry his songs.

Two noteworthy poets, Mitre and Obligado, have treated this theme in Argentine literature. Ascasubi also wrote a poem entitled *Santos Vega,* although that poem was a tale told by Vega rather than the story of the singer himself. But this by no means marked the end of Santos Vega in literature. Robert Lehmann-Nitsche has written a masterly study of the Vega theme, in which he lists literally hundreds of poems and titles of fictional and theatrical works which tell of Santos Vega. Aside from its great bibliographical value, an interesting contribution of Dr. Lehmann-Nitsche's study is the author's thesis that Santos Vega represents the American version of the Faust legend, a version in which the original pact with the Devil has been omitted.

The second basic character in gaucho literature was Martín Fierro. Martín Fierro is supposedly the real gaucho, and in some respects his portrayal may have been true to life. José Hernández—in his two poems, *Martín Fierro* and *La vuelta de Martín Fierro*—described excellently the wretched lot of the militiaman drafted for duty in the frontier forts. This portrayal was real. But whether his Martín Fierro ever was a proper gaucho or not is another matter; he was too tame an individual to be convincing.

But this makes the poem of *Martín Fierro* no less valuable as an historical and literary document. The description of frontier life, the relationship of Spaniard and Indian, and that persecution of the gaucho class which led either to the extinction of the rebels or to a necessary reformation in those who would survive—all have historical significance. As a literary document the work is of value in its synthesis of the various "stock" elements of the gaucho theme. Such folklore elements as those reflected in its quoted proverbs, the motif of the contest in verse already told in *Santos Vega,* the persecuted gaucho and the loyal friend motifs which were to be developed later in connection with Juan Moreira—all are included in the poem of *Martín Fierro.*

And, finally, we have Juan Moreira and all his friends, who are only other Moreiras thinly disguised by other names. Just as Martín Fierro was the reformed gaucho, Juan Moreira was the outlaw who must perish. He has been perishing practically continuously in Argentine literature ever since Eduardo Gutiérrez first told his story. Regardless of any individual title, that story was of two loyal and noble friends, unjustly persecuted by local civil and military authorities, and of the remarkable success of their fight with society. Just as the essential elements of our Wild West tales are a man, a horse, and a gun, so the sanguinary novels of Gutiérrez turned on two men, their horses, and their knives. Unfortunately, like Santos Vega, Juan Moreira became a symbol; he has come to represent the righteous man unjustly persecuted by those in authority. His appeal is the appeal of tragedy. That the gaucho was far from righteous and that his persecution by society was an eminently proper procedure, are facts utterly ignored in Juan Moreira's story.

This theme is the one which attained the greatest popularity in Argentine literature. In the field of prose fiction, Eduardo Gutiérrez wrote, and sold, many a novel retelling the story of Juan Moreira. Coupled with the riding acts of the circus and the work of the famous Podestá family of actors, the Juan Moreira theme formed the basis of the Argentine national theater.[2] Publishing houses then hired professional "poets" to transpose the Gutiérrez novels into "Poems written in verse," and this literary trash found a market justifying repeated editions. The Salvador Matera house of Buenos Aires and that of Alberto Longo in Rosario have been leading offenders in this respect.[3] The poets who are involved frequently, wisely refrain from signing their work.

But there has been other gaucho literature besides that about our three main characters. Of outstanding importance is the gaucho folklore. This usually took the form of popular song, proverb, riddle, or fable. Here it is almost impossible, however, to determine what is gaucho, what is Indian, what is Spanish, and what may be even international. Folk themes have such a disconcerting habit of travel. In all probability, much of this folk literature is fundamentally Spanish with local adaptations and decorations. For example, here is a gaucho song which is Andalusian in character:

> Windows to the street
> never are good
> for mothers who have
> marriageable daughters.[4]

[2] See Madaline Wallis Nichols, "The Argentine theatre," *Bulletin hispanique,* XLII, 1-15.
[3] See bibliographical items 527, 528, 529.
[4] Ventanas en la calle
nunca son buenas
para madres que tengan
hijas solteras.

The following two songs might be either Spanish or gaucho:

> All good girls
> are pursued
> Even as tender little trees
> by the ants.[5]

> All men are devils
> So women say
> But they wait for the devils
> To carry them away.[6]

In its mockery and in the condescension of its attitude toward women, the following verse is as typically gaucho as it is typically Andalusian:

> If you think that I love you
> Because I look at your face,
> Think how many go to the market,
> Look, and buy nothing.[7]

Another, and one of the best known of gaucho songs, is the lament of a man whose horse and whose woman have left him and have gone away to the town of Salta. The verse ends with a prayer for the speedy return of the horse.

Proverbs and riddles were other forms of gaucho folklore. The first gave expression to a simple philosophy: Early rising brings no earlier dawn; God gives bread to the man who has no teeth; To a thin dog, all is fleas. As for the gaucho riddle, it was humorous and direct. If one asked a gaucho, "What does a burro look like?" his answer came quickly: "Another burro." When asked, "In what month do women talk the least?" a gaucho would make the proper reply: "In February."

Besides the several treatments of the three main gaucho themes and this gaucho folklore, there are early gaucho "classics" which should be mentioned: Bartolomé Hidalgo's *Diálogos patrióticos,* in which two gauchos discuss their impressions of the social and political misfortunes of the country; Hilario Ascasubi's delightful picture of country life in his misnamed *Santos Vega;* Estanislao del Campo's *Fausto,* famous not for its gaucho description of the opera, but for its incidental portrayal of the pampa and its life; and Domingo Faustino Sarmiento's *Facundo,* with its descriptions of gaucho types—singer, knife fighter, tracker, pathfinder. There are also numerous historical novels with gaucho characters; those by Eduardo Acevedo Díaz may serve as examples.

Modern gaucho literature—and it is continually being written—is generally merely a portrayal of country life with gaucho decorations. This would be true of the works of the dramatist Florencio Sánchez;

[5] Todas las buenas mozas
son perseguidas
como arbolitos tiernos
de las hormigas.

[6] El demonio son los hombres
Dicen todas las mujeres,
Y sólo están deseando
Que el demonio se las lleve.

[7] Si piensas que yo te quiero
Porque te miro a la cara
¡Cuántos van a la recoba
Miran y no compran nada!

of the poets Regules and Trelles; of Fray Mocho and Javier de Viana in the field of the short story; of Güiraldes, Payró, Hugo Wast, and Benito Lynch[8] in the novel. Exceptions to this general tendency, because of their insistence on the gaucho, are to be found in *El gaucho Florido* by Carlos Reyles, in *El romance de un gaucho* by Benito Lynch, in *Los cuentos del viejo Quilques* by Santiago Maciel, and in the three *Crónicas* by Justino Závala Múñiz.

After the real gaucho died, he experienced at least two interesting reincarnations. One was the literary reincarnation which has been described. The second was a kind of social reincarnation, which, in its turn, was reflected in literature. The gaucho locale changed from country to city; the urban middle and lower classes, usually the descendants of Italian immigrants, apparently began to "play gaucho." This was an extremely popular procedure between the years 1900 and 1920, when it ran a course parallel to that of such North American peculiarities as the "drugstore cowboy," the dude ranch, and the Wild West tale.

But the Argentine Italians took their gauchos with alarming seriousness. As late as 1914 there were over two hundred small clubs, the avowed intent of which was to perpetuate the gaucho tradition. More than fifty of these clubs were in Buenos Aires alone. Members met occasionally of an evening, played the guitar, sang gaucho songs, read gaucho stories, wrote gaucho newspapers, acted in gaucho plays. On Sundays, they went on picnics, built bonfires, roasted steaks, drank *mate*. Members prided themselves on the possession of authentic gaucho costumes, on their riding ability, on their skill in verse composition. Payadas were held, and the newspaper *La Prensa* noted at least one sorrowful occasion when five hundred potential customers battled the police in hot fury because not even standing room was left in the theater where one such payada was to take place.

The names of these clubs are indicative of their character: Desert Bandits, Cubs of the Pampa, The Descendants of the Ombú of the Pampa, Gauchos and Indians, Pampa Brothers, Orphans of the Plain, The Tracker and His Men, Memories of Santos Vega, Pampa Tiger and His Men, The Old Outlaw and His Cubs. One of the main activities of such clubs was the publication of gaucho newspapers which should contain the gaucho stories and verse of club members. More than fifty such newspapers have been listed.

The interesting fact about all this gaucho literature is that none of it has portrayed the original gaucho—the vagrant, generally mestizo, cow hunter. There is a similar unreality in music which has utilized the gaucho as theme. Arturo Berutti has written several gaucho operas,

---

[8] Except for his *El romance de un gaucho*.

despite the fact that gauchos and operas do not seem to belong together. It is only when utilized in art that the gaucho has been portrayed with some measure of reality. Here the paintings of Cesáreo Bernaldo de Quirós may serve in illustration. But whether portrayed as he really was, or as Argentine and Uruguayan citizens have wistfully imagined him to be, the gaucho refuses to die. He has been quite as recalcitrant in this respect as he was in his obedience to every kind of law in life.

The final metamorphosis of the gaucho would seem to be this change into the symbol of patriotic romance. He has come to express a romantic nostalgia for the past. Rubén Darío, the great Nicaraguan poet, has excellently expressed this gaucho symbolism:

> Who are you, solitary wanderer of the night?
> I am that Poesy which once reigned here,
> I am the last gaucho who, departing forevermore,
> Bears away the soul of our old land.[9]

Only the gaucho does not seem to be "departing forevermore." He is still very much alive in modern La Plata literature, music, and art. The real gaucho long since disappeared, but the imaginary gaucho, and the ideals he has come to typify, still live on.

[9] ¿Quién eres, solitario viajero de la noche?
Yo soy la poesía que un tiempo aquí reinó:
¡Yo soy el postrer gaucho que parte para siempre,
De nuestra vieja patria llevando el corazón!

BIBLIOGRAPHY

Essay on Authorities

The study of the origin, development, and history of a class of society, together with the portrayal of that class in literature, must be based upon an exceedingly extensive bibliography if it is to be well done.

The consideration of the economic and social background from which the gaucho emerged, involves a study of the colonial life of the present countries of Brazil, Uruguay, Paraguay, Argentina, and, to a lesser degree, the histories of Peru, Bolivia, and Chile, in so far as they are related to that of the Plata region. Such materials as the laws which regulated La Plata life and the reports on conditions there, involve the national archives of Spain and Portugal as well. In this colonial period, such items are important as those dealing with the introduction of livestock, the ways in which people earned a living, what happened to those who were not interested in work, the lines followed by legitimate and illegitimate trade, where Indian invasions were to be found and why they were there, the racial mixture of society, and the social conditions under which the new mestizos lived.

For the period of the wars with the Portuguese in southern Brazil to that of General Roca's final campaign against the Pampas Indians, gaucho forces almost exclusively formed the national armies, and through their caudillo leaders those armies very largely dictated political policies as well. Again, this long period of caudillism marked an early social revolution. Since this is the period when the gaucho has emerged from his pastoral background and is playing a very active and imposing role in the new national histories, the descriptions of the new character, as encountered in the writings of the many travelers of the time, form one of the most valuable of sources for our study of the real gaucho.

The gaucho of romance is the gaucho utilized in works of art, literature, and music. Here the difficulties in collecting material are tremendous. First, there is the problem as to what is and what is not gaucho literature. Many a work which does not even mention the gaucho gives a far better portrayal of his life and manners than other works where a few gauchos ride across the stage in emphasis of a rural background of an otherwise non-gaucho work. Again, there are many works of identical title; they are frequently unsigned and not dated. This is especially true of the various versifications of the Gutiérrez novels. Editions are often repeated, but they are remarkably difficult to obtain. For example, gaucho periodical literature is even now largely lost, and there is no collection of it in the United States.[1] The fact that it is largely literary trash does not lessen its historical and sociological value. In the theater the *género chico* and gaucho literature run side by side, and the titles of works are often deceptively similar.

In the presence of these difficulties, the policy pursued in this second part of the bibliography has been to include only those works read and so known to contain gauchos, or those works which have been definitely reported to contain gauchos or the titles of which seem to have indicated that they really do treat of gauchos. This has meant the omission of many a suspiciously gaucho title, even by authors known to have written at least one gaucho work. In view of the fact that so many authors have written an occasional gaucho work, it has seemed safer, however, to begin with a smaller and more certain list, to which other items may gradually be added.

PART I

THE REAL GAUCHO

This section deals with the materials for a historical study of the emergence of the gaucho from his pastoral background, a description of the new social type and of its role in La Plata history—notably in La Plata wars.

The arrangement of the material in the section is alphabetical within the broad divisions of Bibliographical Aids, Atlases, Documents, Manuscripts, Periodical Literature, and Books. While materials might be subdivided under such headings as economic, social, historical, descriptive, etc., it was felt that such division would involve a needless repetition of many items; for this reason it was not attempted. After all, the value of our picture must be in its synthetic portrayal of society, not in an elaborate analysis of the component parts. This does not mean, however, that those parts have been neglected. An indication of such study may be found in the footnotes which outline the materials for the several chapters.

[1] Dr. Lehmann-Nitsche seemed to have the most complete collection of the periodical material. Partial collections may still be found in the national libraries, and there are a few small private collections in the Plata countries.

Bibliographical Aids

This study of the gaucho is based upon an examination of the colonial documents, histories, and descriptive writings of Brazil, Uruguay, Paraguay, and Argentina, and upon the materials covering the nineteenth century in Argentina, Uruguay, and Brazil. Naturally, many volumes of bibliography deal with this broad field. While the items listed below are only a few of those which might have been selected, it is believed that they are of such a character that their use should lead a student to the other and less important items which have not been listed.

BIBLIOGRAPHIES

1 "Agencias de publicidad en Buenos Aires," *Revista americana de Buenos Aires,* XXXVI, 115-116.
   A valuable list.

2 Argentine Republic. Ministerio de relaciones exteriores y culto. *Catálogo de documentos del Archivo de Indias en Sevilla referentes a la historia de la República Argentina, 1514-1810.* 2 vols. Buenos Aires, 1901, 1902.
   A bibliographical list of documents, arranged by date.

3 Binayán, Narciso. *Bibliografía de bibliografías argentinas.* Buenos Aires, 1919.

4 Buenos Aires. Biblioteca nacional. *Catálogo por orden cronológico de los manuscritos relativos a América existentes en la Biblioteca Nacional de Buenos Aires.* 2 vols. Buenos Aires, 1905, 1906.

5 Buenos Aires. Museo Mitre. *Catálogo de la biblioteca.* Buenos Aires, 1907.

6 California. University. *Spain and Spanish America in the libraries of the University of California: a catalogue of books.* 2 vols. Berkeley, 1928, 1930.
   This list of the works on Spain and Spanish America in the University of California is of especial value due to the relative completeness of the collection of materials on the Plata region.
   A supplement, "Some recent additions to the South American collection in the University of California libraries," was published by Lewis Winkler Bealer in *The Hispanic American historical review,* XII, 103-106 (Feb., 1932).

7 Desdevises du Dézert, Gaston. *Les sources manuscrites de l'histoire de l'Amérique Latine à la fin du XVIIIᵉ siècle (1760-1807).* Paris, 1914.

8 Estrada, Dardo. *Historia y bibliografía de la imprenta en Montevideo. 1810-1865.* Montevideo, 1912.

9 Falcao Espalter, Mario. "Bibliografía del periodismo uruguayo:

El Universal de Montevideo (1829-1838)," *Humanidades,* IX, 271-316; X, 127-164; XI, 397-431; XII, 285-313.

A very useful annotated bibliography of a newspaper which was published during critical years in La Plata history. Useful information is given in regard to economic conditions, the existence of a disturbing rural class, and much historical information, notably about Lavalleja.

10 Fernández y Medina, Benjamín. *La imprenta y la prensa en el Uruguay desde 1807 a 1900.* Montevideo, 1900.

11 Garraux, Anatole Louis. *Bibliographie brésilienne.* Paris, 1898.

12 Hanke, Lewis, ed. *Handbook of Latin American studies.* 1935—.

A useful guide to current literature in numerous fields. An annual publication.

13 *Ibero-amerikanisches Archiv.* Berlin and Bonn, 1924—.

An excellent guide to the new works being published on Hispanic America. Useful bibliographical information.

14 "Inventario del archivo," Uruguay, Archivo y museo histórico nacional, *Revista histórica,* XII, 5-47, 357-403, 701-747.

15 Jones, Cecil Knight. *Hispanic American bibliographies, including collective bibliographies, histories of literature, and selected general works . . . with critical notes on sources by José Toribio Medina.* Baltimore, 1922.

This collection of bibliographies is a tool of fundamental importance to any student in the field of Hispanic American history.

16 "Latin American libraries," *Library journal,* XLIV, 201-272.

17 "Lista general de bibliotecas populares," *Revista americana de Buenos Aires,* XLII, 140-172.

A very valuable list giving names and addresses. The arrangement is primarily by location; that is, a list is given for the Federal District of Buenos Aires, and this is followed by lists for the several provinces and territories.

18 Medina, José Toribio. *Biblioteca hispano-americana (1493-1810).* 7 vols. Santiago de Chile, 1898-1907.

An excellent and thorough bibliography of the materials on the colonial period.

19 ——— "La imprenta en la América Española," *Anales del Museo de la Plata.* Buenos Aires, 1892.

20 Moses, Bernard. *Spanish colonial literature in South America.* London and New York, 1922.

An annotated bibliography of the works of the colonial period.

21 Museo-Biblioteca de Ultramar en Madrid. *Catálogo de la biblioteca.* Madrid, 1900.

22 New York public library. *Latin-American periodicals current in the reference department.* New York, 1920.

23 Phillips, Philip Lee. *A list of books, magazine articles, and maps relating to Brazil. 1800-1900.* Washington, 1901.

24 "La prensa ibero-americana," *Revista americana de Buenos Aires,* XLII, 5-123.

A valuable bibliography of newspapers and magazines in the several countries of South and Central America. Sections also are devoted to Mexico, Cuba, the Dominican Republic, and Spain.

25 Quesada, Ernesto. "La bibliografía argentina," *Nueva revista de Buenos Aires,* III, 258-278.

A consideration of Argentine bibliographical studies, in connection with a review of the *Anuarios bibliográficos* of Alberto Navarro Viola.

26 ——— "El periodismo argentino. 1877-1883," *Nueva revista de Buenos Aires,* IX, 72-101.

A valuable bibliographical article in that it contains useful material not easily found in other places.

27 ——— "El periodismo argentino en la capital de la república (1877-1883)," *Nueva revista de Buenos Aires,* IX, 425-447.

A valuable bibliographical aid.

28 Quesada, Vicente Gaspar. "Estudios sobre las bibliotecas europeas," *Revista del Río de la Plata* (Buenos Aires).

A study of Hispanic American materials in five European libraries: Biblioteca nacional de París (VIII, 459-478); Biblioteca nacional de Madrid (IX, 159-191); Sevilla, El archivo de Indias (IX, 668-692); La dirección de hidrografía de Madrid (X, 119-159); La biblioteca de la Real Academia de la historia en Madrid (X, 295-327 and 470-489).

29 "Revista bibliográfica," *Nueva revista de Buenos Aires,* V, 454-475.

Included in this section are two useful articles: "Las revistas en América" (pp. 454-461) and "El movimiento intelectual argentino; revistas y periódicos" (pp. 462-475).

30 Rich, Obadiah. *Biblioteca americana nova.* 2 vols. London, 1846.

These volumes cover the years from 1701 to 1800 and from 1801 to 1844. Items are arranged by date of publication and are often annotated.

31 Robaina, Vicente S. "Archivos portugueses," Uruguay, Archivo y museo histórico nacional, *Revista histórica,* IX, 629-638.

This article deals only with those materials which treat of South American matters.

32 Streit, Robert. *Bibliotheca missionum.* 8 vols. Münster-Aachen, 1916—.

One of the most useful of bibliographical guides.

33 Torre Revello, José. *Los archivos de la República Argentina.* Sevilla, 1925.

34 Torres, Luis María. "Cuestiones de administración edilicia de la ciudad de Buenos Aires," Buenos Aires, Universidad nacional, Facultad de filosofía y letras, *Documentos para la historia argentina,* IX, ix-cxli.

Part V of this *Introduction* is entitled "La ciudad de Buenos Aires durante el siglo XVIII: juicios de los contemporáneos." It is useful for its bibliography of early travelers.

35 Wilgus, Alva Curtis. *Histories and historians of Hispanic America.* Washington, 1936.

Arranged by centuries and by localities, this work is an excellent general guide to the historical materials on Hispanic America.

36 Wise, Murray, ed. *Latin American periodicals currently received in the Library of Congress.* Washington, 1941.

Excellent guide to current periodical literature in Hispanic America.

37 Zinny, Antonio. *Bibliografía histórica de las Provincias Unidas del Río de la Plata desde 1780 hasta 1821.* Buenos Aires, 1875.

38 —— *Gaceta de Buenos Aires desde 1810 hasta 1821.* Buenos Aires, 1875.

"The condensed essence" of the entire contents of the newspaper in an eleven-year period.

39 —— *La prensa periodística en el Uruguay.* Buenos Aires, 1883.

ATLASES

Although the atlas by Biedma represents a start in the right direction, there is a decided need for more and better material in this class. More detailed maps showing settlements, roads, frontiers—at different periods —would be decidedly useful. The inclusion of maps showing local rainfall and vegetation conditions (and in an atlas which should be both easily available and of comfortable size) would also be a decided boon to the student.

See, however, item 147, for useful periodical material.

ATLASES

40 Biedma, José Juan. *Atlas histórico de la República Argentina.* Buenos Aires, 1909.

41 General drafting company. *Atlas América Latina.* New York, 1919.

DOCUMENTS

Under this heading are listed printed official records, diaries, reports, or other materials not originally designed as formulated accounts to be published as periodical articles or books.

Only two divisions of this material are attempted: Collections of Documents and Documents Which Refer to One Event, Individual, or Topic.

COLLECTIONS OF DOCUMENTS

42 Angelis, Pedro de. *Colección de obras y documentos relativos a la historia antigua y moderna de las provincias del Río de La Plata.* 5 vols. Buenos Aires, 1910.

The works included in this collection are valuable for material on early travel and settlement in the Plata region; the introduction of livestock into the country; the growth of a frontier mestizo class; contraband trade. See items 69, 70, 73, 74, 78, 79, 87, 100, 104, 106, 107.

43 Argentine Republic. Archivo general. *Archivo de la nación argentina. Época colonial. Reales cédulas y provisiones. 1517-1662.* Buenos Aires, 1911.

Included are numerous cedulas on economic matters: that of 1602, permitting the exportation to Brazil; those of 1604 and 1610 on contraband in connection with the Negro slave trade; one of 1661 establishing the Córdoba customs to prevent the introduction of goods to Peru via Buenos Aires.

44 Argentine Republic. Archivo general. *Partes oficiales y documentos relativos a la guerra de la independencia argentina.* 4 vols. 2d ed. Buenos Aires, 1900-1903.

Gaucho war technique and the gaucho role in the wars of independence are described. It is noteworthy that in the official war despatches, gauchos are named only in Upper Peru, though the *montoneros* are noted in Uruguay; otherwise, cavalrymen ride under names of strangely European connotation: "granaderos a caballo," "cazadores," "dragones," and "húsares."

45 Buenos Aires. Archivo nacional. *Acuerdos del extinguido cabildo. 1589-1820.* 45 vols. Buenos Aires, 1907-1934.

Excellent for material on economic conditions, Indian invasions, and the growth of an outlaw class.

46 Buenos Aires. Archivo general. *Revista.* 4 vols. Buenos Aires, 1869-1872.

Colonial documents dealing largely with such economic matters as the numbers and value of livestock, legitimate and contraband trade, and the Indian and Portuguese troubles arising from their interest in the acquisition of Spanish cattle. The growth of a new frontier vagabond social class is also mentioned; frontier forts and army life there are described. Gauderios are reported in Uruguay.
See items 92, 101, 105, 110.

47 Buenos Aires. Biblioteca nacional. *Anales de la biblioteca.* 10 vols. Buenos Aires, 1900-1915.

Ten volumes, largely of unpublished documentary materials, which, for the purposes of this study, are useful for a consideration of the economic aspect of La Plata life.
See items 63, 64, 77, 83, 84, 95, 160.

48 Buenos Aires. Biblioteca nacional. *Revista de la biblioteca pública de Buenos Aires.* 4 vols. Buenos Aires, 1879-1882.

A collection of colonial documents: descriptions of the Plata region, a consideration of colonial trade, reports of the viceroys Arredondo and Avilés.
See items 65, 68, 85, 88, 96, 102, 103.

49 Buenos Aires. Museo Mitre. *Documentos y correspondencia.* 28 vols. Buenos Aires, 1911.

These volumes contain numerous descriptions of conditions on the Buenos Aires frontier—the frontier forts, Spanish-Indian relations, means of defense against the Indian, the purchase of Indian peace.

50 Buenos Aires. Universidad nacional. Facultad de filosofía y letras. *Documentos para la historia argentina.* 14 vols. Buenos Aires, 1913-1921.

> Documents dealing largely with early La Plata economic materials: figures for trade in hides and Negro slaves; a discussion of Portuguese contraband, with a description of the gauchos, camiluchos, and gauderios who furthered it. Included, also, are an excellent modern history of Spanish colonial economic policies, official pleas by Lerma and Arredondo for the conservation and protection of cattle, and a useful bibliography of early travelers in the Plata region.
> See items 36, 66, 91, 166, 176.

51 Charcas. Audiencia. *Correspondencia de presidentes y oidores (1561-1600).* 3 vols. Madrid, 1918-1922.

> Many of these early documents are of use in this study because of their treatment of such economic matters as the trade relationships of colonial cities and such social matters as the growth of a large vagabond class in society.

52 *Colección de documentos inéditos para la historia de Hispano-América.* 14 vols. Madrid, 1927-1932.

> Volume XIII was of the greatest use. It lists the various sources for Buenos Aires inhabitants. The poem of Luis de Miranda is also included here.

53 *Colección de libros y documentos referentes a la historia de América.* 21 vols. Madrid, 1904-1929.

> Volumes V and VI give Cabeza de Vaca material.

54 *Documentos inéditos del Archivo de Indias.* 42 vols. Madrid, 1864-1884.

> Volume X contains the *Relación* by Gregorio Acosta; Volume XVIII, material on the Mendoza expedition and on Brazilian trade; Volume XIX, on contraband trade to Peru; Volume XXIII contains documents referring to Zárate and his stocking of the Plata region.

55 Levillier, Roberto, ed. *Antecedentes de política económica en el Río de la Plata.* Madrid, 1915.

> Documents useful in a study of the economic condition of colonial society.

56 Manning, William Ray, ed. *Diplomatic correspondence of the United States concerning the independence of the Latin American nations.* I. New York, 1925.

> In Theodorick Bland's report of 1818 are excellent descriptions of the pampas, of the carreta caravans, and of the gaucho. Joel Poinsett's report of the same year describes the life of a rural landed proprietor, and W. G. D. Worthington (1819) describes the gaucho.

57 —————— *Diplomatic correspondence of the United States. Inter-American affairs. 1831-1860.* I. Washington, 1932.

> Francis Baylies describes the gaucho (1832) and his gaucho leader, Rosas. James A. Paden (1855 and 1856), Benjamin C. Yancey (1859), and John F. Cushman (1860) write of the gaucho in the civil wars of Argentina.

58 Montevideo. Archivo general. *Revista del archivo general administrativo.* 10 vols. Montevideo, 1885-1920.

Documents on the founding of Montevideo and the *Actas* of its Cabildo from 1726 to 1813. Extremely useful material on trade, Indians, the Portuguese, vagabonds, and thieves. Of particular interest are the 1768 expedition of two hundred sent in pursuit of thieves and the depositions taken in regard to their crimes. See Volume VII.

59 Núñez Cabeza de Vaca, Alvar. *Relación de los naufragios y comentarios.* Madrid, 1906.

See item 53. This edition contains other useful documents as well. The *Comentarios* themselves are Secretary Hernández' account of Cabeza de Vaca's experiences in the Plata region. Volume VI contains the *Relación general* by Cabeza de Vaca (pp. 3-98) and the numerous documents growing out of his trial. Also included are Pero Hernández' *Relación de las cosas sucedidas en el Río de la Plata (1545)* (pp. 307-359), the *Relación* left by Yrala when Buenos Aires was abandoned in 1541 (pp. 361-377), and Yrala's letter to the king in 1545. The most important single work on the conquest of the Plata because of the inclusion of the several contemporary reports.

60 Spain. Ministerio de fomento. *Cartas de Indias. 1496-1586.* Madrid, 1877.

Early contemporary accounts of the settlement period.

61 Tucumán. Gobernación. *Correspondencia de los Cabildos en el siglo XVI.* 3 vols. Madrid, 1918.

This collection of documents, edited by Roberto Levillier, is exceedingly useful for an understanding of the procedure of Spanish colonization. The Cabildos are those of colonial Tucumán.

DOCUMENTS WHICH REFER TO INDIVIDUALS OR TO SPECIFIC EVENTS

62 Acosta, Gregorio. *Relación de Gregorio de Acosta sobre el gobierno de las provincias del Río de la Plata, dirigida a su Magestad y a su Real Consejo de Indias,* in *Documentos inéditos del Archivo de Indias,* X, 525-536.

A valuable early account of the Mendoza expedition.

63 Aguirre, Juan Francisco. "Diario," Buenos Aires, Biblioteca nacional, *Anales,* IV, 1-271, and VII, 1-490.

Included is a study of colonial trade with a note on the growth of a new, vagabond class in society.

64 Alvear, Diego de. "Diario de la segunda partida demarcadora de límites en la América Meridional," Buenos Aires, Biblioteca nacional, *Anales,* I, 267-384; II, 288-360; III, 373-464.

This work contains a study of the introduction of horses and cattle into the Plata region and of the colonial legitimate and contraband trade in hides.

65 Arredondo, Nicolás de. "Informe (1795)," Buenos Aires, Biblioteca nacional, *Revista,* III, 309-449.

The viceroy reports contraband trade and a needed decrease in the wasteful slaughter of cattle. Gauderios and changadores are troubling him in their attempts to fill the Brazilian need for cattle.

66 ———— "Memoria," Buenos Aires, Universidad nacional, Facultad de filosofía y letras, *Documentos,* VI, 475-481.

67 Avilés, El marqués de (D. José Ramón de Baravilbaso). "Decreto (1800)," Uruguay, Archivo y museo histórico nacional, *Revista histórica,* I, 508-515.

On the establishment of new towns as a means of quieting a disorderly rural population.

68 ——— "Informe (1801)," Buenos Aires, Biblioteca nacional, *Revista,* III, 450-501.

A description of the condition of the Plata viceroyalty during his administration.

69 Azara, Félix de. "Diario del reconocimiento de las guardias y fortines que guarnecen la línea de frontera de Buenos Aires (1796)," Angelis, V, 57-84.

Excellent for the portrayal of the migration of the Chilean Araucanian Indian to the Argentine pampa; an analysis of their mid-eighteenth-century hostility; the role of the blandengues in the settlement of the frontier.

70 Barco Centenera, Martín del. "La Argentina o La conquista del Río de la Plata. 1601," Angelis, II, 183-332.

One of the early accounts of La Plata settlement. It is written in verse.

71 Caillet-Bois, Ricardo, ed. "Dictamen imparcial sobre los gauchos," Buenos Aires, Universidad nacional, Instituto de investigaciones históricas, *Boletín,* V, 102-105.

An introductory study, including a short bibliography of writers who have left contemporary descriptions of the gaucho, is followed by a copy of a short, but valuable, documentary account of the gaucho.

72 "Confidencias de Don Juan Manuel Rosas en el día en que se recibió, por la primera vez, del gobierno de Buenos Aires," *Revista del Río de la Plata,* V, 596-606.

Santiago Vásquez reports on an interview with Rosas: his analysis of the power of the gauchos and a statement of his policy with regard to them.

73 Cruz, Luis de. "Viaje . . . desde el fuerte de Ballenar, frontera de . . . Concepción de Chile . . . hasta la ciudad de Buenos Aires (1806)," Angelis, I, 121-264.

The author describes the guasos of Chile and the horse-loving Peguenche Indians.

74 Díaz de Guzmán, Rui. "Argentina (1612)," Angelis, I, 11-111.

The grandson of Irala writes of early settlement in the Plata region, of cross-country travel, and of the introduction of horses and cattle into the land.

75 Doblas, Gonzalo de. *Memoria . . . sobra la Provincia de Misiones de Indios Guaranís (1785).* Buenos Aires, 1836.

Contraband trade effected by Spanish and Portuguese gauderios with the co-operation of the Minuanes Indians. Operations center in the land between the Ibicuy and Negro rivers, but contraband also apparently travels via Montevideo and by sea and the Río Pardo.

76 "Documentos inéditos referentes a una negociación de paz entre el gobierno del directorio y las tribus ranqueles de la provincia de Buenos Aires, 1819," *Revista del Río de la Plata,* V, 133-148.

77 Garay, Juan de. "Declaración de Juan de Garay en el pleito de Juan de Torres de Vera y Aragón con el fiscal de S. M., 1583," Buenos Aires, Biblioteca nacional, *Anales,* X, 166-181.

78 García, Pedro Andrés. "Diario de un viaje a Salinas Grandes en los campos del sud de Buenos Aires (1810)," Angelis, III, 197-261.
   The growth of a frontier mestizo class; increased Indian interest in horses.

79 ———— "Nuevo plan de fronteras (1816)," Angelis, V, 313-329.
   Indian cattle stealing with the co-operation of gaucho deserters from frontier posts.

80 García Acevedo, Daniel. "Documentos inéditos de Lozano," Uruguay, Archivo y museo histórico nacional, *Revista histórica,* I, 862-894; II, 147-170.
   A description of the introduction of cattle into Uruguayan cattle country from the Paraguayan missions and of the necessity of the Guaraní vaquerías for the support of the mission Indians. The author then notes the decrease in cattle there, due to Buenos Aires and Brazilian vaquerías with the hide shipments to Peru, Chile, and Brazil, and to the European market. New Guaraní cattle hunting grounds have been opened near the Brazilian frontier; if this land is ceded to the Portuguese, it will mean definitive ruin for the missions.

81 García Ros, Balthasar. "Informe a S. M. . . . sobre la instancia hecha por don José García Inclán, para poblar el paraje de Montevideo, en el Río de la Plata, 1721," Uruguay, Archivo y museo histórico nacional, *Revista histórica,* V, 118-152.
   The probable introduction of cattle into Uruguay from the Guaraní missions and a note of present need for cattle there, largely because of contraband trade which has been aided by the Uruguayan Indians.

82 Grimaldi, El marqués de. "Memoria," Uruguay, Archivo y museo histórico nacional, *Revista histórica,* IV, 516-543.
   On such colonial economic topics as the introduction of stock and the vaquerías.

83 Groussac, Paul. "La expedición de Mendoza," Buenos Aires, Biblioteca nacional, *Anales,* VIII, ix-clxxviii.

84 ———— "Juan de Garay," Buenos Aires, Biblioteca nacional, *Anales,* X, ix-ccc.

85 Guevara, Isabel de. "Carta (1556)," Buenos Aires, Biblioteca nacional, *Revista,* I, 384-388.

86 Haedo, Felipe de. "Descripción de la Colonia del Sacramento y puertos del Río de la Plata al norte y sud de Buenos Aires (1778)," *Revista del Río de la Plata,* III, 436-466.
   How to draft settlers who should open up and hold new lands.

87 Henis, Padre Tadeo Xavier. "Diario histórico de la rebelión y guerra de los pueblos guaranís, situados en la costa oriental del río Uruguay (1754)," Angelis, IV, 231-266.
   This work is notable for the first known definition of the gauderios. "Paulistas who have the property and custom of selling what is not theirs are called . . . gauderios."

88 "Informe del Gobernador de Tucumán al rey, sobre los inconvenientes de subordinar a la audiencia de Chile las gobernaciones de Tucumán y Paraguay. 1808," Buenos Aires, Biblioteca nacional, *Revista*, III, 114-118.

89 Larrañaga, Dámaso. "Apuntes históricos sobre el descubrimiento y población de la Banda Oriental del Río de la Plata y las ciudades de Montevideo, Maldonado, Colonia, etc.," Uruguay, Archivo y museo histórico nacional, *Revista histórica*, VI, 611-627.

90 ———— "Diario desde Montevideo al pueblo de Paysandú," Uruguay, Archivo y museo histórico nacional, *Revista histórica*, III, 103-139, 426-453.
   Good material on uses of hides.

91 Lastarria, Miguel. "Reorganización y plan de seguridad exterior de las muy interesantes colonias orientales del Río Paraguay o de La Plata (1805)," Buenos Aires, Universidad nacional, Facultad de filosofía y letras, *Documentos*, III, 5-480.
   An account of Uruguayan trade in hides and of the disreputable gauchos, camiluchos, and gauderios who further Portuguese contraband and wastefully diminish the number of hides available for legitimate trade.

92 Loreto, El marqués de. "Memoria (1790)," Buenos Aires, Archivo general, *Revista*, IV, 351-558.
   Description of the viceroyalty, largely economic in character.

93 Mendoza, Gonzalo de. "Información de los méritos y servicios," Buenos Aires, Junta de historia y numismática americana, *Biblioteca*, I. Apéndice C, 369-383.

94 Miranda, Luis de. "Poema," *Colección de documentos inéditos*, XIII, 363-365. See item 52.

95 Montalvo, Hernando de. "Carta de Hernando de Montalvo, tesorero del Río de la Plata, haciendo una descripción muy detallada de la desembocadura del Río de la Plata, 1576," Buenos Aires, Biblioteca nacional, *Anales*, X, 88-117.

96 Parras, Fray Pedro José de. "Diario (1753)," Buenos Aires, Biblioteca nacional, *Revista*, IV, 166-347.
   The friar reports conditions, notably economic, encountered during travels in Montevideo, Buenos Aires, Santa Fe, Corrientes, Asunción, and Córdoba.

97 Peña, Enrique. "Una carta inédita de Irala," *Revista de derecho, historia y letras*, XIX, 498-509.

98 ———— "El Padre Luis de Miranda," *Revista de derecho, historia y letras*, XXIV, 514-518.

99 Pernety, Antoine Joseph. "Descripción de Montevideo durante la gobernación del Mariscal don José Joaquín de Viana (1763-1764)," Uruguay, Archivo y museo histórico nacional, *Revista histórica*, VI, 265-282.

100 Quiroga, Padre José. "Descripción del Río del Paraguay . . . 1753," Angelis, II, 361-371.

101 "Registro y desarme de portugueses," Buenos Aires, Archivo general, *Revista,* III, 142-263.

102 Ribera, Alonso de. "Carta al rey representando los inconvenientes de comprender en la jurisdicción de la Audiencia de Chile las provincias de Tucumán y Paraguay, 1607," Buenos Aires, Biblioteca nacional, *Revista,* III, 110-114.

103 Rivadeneyra, Fray Juan de. "Relación de la provincia del Río de la Plata (1581)," Buenos Aires, Biblioteca nacional, *Revista,* III, 14-30.
   A description of the Plata region, with notes on the location of colonial cities and the routes followed by trade.

104 Schmidel, Ulderico. "Viaje al Río de la Plata y Paraguay," Angelis, III, 279-317.
   A noteworthy portrayal of the hunger suffered by the Mendoza settlers. Other editions are those of the Junta de historia y numismática americana, of Buenos Aires (*Biblioteca,* I) and *Ulrich Schmidels Reise nach Süd-Amerika,* edited by Valentin Langmantel in Tübingen, 1889.

105 Vértiz, Juan José de (El marqués de Sobremonte). "Memoria (1784)," Buenos Aires, Archivo general, *Revista,* III, 264-477.
   The viceroy reports a troublesome new social class, Portuguese contraband, and Indian invasions.

106 Viedma, Francisco de. "Descripción . . . de la provincia de Santa Cruz de la Sierra (1788)," Angelis, II, 419-542.
   Notes on the mule and cattle business and also on the growth of a large vagabond class in society.

107 —— "Memoria . . . al Señor Marqués de Loreto (1784)," Angelis, I, 445-461.
   Mention of the Indian interest in Spanish livestock on the southern frontier.

108 Villalta, Francisco de. "Carta," Apéndice a, Buenos Aires, Junta de historia y numismática americana, *Biblioteca,* I, 303-323.

109 Zeballos, Estanislao Severo. "Irala," *Revista de derecho, historia y letras,* XXII, 97-134.
   An account of Irala's nine communications sent to the Spanish court in the years from 1541 to 1555.

110 Zevallos, Pedro de. "Memoria (1778)," Buenos Aires, Archivo general, *Revista,* II, 414-436.
   Need for increase in cattle is reported.

MANUSCRIPTS

There is, of course, much manuscript material in existence which would be of great value in the study of the topic of the gaucho. Unfortunately, it is kept largely in private collections or in the archives of the

Hispanic American countries and of Spain or in the several church archives. While the manuscripts themselves are thus not readily available, guides have been published for the more important collections. See such items as 2 and 5.

Unpublished theses form a second class of manuscript material. There have been many theses on the gaucho, but there has been little attempt to study the gaucho from the viewpoint of his contemporaries or to study either the society from which he came or that of which he formed a part. The existence of the immense amount of possibly useful documentary materials or of the descriptive records left by travelers would seem to have been quite largely and universally ignored.

The section which follows contains a few specimen theses on the social, economic, and historical aspects of the gaucho problem.

111 Hollinger, Frances C. *The gaucho.* M.A., Kansas, 1928.
> A study of the origin of the gaucho, his character, his role in Argentine history, and the gaucho theme in literature.

112 Johnson, H. L. *The life and customs of the gaucho.* M.A., Texas, 1928.

113 Kimball, Reta. *The gaucho in the history of Argentina.* M.A., Columbia, 1931.

114 Nichols, Madaline Wallis. *The gaucho.* Ph.D., California (Berkeley), 1937.
> A study of the economic, social, historical, and literary aspects of the topic.

115 Warren, Vanetta Hosford. *The gauchos of Hilario Ascasubi.* M.A., Kansas, 1916.
> In addition to a study of gaucho literature, this thesis contains a description of the gaucho, a note on the origin of the term, and a consideration of the gaucho role in Argentine history and even in present Argentine economic life.

116 Werner, Gustave Adolph. *Gaucho life and literature.* M.A., University of Southern California, Los Angeles, 1920.
> A definition and a description of the gaucho. This work also gives an account of the gaucho importance in Argentine history—reclaiming the plains from the Indian, serving in the armies, aiding the economic development of the country in its cattle industry.

PERIODICAL LITERATURE

Corresponding to the broad divisions in the section on documentary materials, this section as well is divided into two parts: Periodicals and Individual Articles. Literary periodicals are included in Part II of the bibliography.

In the first section, only those periodicals are listed which contain many articles of use in this study. They are, therefore, really collections of materials.

PERIODICALS

117 Buenos Aires. Universidad nacional. Instituto de investigaciones históricas. *Boletín*. 18 vols. Buenos Aires, 1926-1935.

Two of the most valuable studies on the gaucho are to be found in this *Boletín*. See items 71 and 142. Also, among the many book reviews, there are several of interest in a study of the gaucho.

118 *Colección de papeles públicos*. Vols. 6-7, 9-10. Buenos Aires, 1807-1811.

This material, taken largely from the *Correo de comercio*, is of use in the study of the gaucho because of its accounts of rural society and such economic matters as the raising of horses and cattle, and the legitimate and contraband trade in their hides.

119 *The Hispanic American historical review*. Baltimore, 1918-1922; Durham, North Carolina, 1926—

This is the best periodical in English for the study of Hispanic American questions.

120 *Nueva revista de Buenos Aires*. 12 vols. Buenos Aires, 1881-1884.

While especially good for its literary bibliographical material and for that on inter-American boundary questions, this review also contains articles of value for the purposes of this study. There are descriptions of gaucho warfare, of the cattle and hide industries, of the influence of war and of contraband trade, of rural life, of cross-country travel, of the growth of the gaucho class in society.
See items 25-27, 29, 152-156, 158, 173, and 192.

121 La Plata. Universidad nacional. Facultad de humanidades y ciencias de la educación. *Humanidades*. 24 vols. La Plata, 1921-1934.

This review contains much valuable bibliographical, economic, and literary material; there is also historical material, dealing largely with Lavalleja, and included also are indications of the growth of a new frontier class of society.
For items of especial interest, see 140, 145, 172, 443, 444.

122 *La revista americana de Buenos Aires*. Vols. 24-42. Buenos Aires, 1929-1933.

This review contains articles on the gaucho in literature and art. For the purposes of this study, however, its use is primarily bibliographical.
See items 1, 17, 24.

123 *Revista de derecho, historia y letras*. 76 vols. Buenos Aires, 1898—

In addition to useful material on literature and music (502, 526, and 1419), this review contains several valuable documentary studies, articles on the early history of the Plata settlement, and material useful for an economic study of colonial society.
See items 97, 98, 109, 130, 151, 169, 174, 189, 190.

124 *Revista de estudios hispánicos*. 2 vols. New York, 1928-1929.

A review especially good for bibliography. Its place is now being filled by the *Revista hispánica moderna*.

125 *Revista del Río de la Plata.* 13 vols. Buenos Aires, 1871-1877.

An excellent review containing valuable bibliographical material; accounts of the economic and social phases of La Plata life; descriptions of the gaucho character and life, and of the gaucho role in the Argentine armies. See items 72, 76, 86, 130, 132, 157, 164, 196.

126 Uruguay. Archivo y museo histórico nacional. *Revista histórica.* 12 vols. Montevideo, 1907-1924.

Useful for bibliographical material, for its inclusion of documentary material and for articles on early Uruguayan history. There is also included material on art and literature.
See items 14, 31, 67, 80-82, 89, 90, 99, 128, 131, 175, 176, 188, 191.

ARTICLES

127 Ambrosetti, Juan Bautista. "Viaje a las misiones argentinas y brasileras," La Plata, Universidad nacional, Museo, *Revista,* III, 417-448; IV, 289-336 and 353-368; V, 225-250.

Valuable for its contemporary account of conditions.

128 Araújo, Orestes. "Apuntes sobre geografía histórica del Uruguay," Uruguay, Archivo y museo histórico nacional, *Revista histórica,* V, 153-201.

The disreputable character of the early inhabitants of Río Grande do Sul; Hernandarias and his introduction of cattle into Uruguay; cattle hunting by Jesuits and changadores; the growth of a bandit class.

129 Azara, Félix de. "Apuntamientos para la historia natural de los cuadrúpedos del Paraguay y Río de la Plata," Argentine Republic, Ministerio de agricultura, *Anales,* Buenos Aires, 1900. Pp. 1-18.

The introduction of the horse in Argentina; its increase in the different sections of the country; its uses.

130 ———— "Viajes." See "Geografía física," *Revista de derecho, historia y letras,* XXVIII, 205-212, 363-385, 509-531; and *Revista del Río de la Plata,* V, 455-468, and VII, 3-28.

131 Barbagelata, Lorenzo. "Artigas antes de 1810," Uruguay, Archivo y museo histórico nacional, *Revista histórica,* I, 58-101.

Social and economic inequalities led to the growth of a vagabond class interested in contraband trade.

132 Barros, Alvaro. "Fronteras y territorios federales en las pampas del sud," *Revista del Río de la Plata,* II, 231-247, 451-467, 607-635.

A description of the gaucho army on the frontier and of contraband operations in the neighborhood of Azul.

133 Bauzá, Francisco. "El gaucho," Barbagelata, *Una centuria literaria,* 176-185.

A description of the gaucho class: the economic conditions in society which produced gauchos; gaucho appearance, character, language, and amusements.

134 Bayo, Ciro. "El gaucho y la pampa." An appendix to *Aucafilú,* Madrid, 1916.

135 Bonet, Carmelo M. "Ensayo sobre el gaucho uruguayo," *Nosotros,* XXXIII, 396-404.

The gaucho as the natural outgrowth of the society in which he lived.

136 Bunge, Carlos Octavio. "El derecho en la literatura gauchesca," *Estudios jurídicos,* Madrid, 1926. Pp. 5-30.

Despite its title, this article is a general study of the gaucho as a separate class in Argentine society. After making a distinction between the gauchos of the interior provinces and of the pampa, the author describes the latter. He gives an account of the role played by the gaucho in the various periods of Argentine history, tells of the law by which he lived and his troubles with that made by society, discusses the gradual transformation of the gaucho type and its unreal reflection in Argentine literature.

137 Cardoso, Aníbal. "Antigüedad del caballo en el Plata," Buenos Aires, Museo nacional, *Anales,* XXII, 371-439.

The author's conclusion is that the horse existed on the pampas long before the coming of the Spaniards. While this thesis has been proved inaccurate by Nordenskiöld (see item 331), much incidental information is included which is of value.

138 ———— "Breves noticias y tradiciones sobre el origen de la 'boleadora' y del caballo en la República Argentina," Buenos Aires, Museo nacional, *Anales,* XXVIII, 153-181.

A study of the evolution of the *boleador* from the *bola perdida* of the Patagonian Indians.

139 ———— "Nuevos comprobantes a propósito de la antigüedad del caballo en el Plata," Buenos Aires, Museo nacional, *Anales,* XXIV, 445-460.

A further expression of belief in a pre-Spanish horse.

140 Carrizo, Juan Alfonso. "Nuestra poesía popular," La Plata, Universidad nacional, Facultad de humanidades y ciencias de la educación, *Humanidades,* XV, 241-342.

A study of gaucho origin as well as of the gaucho theme in literature. The author describes the gaucho and differentiates between the gaucho types to be found in the northern and interior provinces and those on the coast.

141 Clulow, Alfredo. "Gauchismo y americanismo," *De la hora que pasa,* Montevideo, 1927.

142 Coni, Emilio Ángel. "Contribución a la historia del gaucho," Buenos Aires, Universidad nacional, Instituto de investigaciones históricas, *Boletín,* XVIII, 48-79. Buenos Aires, July, 1934- March, 1935.

A study of gaucho origin. The author believes that the first gauchos came from Santa Fe and that these were presently followed by gauchos from Entre Ríos and Buenos Aires.   •

143 ———— "Los gauchos de Salta," *La Nación,* August 9, 1936.

The gaucho of the north is agricultural and not nomadic. The gaucho as soldier.

144 ——— "Los gauchos del Uruguay hasta la fundación de Montevideo," *La Nación,* Buenos Aires, September 8, 1935.

A report of a lecture. Due to an early lack of horses in Uruguay, the author believes the first Uruguayan gauchos to have come from Misiones and Santa Fe, and that the Portuguese influence on the development of the gaucho in Uruguay was relatively late.

145 Costa Álvarez, Arturo. "Nuestro preceptismo literario: indianismo, americanismo, gauchismo, criollismo, nacionalismo," La Plata, Universidad, Facultad de ciencias de la educación, *Humanidades,* IX, 85-164.

146 Daireaux, Emilio. "Las razas indias en la América del Sud," Buenos Aires, Sociedad científica argentina, *Anales,* IV, 37-48, 103-110, 148-149, 208-223.

147 Delachaux, Enrique. "Las regiones físicas de la República Argentina," La Plata, Universidad nacional, *Revista del museo de la Plata,* XV, 102-131.

Useful for its lists of early travelers.

148 Falcao Espalter, Marco. "Génesis del tipo gaucho en el siglo XVIII," *La Prensa,* October 14, 1928.

149 ——— "Nacimiento del tipo gaucho en el siglo XVIII," *La Prensa,* May 27, 1928.

150 Franco, Luis. "El genio gaucho," *Babel,* XXI, no. 17, pp. 23-28.

151 Fregeiro, Clemente L. "Antecedentes de las invasiones inglesas en el Río de la Plata," *Revista de derecho, historia y letras,* I, 365-378.

Useful in an economic study.

152 ——— "San Martín, Guido y la espedición a Chile y el Perú," *Nueva revista de Buenos Aires,* IV, 291-315.

This article includes a description of gaucho warfare technique.

153 Gálvez, Víctor. "Las ciudades del interior. Provincia de Jujuy," *Nueva revista de Buenos Aires,* X, 263-267.

154 ——— "Mi tierra," *Nueva revista de Buenos Aires,* IX, 345-374 and 560-582.

A description of rural life in the interior provinces. Its economic aspects are stressed. There is also included a description of the gradual transformation of the gaucho type.

155 ——— "Recuerdos de Tucumán y Salta," *Nueva revista de Buenos Aires,* X, 443-466.

156 ——— "Treinta años antes," *Nueva revista de Buenos Aires,* IX, 204-236.

This article contains a description of the gaucho in the interior provinces.

157 García, Manuel Rafael. "Apuntamientos para la historia colonial del Río de la Plata," *Revista del Río de la Plata*, I, 635-647; II, 39-54; IV, 354-369.
   A picture of the economic condition of the Plata region in the colonial period; a description of the rural towns with their growing vagabond class; an account of frontier army life.

158 Garmendia, José Ignacio. "El fogón," *Nueva revista de Buenos Aires*, VII, 329-340.
   A picture of gaucho army life.

159 Girosi, Pablo. "Un tipo: dos momentos," *Nosotros*, LXX, 196-208.
   A study of the influence of the gaucho on present-day Argentine character, with emphasis on such elements as the feeling of the importance of the individual and that of racial superiority.

160 González Arrili, Bernardo. "Güemes," *Nosotros*, XXXVIII, 204-220.
   The source and character of the gaucho are discussed incidentally in this article.

161 Groussac, Paul. "El gauchismo," Buenos Aires, Biblioteca nacional, *Anales*, I, 414.

162 —————— "El gaucho," *El viaje intelectual*, Buenos Aires, 1904. Pp. 47-75.

163 Gutiérrez, Bartolomé. "Del folklore de la pampa, los deportes del gaucho," *La Nación*, July 16, 1927.

164 Gutiérrez, Juan María. "El vireinato del Río de la Plata durante la administración del Marqués de Loreto," *Revista del Río de la Plata*, VIII, 212-240.
   This article contains material on the mule trade with Peru.

165 Lehmann-Nitsche, Robert. "La bota de potro," Academia nacional de ciencias, Córdoba, *Boletín*, XXI, 183-300.
   A study of a characteristic article of gaucho dress.

166 —————— "El chambergo," Academia nacional de ciencias, Córdoba, *Boletín*, XXI, 1-99.
   An article on another item of the gaucho dress.

167 —————— "Noticias etnológicas sobre los antiguos Patagones, recogidas por la expedición Malaspina en 1789," Academia nacional de ciencias, Córdoba, *Boletín*, XX, 103-112.

168 Levene, Ricardo. "Introducción," Buenos Aires, Universidad nacional, Facultad de filosofía y letras, *Documentos*, IV, vii-cxvi.
   An excellent study of the changes in royal policy in the economic control of the Plata region.

169 —————— "Los orígenes de la revolución argentina de 1810," *Revista de derecho, historia y letras*, XXXIV, 549-559.

170 Lugones, Leopoldo. "A campo y cielo," *Nosotros,* X, 225-235.
Ideas on the gaucho: his origin, life, "calamities," and disappearance.

171 Lynch Arribalzaga, Enrique. "Origen y carácteres del caballo criollo," Argentine Republic, Ministerio de agricultura, *Anales,* 86-131 (Buenos Aires, 1900).
The peculiar value of this article is to be found in its listing of many early references to the horse in the Plata region.

172 Marfany, Roberto H. "El cuerpo de blandengues de la frontera de Buenos Aires (1752-1810)," La Plata, Universidad nacional, Facultad de humanidades y ciencias de la educación, *Humanidades,* XXIII, 313-374.
Useful for its study of frontier society.

173 Martínez, Benigno T. "Conquista y fundación de los pueblos de Entre Ríos," *Nueva revista de Buenos Aires,* X, 94-128.
War and contraband trade in their influence on the development of the gaucho outlaw in the lairs of the Montiel district.

174 Mendoza, Prudencio de la C. "La ganadería colonial en el siglo XVIII," *Revista de derecho, historia y letras,* LXXIII, 622-634.
Useful material on the introduction of cattle.

175 Miranda, Julián O. "Maldonado antiguo," Uruguay, Archivo y museo histórico nacional, *Revista histórica,* VI, 319-349, and IX, 122-141.

176 ———— "Población definitiva de la Banda Oriental," Uruguay, Archivo y museo histórico nacional, *Revista histórica,* VII, 779-793.

177 Mitre, Bartolomé. "La sociabilidad argentina," *Revista chilena,* VII, 45-69, 161-184.
The author notes the beginning of the "useful occupation" of Argentine soil which started with the importation of stock, "brought overland from Peru and from Brazil."

178 Molinari, Diego Luis. "Introducción," Buenos Aires, Universidad nacional, Facultad de filosofía y letras, *Documentos,* VII, ix-xcviii.
A study of the Negro slave trade.

179 Moreno, Francisco. "Viage a la Patagonia Setentrional," Buenos Aires, Sociedad científica argentina, *Anales,* I, 182-197.

180 Nichols, Madaline Wallis. "The Argentine gaucho," *The bulletin of the Pan American Union* (May, 1941), pp. 271-275.

181 ———— "Colonial Tucumán," *The Hispanic American historical review* (November, 1938), pp. 461-485.

182 ———— "The gaucho," *The Pacific historical review* (March, 1935), pp. 61-70.

183 ———— "The gaucho," *The Hispanic American historical review* (November, 1937), pp. 532-536.

184 ——— "El gaucho argentino," *Revista ibero-americana,* I, no. 1, pp. 153-158, 161-164.

185 ——— "The gaucho 'motif' in Río de la Plata life," *The Spanish review* (November, 1935), pp. 87-89.

186 ——— "Pastoral society on the pampa," *The Hispanic American historical review* (August, 1939), pp. 367-371.

187 ——— "The Spanish horse of the pampas," *The American anthropologist* (January-March, 1939), pp. 119-129.

188 Palomeque, Alberto. "La revolución de mayo," Uruguay, Archivo y museo histórico nacional, *Revista histórica,* IX, 287-326, 667-703.

189 Peña, Enrique. "La despoblación de Buenos Aires en 1541," *Revista de derecho, historia y letras,* XIX, 178-186.

190 ——— "Irala," *Revista de derecho, historia y letras,* XX, 345-366.

191 Pérez Castellano, José Manuel. "La Banda Oriental en 1787," Uruguay, Archivo y museo histórico nacional, *Revista histórica,* V, 661-688.
    Wild cattle and horses; the mule trade; the business of dealing in hides.

192 Quesada, Vicente Gaspar. "Noticias sobre la antigua provincia del Río de la Plata," *Nueva revista de Buenos Aires,* IV, 442-463.
    On the economic aspect of the problem.

193 Sagarna, Antonio. "El hombre del pronunciamiento de la liberación y de la organización," *Nosotros,* LXVIII, 5-16.
    Urquiza and his relation to the gaucho are discussed.

194 Saint Robert, M. Chevalier. (Quoted in Washburn, Charles, *History of Paraguay,* Boston, 1871.)
    A contemporary description of the gaucho.

195 Spegazzini, Carlos. "Costumbres de los patagones," Buenos Aires, Sociedad científica argentina, *Anales,* XVII, 221-240.

196 Vicuña Mackenna, Benjamín. "Buenos Aires, mercado americano," *Revista del Río de la Plata,* IV, 80-97.
    An account of early vaquerías and of the mule trade with Peru.

Books

The following bibliography is a highly selected list of those books found most valuable either for an actual portrayal and study of the gaucho or for a study of the society from which he emerged and in which he lived. The emphasis in this list is on the descriptive works of travelers, on studies of the economic and social aspects of La Plata life, on histories of the gaucho role in La Plata wars. While no such subdivisions are attempted in the bibliography, see such several chapter footnotes as those on travel literature (Chapter I) and on economic literature (Chapter V).

197 Acarete du Biscay. *Account of a voyage up the River de la Plata and thence overland to Peru (1658),* in D'Acugna, Christopher, *Voyages and discoveries in South America.* London, 1698.

> This work contains an account of the condition of the livestock industry at the time of the author's visit. Included are statistics on contraband trade and descriptions of various uses for cattle hides.

198 Acevedo, Eduardo. *Historia del Uruguay.* 9 vols. Montevideo, 1916-1929.

> A work useful for its account of the Spanish-Portuguese struggle for the possession of the Banda Oriental. Spain's economic policy is discussed in its relation to the Plata region. Between 2,000 and 3,000 cattle hunters are reported in the Banda Oriental in 1793-1794.

199 Acevedo Díaz, Eduardo. *El mito del Plata.* Buenos Aires, 1917.

> A study of the gaucho as a soldier. There are also included an analysis of gaucho character and an indication of the necessary disappearance of the gaucho as a separate class of society.

200 Alais, Octavio P. *Libro criollo. Costumbres nacionales.* Buenos Aires, 1903.

201 Álvarez, Juan. *Ensayo sobre la historia de Santa Fe.* Buenos Aires, 1910.

> Primarily an analysis of the reasons for Spain's economic orientation of South America towards Peru, with the corresponding growth of La Plata contraband trade. The work also includes a consideration of the gaucho as a soldier and a note on the social transformation of the gaucho type.

202 ———— *Estudio sobre las guerras civiles argentinas.* Buenos Aires, 1914.

> The book includes a description of the economic condition of colonial society in the Plata region and an analysis of the economic reasons for the formation of the gaucho class.

203 Andrews, Captain Joseph. *Journey from Buenos Aires through the provinces of Córdova, Tucumán, and Salta, to Potosí.* London, 1827.

> An account of traveling conditions—carriages used, provisions that are taken, bugs encountered in post-houses, Indian dangers. The author also describes the gaucho method of travel and he includes a description of a "gaucho dandy."

204 Arago, Jacques Étienne Victor. *Promenade autour du monde, pendant les années 1817, 1818, 1819 et 1820, sur les corvettes du roi, l'Uranie et la Physicienne, commandées par M. Freycinet.* Paris, 1822.

> A ten-page contemporary description of the gaucho is included (pp. 433-443).

205 Arata, Pedro M. *El mate en nuestras costumbres.* Buenos Aires, 1881.

206 Araújo, Orestes. *Diccionario popular de historia de la República Oriental del Uruguay.* 3 vols. Montevideo, 1901-1903.

Under the headings *Comercio, Changadores, Ganado,* and *Industrias,* there is a description of the economic aspect of life in the Plata region. The growth and the necessary social transformation of the gaucho class are described under the heading *Gaucho.*

207 ——— *Historia compendiada de la civilización uruguaya.* 2 vols. Montevideo, 1907.

The introduction of livestock into the Plata region, Spanish and Portuguese occupation of the Banda Oriental, and cattle hunting there.

208 Arcos, Santiago. *La Plata.* Paris, 1865.

Artigas, Rivera, Rosas, and Urquiza as gaucho leaders. There is note of the gaucho idea of war as being both pleasant and profitable.

209 Argentine Republic. Ministerio de agricultura. *El caballo argentino.* Buenos Aires, 1900.

The introduction and increase of the horse in Argentina. Among the many articles included in this work, those by Azara and Lynch are of most value. See items 129 and 171.

210 Arias y Miranda, José. *Examen crítico-histórico del influjo que tuvo en el comercio, industria y población de España su dominación en América.* Madrid, 1854.

Reasons for contraband trade.

211 Arreguine, Víctor. *Estudios históricos.* Montevideo, 1913.

This work contains a study of the gaucho as soldier and of the type of leader the gaucho would follow.

212 ——— *Historia del Uruguay.* Montevideo, 1892.

Of especial interest for the purposes of this study are the accounts of the introduction of cattle in Uruguay and of the influence of the expulsion of the Jesuits upon the mixing of Spaniards with the mission Indian. A description of the gaucho is also included.

213 ——— *Los orientales. Tierra salvaje.* Buenos Aires, 1924.

There is included in this work a description of the gaucho as a soldier.

214 *An authentic narrative of the proceedings of the expedition under the command of Brigadier-General Craufurd, until its arrival at Montevideo; with an account of the operations against Buenos Aires under the command of Lieutenant General Whitelocke.* London, 1808.

Included in this narrative is an account of Argentine economic life.

215 Ayarragaray, Lucas. *La anarquía argentina y el caudillismo.* 2d ed. Buenos Aires, 1925.

A study of the part played by the gaucho and his caudillo leaders in the post-Independence period of Argentine history.

216 Azara, Félix de. *Descripción e historia del Paraguay and del Río de la Plata.* 2 vols. Madrid, 1847.

A study, valuable for its descriptions of the Pampas Indians and of the rural classes of the Plata society.

217 ——— *Geografía física y esférica de las provincias del Paraguay y Misiones Guaraníes (1790),* in Montevideo, Museo nacional, *Anales del museo de Montevideo,* I, 11-468. Montevideo, 1904.

This work is of value for the purposes of this study because of its descriptions of the importance in the country of the horse and cow, its notations indicating just where they are to be found, and its account of an early cow hunt or vaquería. Of the eleven journeys covered, the material of most use came from the third trip, that of 1784 to the Misiones pueblos.

218 ——— *Memorias póstumas.* Madrid, 1847.
In the "Memoria rural del Río de la Plata" the author discussed the trade in hides.

219 Barbagelata, Hugo David. *Sobre la época de Artigas.* Paris, 1930.
Included is a description of the gaucho as soldier.

220 Barbará, Federico. *Usos y costumbres de los pampas y algunos apuntes históricos sobre la guerra de la frontera.* 1st ed. Buenos Aires, 1856.

221 Bates, Henry Walter, ed. *Central America, the West Indies, and South America.* London, 1878.
Included are descriptions of the Tehuelches Indians and of the gaucho.

222 Beerbohm, Julius. *Wanderings in Patagonia.* London, 1881.
Descriptions of gauchos are included.

223 Bishop, Nathaniel Holmes. *A thousand miles' walk across South America.* Boston, 1881.
An account of a trip taken with a caravan of carts from Buenos Aires to Mendoza. The description of the gaucho is most uncomplimentary.

224 Bonnycastle, Sir Richard Henry. *Spanish America.* London, 1818.
A brief account of the economic conditions in the Plata is included.

225 Bosque, Carlos. *Compendio de historia americana y argentina.* Buenos Aires, n.d.
Economic conditions in the Plata region are discussed.

226 Bougainville, Louis Antoine de. *Voyage autour du monde,* Paris, 1771, in Berenger, Jean Pierre, *Collection de tous les voyages faits autour du monde.* Paris, 1789.
Note of the growth of a brigand people on the Banda Oriental.

227 Brackenridge, Henry Mario. *Voyage to Buenos Aires, in 1817 and 1818* (London 1820), in Sir Richard Phillips, *New voyages and travels,* III.
Descriptions of gauchos; a party of Pampas Indians ride into town; the frontier line of forts "originally built as defense against the Indian who of late has been causing no trouble."

228 Brand, Lieutenant Charles. *Journal of a voyage to Peru; a passage across the Cordillera of the Andes, in the winter of 1827, performed on foot in the snow; and a journey across the pampas.* London, 1828.
The author describes the Uruguayan gaucho patriot troops as of disreputable appearance. In connection with his trip across the pampa, he writes of post-houses; of gaucho character, appearance, and amusements; and he lists the many strange uses for hides which he had noted.

229 Brossard, Alfred de. *Considérations historiques et politiques sur les Républiques de la Plata dans leurs rapports avec la France et l'Angleterre.* Paris, 1850.
This work contains a brief description of the gaucho and of such leaders as López, Rivera, and Rosas.

230 Burmeister, Hermann. *Reise durch die La Plata-Staaten, mit besonderer Rücksicht auf die physische Beschaffenheit und den Culturzustand der Argentinischen Republik. Ausgeführt in den Jahren 1857, 1858, 1859, und 1860.* 2 vols. Halle, 1861.
While primarily geographical in character, this work nevertheless contains a valuable contemporary description of the gaucho.

231 Burton, Captain Richard Francis. *Letters from the battlefields of Paraguay.* London, 1870.
Describes the gaucho of Corrientes and the methods of gaucho warfare.

232 Bustamante Carlos, Calixto ("Concolorcorvo"). *El lazarillo de ciegos caminantes desde Buenos Aires hasta Lima. 1773,* in Buenos Aires, Junta de historia y numismática americana, *Biblioteca,* IV, 3-324. Buenos Aires, 1908—.
Written at the crucial period in gaucho history, when the type was just coming into being, the description of the gauderios included in this work is of singular importance. The gauderio is defined as "a young man born in the neighborhood of Montevideo," but the type was also reported as found singing "horrible songs" in Tucumán.

233 Caldcleugh, Alexander. *Travels in South America during the years 1819-1820-1821.* London, 1825.
Useful for a study of Indians and of economic conditions.

234 Campbell, John. *A concise history of the Spanish America.* London, 1741.
Useful only for its account of economic conditions.

235 Cárcano, Ramón J. *Historia de los medios de comunicación y transporte en la República Argentina.* Buenos Aires, 1893.

236 Cervera, Manuel M. *Historia de la ciudad y provincia de Santa Fe. 1573-1853.* Santa Fe, 1908.
A useful book for any study of the conquest and occupation of the Plata region. It is particularly valuable for the study of the Indian invasions from the Chaco and in Santa Fe, the occupation of the Entre Ríos, and the growth of a vagabond class. Included are 134 pages of documents.

237 Charlevoix, Padre Pedro Francisco Javier de. *Historia del Paraguay.* 6 vols. Madrid, 1910, 1916.

238 Coni, Emilio Ángel. *Historia de las vaquerías del Río de la Plata.* Madrid, 1930.

239 Corbière, Emilio P. *El gaucho. Desde su origen hasta nuestros días.* Buenos Aires, 1929.
Distinctive elements of this general study are the author's apparent identification of the terms *gaucho* and *mestizo;* his consideration of urban gauchos specializing in law, politics, and general corruption; his belief in

the totally negative contribution to society of the gaucho type. The truth of literary portrayals of the gaucho is described as comparable to the truth of funeral orations; the author also expresses disapproval of the nonsocial ideals expressed in that literature.

240 Coroleu, José. *América. Historia de su colonización, dominación e independencia.* Barcelona, 1895.

This work describes the gaucho, and particularly the gaucho soldier of Güemes.

241 Costa, Alfredo R. da. *O Rio Grande do Sul.* 2 vols. Porto Alegre, 1922.

242 Daireaux, Emilio. *Vida y costumbres en el Plata.* 2 vols. Buenos Aires, 1888.

Stating his belief that the term *gaucho* denotes a social class and not a race, Daireaux stresses the influence of the Arab on that class, due to an emigration of the Moors from southern Spain after the completion of the reconquest. He then describes the gaucho and the fighting skill he displayed in cattle hunt, contraband trade, and war.

243 Darwin, Charles. *Journal of researches into the natural history and geology of the countries visited during the voyage round the world of H.M.S. "Beagle."* 2d ed. London, 1913.

Included are descriptions of gauchos and Indians on the Buenos Aires frontier.

244 Dávalos, Juan Carlos. *Los gauchos.* Buenos Aires, 1928.

A description of the gaucho of Salta; his Spanish and his Indian characteristics; the clothes he wore, the kind of saddle he used.

245 Davie, John Constance. *Letters from Buenos Ayres and Chili.* London, 1819.

While the gaucho does not figure in this work, it is of use for the purposes of this study because of notes on economic conditions influenced by the gaucho; trade in hides; the making of by-products.

246 De-María, Isidoro. *Compendio de la historia de la República Oriental del Uruguay.* 6 vols. in 3. Montevideo, 1895-1901.

Useful for a study of the introduction of cattle, the cattle hunts, and the Indians of Uruguay.

247 Dobrizhoffer, Martín. *An account of the Abipones, an equestrian people of Paraguay.* London, 1822. 1st ed., 1784.

A study useful for its treatment of such items of early colonial trade as the numbers of horses and cattle on the plains, the results of waste in their slaughter, and the mule trade with Peru. The migration of the Abipones in from the north Bermejo frontier is also noted.

248 Estrada, José Manuel. *Fragmentos históricos.* Buenos Aires, 1901.

A study of the influence of social institutions and of geography on the creation of human types. Gaucho character is described as predicated by life in an open country, away from towns. The gaucho role in the wars is portrayed as a social, class struggle.

249 ———— *Lecciones sobre la historia de la República Argentina.* Buenos Aires, 1898.

The role of the gaucho in the Argentine civil wars and a description of several gaucho leaders.

250 Falkner, Padre Tomás. "Descripción de la Patagonia," La Plata, Universidad nacional, *Biblioteca centenaria,* I, 21-126.

Originally published in 1774 as *A description of Patagonia and the adjoining parts of South America,* this work emphasizes economic conditions in the Plata region, including the interior provinces. It also treats of Indian tribes. It does not specifically mention the gaucho, though content is such that there would be every reason for such mention were the term in use at the time.

251 Fontpertius, A. F. de. *Les états latins de l'Amérique.* Paris, 1882.

This work includes a description of the gaucho.

252 Fraser, John Foster. *The amazing Argentine. A new land of enterprise.* London and New York, 1914.

This book contains a brief account of the introduction of horses and cattle into Argentina and a description of the modern gaucho as seen at his horse races.

253 Frías, Bernardo. *Historia de Güemes y de la provincia de Salta.* 3 vols. Salta, 1902, Buenos Aires, 1907, and Salta, 1911.

An excellent description of the gaucho, and especially of the gaucho as soldier. There is also included an account of colonial trade.

254 Friederici, Georg. *Der Charakter der Entdeckung und Eroberung Amerikas durch die Europäer.* Stuttgart-Gotha, 1925.

One of the best works on the general technique of the Spanish conquest.

255 Gandía, Enrique de. *Historia de la conquista del Río de la Plata y del Paraguay. 1535-1556.* Buenos Aires, 1932.

An excellent work, useful for the purposes of this study because of its well-documented treatment of the subject of the introduction of horses into the Plata region. This study rather destroys the myth of those Mendoza horses which for so many years have been held responsible for stocking the pampa.

256 García, Juan Agustín. *La ciudad indiana.* Buenos Aires, 1900.

An excellent study of the economic reasons for the formation of the vagabond gaucho class. In civil life the gaucho might only be either a gatherer of hides, generally for use in contraband trade, or a temporary settler on the frontier from which he would be driven because of his lack of legal title to the land. The author describes the resultant contempt for law and analyzes other aspects of Spanish character, notably the worship of courage.

257 García Al-Deguer, Juan. *Historia de la Argentina.* 2 vols. Madrid, 1902-1903.

Useful for a study of economic conditions.

258 García Camba, Andrés. *Memorias del general García Camba para la historia de las armas españolas en el Perú (1809-1821).* Madrid, 1916.

A Spanish report on the gaucho success in war.

259 Gelpi y Ferro, Gil. *Estudios sobre la América.* Habana, 1864.

Of use for the period of the settlement of the Plata region.

260 Gerstaecker, Friedrich Wilhelm Christian. *Narrative of a journey round the world.* New York, 1853.

The author describes the appearance of several gaucho types encountered in his journey; the red, ruffian follower of Rosas; the old gaucho worker in the Buenos Aires slaughterhouse; the payador. He also writes of the gaucho mode of life in the country huts and of the manifold uses found for cattle hides.

261 Gillespie, Major Alexander. *Gleanings and remarks: collected during many months of residence at Buenos Ayres and within the upper country.* London, 1818.

One of the significant things about this work is that the word *gaucho* is *not* used in it, despite the fact that after the English invasions the author and several fellow officers had been sent across country and exiled to the province of Rioja, where conspiracy and escape would be difficult. The Argentine peon soldier is described at length in an account which would exactly fit the gaucho; "vagrant horsemen" and "the lower orders" are frequently mentioned. According to this work, then, the gaucho type was in existence, but the word *gaucho* would not seem to have been in general use in the interior provinces around 1810.

Major Gillespie describes as well the mode of life encountered and the economic condition of the country.

262 Gómez, Hernán Félix. *Historia de la provincia de Corrientes.* 2 vols. Corrientes, 1928, 1929.

This work contains material on the uses for hides and on the economic situation in the Plata region.

263 González, Joaquín Víctor. *Mis montañas.* Buenos Aires, 1925.

This work includes a description of the gaucho type existing in the southwestern part of Argentina.

264 Goycochea, Castilhos. *A alma heroica das coxilhas.* Rio de Janeiro, 1935.

An account of the origin of the Portuguese gaucho, together with a description of the Portuguese advance into the Banda Oriental.

265 ———— *O gaucho na vida politica brasileira.* Rio de Janeiro, n.d.

266 Graham, Robert Bontine Cunninghame. *The horses of the conquest.* London, 1930.

This work treats of such matters as the various styles of riding, the shipment of horses from Spain, and names given to horses on the pampas.

267 ———— *The Ipané.* New York, 1925.

Good for material on the history of the lasso and the bolas. The author also describes the curious gaucho-Indian custom of having a dance in honor of the death of a child and in celebration of its presumable entrance to heaven.

268 ———— *Pedro de Valdivia, conqueror of Chile.* London, 1926.

Useful for its reproduction of Valdivia's five letters to Charles V, and for the other indications of the introduction of livestock into the Tucumán country.

269 Granada, Daniel. *Vocabulario rioplatense razonado.* Montevideo, 1890.

A description of the gaucho in 1890, with an indication of the changes in type which had taken place after the civil wars. Included also are quotations from descriptions by early writers, notably from Pedro Estala's *El viajero universal.*

270 Groussac, Paul, *et al.* *Memoria histórica y descriptiva de la provincia de Tucumán.* Buenos Aires, 1882.

This work is useful for the purposes of this study because of its indications of the influence of geography on the evolution of the gaucho type and its considerations of the gaucho role in Argentine wars. There is also included much material on cattle and hides.

271 ——— *El viaje intelectual.* 2 vols. Madrid and Buenos Aires, 1904.

Three studies of the gaucho are included in this collection: *A propósito de americanismos, Calandria,* and *El gaucho.* The first, though primarily philological in character, also contains material on the origin of the gaucho type; the second is a portrayal of a famous gaucho outlaw.

The third study, a lecture delivered at the World's Folklore Congress meeting at Chicago in 1893, is a description of two varieties of gaucho—those from around Buenos Aires and those from the interior provinces, between the Salado and Dulce rivers. The part played by the gaucho in Argentine wars is discussed.

Groussac defines the gauchos as "men clever in the use of lasso and horse"; they are also "vagabond" and "outlaw."

272 Guevara, Padre José. *Historia de la conquista del Paraguay, Río de la Plata, y Tucumán.* Buenos Aires, 1882.

With those by Lozano, Funes, Dobrizhoffer, and Charlevoix, this is one of the five great Jesuit histories of the Plata region.

273 Guinard, M. *Trois ans d'esclavage.* Paris, 1845.

A description of the Pampas Indians is included.

274 Haigh, Samuel. *Sketches of Buenos Aires, Chile, and Peru.* London, 1831.

This work contains excellent descriptions of the gaucho, of the frontier forts, and of the caravans of *carretas* used in trade.

275 Hakluyt society. *The conquest of the River Plate (1535-1555).* London, 1891.

See item 333.

276 Hauff, Walter von. *Im Kampf mit Indianer und Gaucho.* Leipzig, 1925.

The author of this work describes the gaucho and discusses his relationship to the Indian.

277 Head, Captain Francis Bond. *Rough notes taken during some rapid journeys across the pampas and among the Andes.* Boston, 1827.

A description of the gauchos, and of the huts in which they lived, by a man who had an opportunity to study them in his four rides across the pampa from Buenos Aires to Chile. Captain Head also describes the education of the little gaucho from the time he swings in his hide cradle to the time he learns to ride by climbing up his horse's tail; he tells of carriages that cross the plains, the ravages of the Pampas Indians, and the gaucho role in war.

278 Helms, Anthony Zachariah. *Travels from Buenos Aires, by Potosí, to Lima.* London, 1807.

Principally useful for material on trade, but also included are descriptions of the gaucho and of the Indian.

279 Hernández, José. *Instrucción del estanciero.* Buenos Aires, 1881.

280 Herrera y Tordesillas, Antonio de. *Historia general.* Madrid, 1726-1727.

Useful for the story of the conquest.

281 Hinchliff, Thomas Woodbine. *South American sketches.* London, 1863.

Descriptions of the gaucho are included.

282 Hudson, William Henry. *Far away and long ago.* New York, 1924.

This work contains descriptions of the gaucho.

283 Huret, Jules. *En Argentine. De Buenos Aires au Gran Chaco.* Paris, 1911.

A description of the gaucho; his character, clothes, amusements, equipment, and his custom of drinking *mate.*

284 Hutchinson, Thomas Joseph. *Buenos Aires and Argentine gleanings: with extracts from a diary of Salado exploration in 1862 and 1863.* London, 1865.

This work contains an excellent contemporary description of the gaucho; his clothes; his hut; his food; his equipment; his amusements; an analysis of his character. There is also a remarkable account of the many uses for horses in Argentine rural life, and there are statistics illustrative of the kind, amount, and manner of trade.

285 —— *The Paraná, with incidents of the Paraguayan war and South American recollections from 1861 to 1868.* London, 1868.

Descriptions of gaucho and Indian are included.

286 Ibarguren, Carlos. *De nuestra tierra.* Buenos Aires, 1917.

After a consideration of the importance of the horse to Argentine society and of the influence of geography on character, Ibarguren describes the two Argentine rural social types—the gaucho and the muleteer. He also writes of the latter's value in *montonera* warfare.

287 Jefferson, Mark. *Peopling the Argentine pampa.* New York, 1926.

The gaucho is described as a product of his environment and defined as "a hunter of horses and cows." The author of this work then describes the gaucho and compares him with the guaso of Chile.

288 Kennedy, Albert Joseph. *La Plata, Brazil, and Paraguay, during the present war.* London, 1869.

A contemporary description of the gaucho.

289 King, Colonel John Anthony. *Twenty-four years in the Argentine Republic.* New York, 1846.

A short description of the gaucho is included, and it is of use as another contemporary record.

290 Kühn, Franz. *Grundriss der Kulturgeographie von Argentinien.* Hamburg, 1933.

Primarily a geographical work, but there are included studies of the various Indian tribes and a description of the gaucho.

291 Larden, Walter. *Argentine plains and Andine glaciers.* New York and London, 1911.

    The native peon as representative of the gaucho class of older days.

292 Latham, Wilfrid. *The states of the River Plate.* 2d ed. London, 1868.

    This book contains an excellent description of the gaucho; a study of the influence of economic and political uncertainty upon his life and character; a study of trade.

293 Leguizamón, Martiniano. *La cuna del gaucho.* Buenos Aires, 1935.

    A study of gaucho origin and of the gaucho soldier. Other studies in this work are on the *boleadora indígena* (pp. 53-77), the Charrúas of Entre Ríos (pp. 79-87), Hidalgo (pp. 89-96). The work concludes with a manuscript of 1772 in which the gaucho is described but not named (pp. 145-157).

294 —— *Etnografía del Plata: el origen de las boleadoras y el lazo.* Buenos Aires, 1919.

295 —— *El gaucho.* Buenos Aires, 1917.

296 —— *Páginas argentinas.* Buenos Aires, 1911.

    One of the articles in this collection, "Sobre el criollismo," treats of the gaucho role in history.

297 Lehmann-Nitsche, Robert. "Santos Vega," Academia nacional de ciencias, Córdoba, *Boletín, XXII,* 1-434.

    Besides a scholarly study of a gaucho literary theme, this work contains much valuable information on gaucho clubs and periodicals (pp. 379-382, 392-393) which indicate a reincarnation of gaucho life in the Plata region, even though that life may be even more artificial than the literary reincarnation that preceded it.

298 Levillier, Roberto. *Nueva crónica de la conquista del Tucumán. 1563-1573.* Buenos Aires, 1926, 1930, 1931.

    An excellent study of the conquest and settlement of Tucumán. The military and economic plans behind that conquest are also studied.

299 —— *Les origines argentines.* Paris, 1912.

    An interesting study of the gaucho, with emphasis on his combativity.

300 Lista, Ramón. *Mis esploraciones y descubrimientos en la Patagonia, 1877-1880.* Buenos Aires, 1880.

301 —— *Viaje al país de los Tehuelches.* Buenos Aires, 1879.

302 Livacich, Serafín. *Buenos Aires.* Buenos Aires, 1907.

    Useful for a study of the settlement of Buenos Aires.

303 Long, Professor *(et al.). America and the West Indies.* London, 1845.

    This work contains a description of the Indian and of conditions on the Buenos Aires frontier.

304 López, Vicente Fidel. "El año XX," *Revista del Río de la Plata,* V, 45-132, 252-311, 399-454; VII, 29-110; VIII, 241-305; IX, 103-158, 363-440; X, 491-592; XI, 566-663.

    This work includes descriptions of the gaucho; of the geographical, social, and economic factors which influenced his development; of his role in Argentine history; and of his caudillo leaders.

305 Lozano, Pedro. *Historia de la conquista del Paraguay, Río de la Plata y Tucumán. 1745.* Buenos Aires, 1873-1875.

306 Lugones, Leopoldo. *La guerra gaucha.* 2d ed. Buenos Aires, 1926.

While primarily a literary work, this collection of sketches nevertheless gives an excellent account of gaucho war technique.

307 —— *El payador. Hijo de la pampa.* Buenos Aires, 1916.

A study of the origin of the gaucho, a description of his character, and, especially, an analysis of his important contributions to many phases of Argentine life.

308 Lynch, Ventura R. *Costumbres del indio y el gaucho.* Buenos Aires, 1883.

309 McColl, J. *Guide to Montevideo.* London, 1862.

310 Machado, José Eustaquio. *El gaucho y el llanero.* Caracas, 1926.

311 Madero, Eduardo. *Historia del puerto de Buenos Aires.* Buenos Aires, 1902.

On the discovery of the Plata; useful for its quoted documents.

312 Magariños Cervantes, Alejandro. *Estudios históricos, políticos, y sociales sobre el Río de la Plata.* Paris, 1854.

A definition and an excellent description of the gaucho. This work also describes the gaucho role in Argentine history.

313 Mansilla, Lucio Victorio. *Una excursión a los indios ranqueles.* Buenos Aires, 1928. 1st ed., 1870.

An account of the author's visit in the Indian villages beyond the frontier. The work contains many comparisons of the Indian and gaucho—to the disadvantage of the latter.

314 Mantegazza, Paolo. *Viajes por el Río de la Plata.* Buenos Aires, 1916. 1st ed., 1867.

This work contains descriptions of the gaucho—his character, home, food, and amusements. It also includes an account of the movements of trade in the midnineteenth century and a description of the Pampas Indians.

315 Marmier, Xavier. *Lettres sur l'Amérique.* 2 vols. Paris, 1881.

This work contains a definition and a description of the gaucho. It also notes the existence of a "gaucho-proprietor" class.

316 Mellet, Julien. *Viajes por el interior de la América Meridional.* Santiago de Chile, n.d.

Useful for a description of the Negro slave trade in America.

317 Miers, John. *Travels in Chile and La Plata.* London, 1826.

A travel work useful for notes on cattle herds, the many local uses found for hides, the mule trade, and the Pampas Indians. It also contains a description of the gaucho and an analysis of the reasons for his success as a fighter in the wars.

318 Miller, John. *Memorias del General Miller.* Madrid, 1829.

An excellent account of the gaucho, especially as a soldier. Included also are descriptions of the Pehuenches and of the vaquerías.

319 Mitre, Bartolomé. *Historia de Belgrano y de la independencia argentina.* 3 vols. Buenos Aires, 1887.
   Besides its value for the descriptions of the gaucho soldier, written by one who knew him personally, this work is exceedingly valuable for its presentation of the economic conditions of La Plata society.

320 —— *Historia de San Martín y de la emancipación.* 4 vols. Buenos Aires, 1890.
   The first volume contains a description of the gaucho soldier of Salta.

321 Moses, Bernard. *The establishment of Spanish rule in America.* New York, 1907.
   Especially useful in a study of trade in hides and Negro slaves.

322 —— *Papers on the southern Spanish colonies of America.* Berkeley, 1911.
   An account of the Spanish-Portuguese relations in the Banda Oriental is included.

323 Moussy, Martín de. *Confédération argentine.* Paris, 1862.

324 Mulhall, Mrs. Michel George. *Between Amazon and Andes.* London, 1881.
   Included are descriptions of the gaucho and of the carreta caravans.

325 Muñiz, Rómulo. *El gaucho.* Buenos Aires, 1934.

326 —— *Los indios Pampas.* Buenos Aires, 1929.

327 Murray, John Hale. *Travels in Uruguay, South America.* London, 1871.
   Included are descriptions of the gaucho.

328 Museo colonial e histórico de la provincia de Buenos Aires. *Guía descriptiva.* 2d ed. Buenos Aires, 1926.

329 Musters, George Chaworth. "At home with the Patagonians," La Plata, Universidad nacional, *Biblioteca centenaria,* I, 127-388.
   A Spanish translation of a book published in English in London (1873). Useful for this study because of notes on the early horses of Patagonia, a comparison between gaucho and Indian methods of horse-breaking, and indications of the growth of a mestizo race due to the Araucanian fondness for Spanish captives and to Spanish desertions from frontier armies.

330 Niles, John Milton. *South America and Mexico.* Hartford, 1844.
   Contains a contemporary description of the gaucho.

331 Nordenskiöld, Erland. *Deductions suggested by the geographical distribution of some post-Columbian words used by the Indians of South America,* in his *Comparative ethnographical studies.* 9 vols. Göteburg, 1919-1931.
   The third chapter of this work is entitled "The introduction of horses and cattle into South America." Its thesis is that the pampa herds of wild horses owe their origin not to the Mendoza mares, but to the horses stolen from the Spaniards in Chile by the Araucanian Indians. The author also believes that cattle as well were more likely to come from Spanish settlements in the western country of Tucumán than from the east where settlement was relatively late.

332 Núñez, Ignacio. *An account, historical, political, and statistical, of the United Provinces of Río de la Plata.* London, 1825.

Useful in a study of economic conditions.

333 Núñez Cabeza de Vaca, Alvar. *Commentaries.* Vol. 81. Hakluyt society publications. London, 1891.

An English translation of one of the first accounts of the Plata region. See item 53.

334 Orbigny, Alcide Dessalines d'. *L'homme américain.* Paris, 1839.

Useful in the study of the Indians of Argentina and Uruguay.

335 ———— *Voyage pittoresque dans les deux Amériques.* Paris, 1836.

Included are descriptions of the gaucho, particularly of the gaucho militiaman. This work also contains material on the Pampas Indians and on their relationship to the gaucho.

336 Ovalle, Alonso de. *Histórica relación del Reyno de Chile.* Rome, 1646.

A description of the Pampas Indians is included.

337 Oviedo y Valdés, Gonzalo Fernández de. *Historia general y natural de las Indias.* Madrid, 1851-1855.

338 Pauw, Cornelius de. *Recherches philosophiques sur les Américains.* London, 1770.

Pages 281-326 treat of the Patagonians and of the travelers who have been calling on them.

339 Page, Frederick Mann. *Los payadores gauchos.* Darmstadt, 1897.

Primarily a study of gaucho literature and language, nevertheless this work contains material on the origin and on the character of the gaucho.

340 Page, Thomas Jefferson. *La Plata, the Argentine Confederation, and Paraguay.* London, 1859.

A general account of the conditions noted between the years 1853 and 1856. The book contains economic material on the cattle industry, trade, and uses of hides; descriptions of the gaucho, of his practical education and his life; notes on his relationship to the Indian and on the gaucho career in war.

341 Parish, Woodbine. *Buenos Aires and the provinces of the Río de la Plata.* London, 1852.

A description of the gaucho and of his mode of life; the influence of the Ranqueles and the gaucho deserters from the army in the formation of a new frontier race. Woodbine Parish notes a similarity in gaucho and Indian attitude toward mares, and he also records the curious fact that in Tucumán the gaucho is known as the *mamelucho* (who belongs in Brazil). Another interesting feature of this work is the account of the many strange uses found for horses in the Plata region.

342 Paz, General José María. *Memorias póstumas.* Buenos Aires. 2d ed., 1917.

The first volume contains a contemporary account of the gaucho soldiers of Güemes.

343 Pelliza, Mariano A. *Historia argentina.* 3 vols. Buenos Aires, 1888-1889.

The origin of the gaucho, a comparison of gaucho life with that of the Indian, and the growth of the *matrero,* or gaucho outlaw, class. This work also contains excellent economic material on the hide industry.

344 ——— *El país de las pampas (1516-1780)*. Buenos Aires, 1887.
Much of the descriptive material on gaucho life in this book is to be found also in the author's *Historia argentina*. One of the additional items of interest, however, is a note of the Paulista need for mules and horses, a need which would possibly seem to indicate the improbable origin of the gaucho type in Brazil.

345 Pernety, Antoine Joseph. See item 338.

346 Proctor, Robert. *Narrative of a journey across the Cordillera of the Andes and of a residence in Lima and other parts of Peru in the years 1823 and 1824.* London, 1825.
A contemporary description of the gaucho. This work is also useful for its indications of the many uses found for hides.

347 Quesada, Ernesto. *El "criollismo" en la literatura argentina.* Buenos Aires, 1902.
A valuable study of the transformation in gaucho literature due to the transformation in society and the influence of the immigrant. Quesada notes such evidences of the popularity of the gaucho theme in middle-class urban society as the versification of many of the gaucho novels, the public contests between modern imitation payadores serving as a theater attraction, and the large libraries of gaucho works which were being published. Together with the Santos Vega study by Lehmann-Nitsche (see item 297), this work demonstrates the Italian immigrant's interest in "playing at being a gaucho."

348 Quesada, Vicente Gaspar. *La Patagonia.* Buenos Aires, 1875.
This book contains useful material on the Patagonian Indians.

349 Radaelli, Sigfrido A. *Capítulos de historia argentina.* Buenos Aires, 1931.
A work very useful in a study of colonial economic life.

350 Rickard, Major Francis Ignacio. *A mining journey across the great Andes, with explorations in the silver mining districts of the provinces of San Juan and Mendoza, and a journey across the pampas to Buenos Aires.* London, 1863.
A few contemporary references to the gaucho.

351 Robertson, John Parish (with William Parish Robertson). *Letters on South America.* 3 vols. London, 1843.
This work contains descriptions of the gaucho of Corrientes and of the business of catching, treating, and shipping the hides of cattle and horses.

352 Rojas, Ricardo. *La literatura argentina.* 8 vols. Buenos Aires, 1924-1925.
Two volumes (I and II) are devoted to a study of gaucho literature. The work, however, also contains excellent material on the origin of the gaucho; on the influence of landscape and climate upon the gaucho, with several resultant types; and, especially, on the gaucho role in history and the many leaders he followed in the wars.

353 Rolt, Richard. *A new and accurate history of South America.* London, 1756.
Useful in a study of economic conditions.

354 Ross, Gordon. *Argentina and Uruguay.* London, 1917.

Peon, soldier, policeman, and fireman are named as the modern descendants of the gaucho whom the author encountered actually surviving only in the province of Salta. The gaucho is described and also the role he played in La Plata history and in the economic development of the country.

355 Rossi, Vicente. *El gaucho. Su origen y evolución.* Río de la Plata, 1921.

The author's thesis is that the real gaucho is fundamentally a warrior and that he originated in Uruguay.

356 Rumbold, Sir Horace. *The great silver river. Notes of a residence in Buenos Ayres in 1880 and 1881.* London, 1887.

This work contains descriptions of the Pampas Indians and of the gaucho.

357 Salaverría, José María. *Vida de Martín Fierro, el gaucho ejemplar.* Madrid, 1934.

In addition to a study of the poem of *Martín Fierro,* this work contains an analysis of gaucho characteristics and a note on the transformation of the gaucho type.

358 Saldías, Adolfo. *La evolución republicana durante la revolución argentina.* Madrid, 1919.

Useful in a study of economic conditions.

359 Sarmiento, Domingo Faustino. *Civilización y barbarie. Vida de Juan Facundo Quiroga.* Madrid, 1924. 1st ed., 1845.

Included are descriptions of gaucho types.

360 ―――― *Conflicto y armonía de las razas en América.* 2 vols. Buenos Aires, 1883.

Useful in a consideration of Indian influence on Argentine society.

361 Scalabrini, Ángel. *Sul Rio della Plata.* Como, 1894.

This work contains an analysis of the character of gaucho leaders and a description of the gaucho as a soldier. Claiming that animals were the "pioneers of colonization," the author of this work notes the importance of horses and cattle in colonial life.

362 Scarlett, Peter Campbell. *South America and the Pacific.* 2 vols. London, 1838.

A contemporary account of the gaucho is included in this work.

363 Scarone, Arturo. *El gaucho.* Montevideo, 1922.

A general description of the gaucho; the origin of the term and of the class; gaucho character, dress, homes, amusements; the gaucho role in Argentine history.

364 Schoo Lastra, Dionisio. *El indio del desierto, 1535-1879.* Buenos Aires, 1928.

365 Serrano, Antonio. *Los primitivos habitantes del territorio argentino.* Buenos Aires, 1930.

A study of the Argentine Indians.

366 Southey, Robert. *History of Brazil.* 3 vols. 2d ed. London, 1822.

An excellent account of the settling of the Plata lands.

367 Strain, Lieutenant Isaac G. *Cordillera and pampa, mountain and plain. Sketches of a journey in Chili and the Argentine provinces, in 1849*. New York, 1853.

In this work there is a good comparison of the guaso with the gaucho. Included, also, are such miscellaneous items as a description of the frontier forts, notes on the extent of the cattle industry, and the explanation that the growth of the gaucho power was due to the division of society into parties and cliques in the principal cities.

368 Techo, Nicolás del. *The history of Paraguay, Tucumán, and the adjacent provinces in South America*, in Churchill: *A collection of voyages and travels*, VI. London, 1752.

Del Techo came in 1675. This work contains a good description of the Abipones Indians.

369 Tschudi, Johann Jakob von. *Travels in Peru*. New York, 1854.

The word *gaucho* is not specifically mentioned, but the descriptions of the character of *montonera* forces and of the Buenos Aires-Peruvian mule trade are useful for the purposes of this study.

370 Valdés, Carmelo B. *Tradiciones riojanas. Blancos y negros.* Buenos Aires, 1916.

Useful for its descriptions of the gaucho soldier.

371 Vianna, Oliveira [Oliveira Vianna, Francisco José de]. *Populacoes meridionaes do Brasil*. 3 vols.

Volume I is reported to contain material on the gaucho of Rio Grande do Sul.

372 Vidal, E. E. *Picturesque illustrations of Buenos Aires and Montevideo*. London, 1820.

373 Washburn, Charles. *The history of Paraguay*. New York, 1871.

See item 194.

374 Watson, Robert Grant. *Spanish and Portuguese South America during the colonial period*. London, 1884.

Useful for a study of economic conditions.

375 Ybarra, Gregorio. *Trages y costumbres de la provincia de Buenos Aires*. Buenos Aires, 1839.

376 Zeballos, Estanislao Severo. *Descripción amena de la República Argentina*. 3 vols. Buenos Aires, 1881, 1883, 1888.

This work is valuable for its description of the gaucho as soldier, defender, and settler of the frontier. The introduction of livestock from Peru and Tucumán is also noted.

377 ———— *Viaje al país de los araucanos*. Buenos Aires, 1881.

378 Zum Felde, Alberto. *Proceso histórico del Uruguay*. Montevideo, 1930.

In opposition to the thesis of Rossi (see item 355), Zum Felde notes the lack of Charrúa influence on Uruguayan rural life and stresses, instead, the importance of Spanish and of the Guaraní-Quechuan elements which entered by way of the Paraguayan missions. The author then states and develops the thesis that cattle have been responsible for the estancia, the gaucho, the montonera, and the caudillo; he describes gaucho character and life, and the influence of the gaucho on even modern Uruguayan society.

PART II

THE GAUCHO OF ROMANCE

The gaucho of romance is the gaucho utilized in works of fantasy. This section falls into the broad groupings of Literature, Art, Music. The first section is subdivided under the following headings: Bibliographies of Literature, Histories of Literature, Folklore, Critical Works, Literature, and Language.

LITERATURE

BIBLIOGRAPHIES OF LITERATURE

While there are many general bibliographical studies of Argentine, Uruguayan, and Brazilian literature, specific bibliographies of gaucho literature have been few in number and remarkably incomplete. (See, however, Domingo Caillava's study of the gaucho literature of Uruguay —item 379—and the general bibliography of gaucho literature by Madaline W. Nichols—item 385.) Lists of a few of the better-known works of gaucho literature may also be found in the several theses on the topic. Other studies of bibliographical value for the topic of gaucho literature are such general accounts as those by Ricardo Rojas (item 398) and Robert Lehmann-Nitsche (item 472).

379 Caillava, Domingo. *La literatura gauchesca en el Uruguay*. Montevideo, 1921.

380 Coester, Alfred. *Bibliography of Uruguayan literature*. Cambridge, Massachusetts, 1931.

381 —————— *A tentative bibliography of the belles-lettres of the Argentine Republic*. Cambridge, 1933.

382 Ford, Jeremiah Denis Matthias. *A tentative bibliography of Brazilian belles-lettres*. Cambridge, 1931.

383 Gutiérrez, Juan María. "Ensayo de una biblioteca, o catálogo bibliográfico-crítico, con noticias biográficas, de las obras en verso, con forma o con título de poemas, escritas sobre América o por hijos de esta parte del mundo," *Revista del Río de la Plata*, VIII, 549-579.

384 Leavitt, Sturgis Elleno. *Argentine literature. A bibliography of literary criticism, biography, and literary controversy*. Chapel Hill, North Carolina, 1924.

385 Nichols, Madaline W. "Der Gaucho als literarische Figur: Eine bibliographische Studie," *Ibero-Amerikanisches Archiv*, XIII, April, 1939, pp. 22-43.

HISTORIES OF LITERATURE

Much material on gaucho literature is to be found in the general literary histories of Argentina and Uruguay. Of such studies, that by Ricardo Rojas, with two of its eight volumes devoted specifically to gaucho literature, is, perhaps, of the greatest value.

386 Alonso Criado, Emilio. *Literatura argentina*. Buenos Aires, 1916.

387 Ayala Duarte, Crispín. *Resumen histórico-crítico de la literatura hispano-americana*. Caracas, 1927.

388 Barbagelata, Hugo David. *Una centuria literaria, 1800-1900*. Paris, 1924.

389 ———— (with Ventura García Calderón). "La literatura uruguaya, 1757-1918," *Revue hispanique*, XL, 415-524.

390 Blixen, Samuel. *Estudio compendiado de obras de la literatura contemporánea desde 1789-1893*. Montevideo, 1894.

391 Coester, Alfred. *The literary history of Spanish America*. 2d ed. New York, 1928.

392 Daireaux, Max. *Littérature hispano-américaine*. Paris, 1930.

393 Fernández y Medina, Benjamín. "Síntesis de historia literaria," Uruguay, Archivo y museo histórico nacional, *Revista histórica*, VI.

394 García Velloso, Enrique. *Historia de la literatura argentina*. Buenos Aires, 1914.

395 Martínez, Felipe. *La literatura argentina desde la conquista hasta nuestros días, seguida de un estudio sobre la literatura de los demás países hispano-americanos*. Buenos Aires, 1905.

396 Montero Bustamante, Raúl. *Historia de la literatura uruguaya*. Montevideo, 1910.

397 Reyles, Carlos, ed. *Historia sintética de la literatura uruguaya*. 3 vols. Montevideo, 1931.

398 Rojas, Ricardo. *La literatura argentina*. 8 vols. Buenos Aires, 1924-1925.

399 Roxlo, Carlos. *Historia crítica de la literatura uruguaya*. 7 vols. Montevideo, 1912-1916.

400 Zum Felde, Alberto. *Crítica de la literatura uruguaya*. Montevideo, 1921.

FOLKLORE

Much interesting and valuable work has been done in the field of La Plata folklore. The items which follow are only a few, selected because of their illustrative value of the various types of such studies. See also items 443-445 and 532.

401 Ambrosetti, Juan Bautista. *Supersticiones y leyendas.* Buenos Aires, 1917.

402 Bayo, Ciro. *Romancerillo del Plata.* Madrid, 1913.

403 De-María, Isidoro. *Tradiciones y recuerdos. Montevideo antiguo.* Montevideo, 1889.

404 Furt, Jorge M. *Arte gauchesco. Motivos de poesía.* Buenos Aires, 1924.

405 Granada, Daniel. *Reseña histórico-descriptiva de antiguas y modernas supersticiones del Río de la Plata.* Montevideo, 1896.

406 Lehmann-Nitsche, Robert. "Adivinanzas ríoplatenses," La Plata, Universidad nacional, *Biblioteca centenaria,* Buenos Aires, 1911. VII, 9-493.

407 Martínez, Benjamín Demetrio. *Folk-lore del litoral.* Buenos Aires, 1924.

408 Rojas, Ricardo. See item 398.

409 Rossi, Vicente. *Cosas de negros.* Córdoba, 1926.

CRITICISM

To be complete, a bibliography of critical literature on the gaucho should doubtless contain not only general studies of gaucho literature, but also the studies of the several authors of gaucho works. And a careful perusal of periodical literature would yield hundreds of such titles for even some of the comparatively unimportant authors of gaucho literature. The single review, *Nosotros,*[1] contains over two hundred articles on gaucho literature.

This bibliography, therefore, makes no pretense of such completeness. It notes merely specimen items in the two broad fields: General Critical Works Which Contain Studies of Gaucho Literature and Writers and General Critical Studies of Specifically Gaucho Literature. A few items on writers of gaucho literature are also included.

General

410 Bauzá, Francisco. *Estudios literarios.* Montevideo, 1885.

411 Bonet, Carmelo M. "La literatura nativista y la realidad social ríoplatense," *Palabras,* Buenos Aires, 1935. Pp. 79-110.

412 Bourel, Pedro. *Cartas provincianas. Cartas literarias.* Buenos Aires, 1887.

[1] Published at Buenos Aires since 1907, under the editorship of Alfredo Antonio Bianchi and Roberto Fernando Giusti. An annotated guide to the works on Hispanic American literature in this review was published by the Instituto de las Españas, New York, 1937, with the title *Bibliografía hispánica. Revista "Nosotros." Artículos sobre literatura hispanoamericana,* by Madaline W. Nichols and Lucia Burk Kinnaird.

413 Contreras, Francisco. "De la cultura colonial al modernismo," *Nosotros,* LXX, 26-45.

414 Gálvez, Manuel. *La vida múltiple.* Buenos Aires, 1916.

415 Girosi, Pablo. "La influencia europea en el porvenir de la literatura argentina," *Nosotros,* LXXX, 249-259.

416 Luisi, Luisa. *A través de libros y de autores.* Buenos Aires, 1925.

417 Machali Cazón, R. *Ensayos críticos y literarios.* Paris, 1889.

418 Morales, Ernesto. *El sentimiento popular en la literatura argentina.* Buenos Aires, 1926.

419 Oyuela, Calixto. *Estudios y artículos literarios.* Buenos Aires, 1889.

420 Payró, Roberto Jorge. *Silüetas.* Buenos Aires, 1931.

421 Rohde, Jorge Max. *Las ideas estéticas en la literatura argentina.* 3 vols. Buenos Aires, 1921.

422 Torres Caicedo, J. M. *Ensayos biográficos y de crítica literaria sobre los principales poetas y literatos hispano-americanos.* Paris, 1863.

Gaucho Literature

423 Aita, Antonio. "El significado del modernismo," *Nosotros,* LXXI, 361-375.

424 ———— "El teatro argentino," *Nosotros,* XLVI, 559-561.

425 *Anuario teatral argentino.* Vols. II and III. Buenos Aires, 1925-1926.

426 Bayo, Ciro. "Prólogo y notas." Edition of *Martín Fierro.* Madrid, 1919.

427 Bianchi, Alfredo Antonio. "Nuestro teatro en el año 1916," *Nosotros,* XXV, 125-127.

428 ———— "Pablo Podestá," *Nosotros,* XLIV, 86-88.

429 ———— "Veinte y cinco años de teatro nacional," *Nosotros,* LVIII, 145-167.

430 Bierstadt, Edward Hale. "The drama of the Argentine," *Three plays of the Argentine.* New York, 1920. Pp. xi-xliii.

431 Blanco, Marcos Manuel. "Obligado y su momento histórico," *Nosotros,* XXXIV, 501-513.

432 Borges, Jorge Luis. *Discusión.* Buenos Aires, 1932.
     Includes article on *Martín Fierro.*

433 Bosch, Mariano Gregorio Gerardo. *Historia de los orígenes del teatro nacional argentino y la época de Pablo Podestá.* Buenos Aires, 1929.

434 ——— *Historia del teatro en Buenos Aires.* Buenos Aires, 1910.

435 ——— "Orígenes del teatro nacional argentino," Argentine Republic, *Instituto nacional de estudios de teatro,* Buenos Aires, 1936, I, 51-69.

436 ——— *Teatro antiguo de Buenos Aires.* Buenos Aires, 1904.

437 Buerger, David Bernard. *Fatalism in gauchesca literatura.* M.A. thesis, Pittsburgh, 1928.

438 Bunge, Carlos Octavio. "El derecho en la literatura gauchesca," *Estudios jurídicos,* Madrid, 1926. Pp. 5-30.

439 ———"Introducción." Edition of *Martín Fierro.* Buenos Aires, 1919.

440 Caillava, Domingo. *La literatura gauchesca en el Uruguay.* Montevideo, 1921.

441 Campo, Cupertino del. *Martín Fierro, homenaje al poeta José Hernández en el centenario de su nacimiento.* Rosario, 1934.

442 Carnighan, Margaret. *The gaucho in the literature of Argentina.* M.A. thesis, Arizona, 1933.

443 Carrizo, Juan Alfonso. "Algunos aspectos de la poesía popular de Catamarca, Salta y Jujuy," La Plata, Universidad nacional, Facultad de humanidades, *Humanidades,* XXI, La Plata, 1930. Pp. 195-232.

444 ——— "Nuestra poesía popular," La Plata, Universidad nacional, Facultad de humanidades y ciencias de la educación, *Humanidades,* XV, 241-342.

445 ——— "La poesía popular y el *Martín Fierro," Nosotros,* LIX, 41-60.

446 Crispo Acosta, Osvaldo ("Lauxar"). "La poesía gauchesca," *Motivos de crítica hispano-americanos,* Montevideo, 1914.

447 Díaz Leguizamón, Héctor. "En torno a Juan Moreira," *El signo de Euforión,* Buenos Aires, 1927. Pp. 212-218.

448 Echagüe, Juan Pablo. *Una época del teatro argentino (1904-1918).* 2d ed. Buenos Aires, 1926.

449 ——— "*Martín Fierro* juzgado en el '72," *Nosotros,* LXXXI, 318-321.

450 ——— *Un teatro en formación.* Buenos Aires, 1919.

451 Espinosa, José Edmundo. "Notes on the role of gaucho literature in the evolution of Americanism in Argentina," *Hispania* (February, 1936), pp. 85-92.

452 Falcao Espalter, Mario. "La poesía gauchesca," Reyles, Carlos, *Historia sintética,* I.

453 Filartigas, Juan M. *Literatura nacionalista en el Uruguay.* Montevideo, 1928.

454 Furt, Jorge M. *Lo gauchesco en "La literatura argentina" de Ricardo Rojas.* Buenos Aires, 1929.

455 García Velloso, Enrique. "Los primeros dramas en los circos criollos," Argentine Republic, *Instituto nacional de estudios de teatro,* II, 39-91.

456 Gerchunoff, Alberto. "La vuelta de Juan Moreira," *El hombre que habló en la Sorbona.* Buenos Aires, 1926. Pp. 167-175.

457 Giusti, Roberto Fernando. "El drama rural argentino," Argentine Republic, *Instituto nacional de estudios de teatro,* VII, 9-34.

458 ———— "En el centenario de Hernández," *Nosotros,* LXXXI, 312-317.

459 ———— "La novela y el cuento argentinos," *Nosotros,* LVII, 78-99.

460 ———— "Orígenes del teatro ríoplatense," *Nosotros,* XXVIII, 67-77.

461 González Castillo, José. "El sainete, medio de expresión teatral argentino," Argentine Republic, *Instituto nacional de estudios de teatro,* III, 35-56.

462 Gosnell, Luis. *The Santos Vega legend of H. Ascasubi.* M.A. thesis, George Washington University, 1926.

463 Goyena, Pedro. *Crítica literaria.* Buenos Aires, 1917.

464 Gustafson, B. Gordon. *Fausto. Impresiones del gaucho Anastasio el Pollo, por Estanislao del Campo.* M.A. thesis, Kansas, 1932.

465 Heiskill, M. L. *Martín Fierro, ejemplo del españolismo argentino.* M.A. thesis, Chicago, 1931.

466 Holmes, Henry Alfred. *Martín Fierro. An epic of the Argentine.* New York, 1923.

467 Johnson, Helen Deal. *The gaucho in Argentine literature.* M.A. thesis, Oklahoma Agricultural and Mechanical College.

468 Labarthe, Pedro Juan. *Filosofía del gaucho Martín Fierro.* M.A. thesis, Columbia, 1930.

469 Latorre, Mariano. "El huaso y el gaucho en la poesía popular," *Atenea* (November and December, 1936), pp. 184-205, 380-400.

470 Leguizamón, Martiniano. *El primer poeta criollo del Río de la Plata.* Buenos Aires, 1917.

471 ———— *El trovero gauchesco.* Buenos Aires, 1922.

472 Lehmann-Nitsche, Robert. "Santos Vega," Córdoba, Argentina, Universidad, *Boletín de la Academia Nacional de Ciencias,* XXII, Buenos Aires, 1917. Pp. 1-434.

473 Menéndez y Pelayo, Marcelino. *Historia de la poesía argentina.* 2 vols. Madrid, 1911-1913.

474 Muiño, Enrique. "El compadrito y el gaucho," Argentine Republic, *Instituto nacional de estudios de teatro,* III, 9-25.

475 Nichols, Madaline Wallis. "The Argentine theatre," *Bulletin hispanique,* XLII, no. 1, January-March, 1940. Pp. 1-15.

476 ———— "El gaucho en la literatura," *La revista americana de Buenos Aires* (May, 1938), pp. 33-43.

477 ———— "The gaucho in literature," *The Moraga quarterly* (Winter, 1936), pp. 73-82.

478 ———— "Santos Vega," *Hill Trails* (January-February, 1939), p. 34.

479 Page, Frederick Mann. *"Fausto,—a gaucho poem," Publications of the Modern Language Association,* XL (1896), pp. 1-62.

480 ———— *Los payadores gauchos.* Darmstadt, 1897.

481 Pereira Rodríguez, José. "Nuevo sentido de la poesía gauchesca," Reyles, *Historia sintética,* III.

482 Pi, Wifredo. "La poesía gauchesca," Salaverri, *Florilegio de prosistas uruguayos,* pp. 93-96.

483 Podestá, José J. *Medio siglo de farándula.* Río de la Plata, 1930.

484 Princivalle, Carlos María. "Florencio Sánchez, su obra y el teatro nacional," Reyles, *Historia sintética,* II.

485 Quesada, Ernesto. *El "criollismo" en la literatura argentina.* Buenos Aires, 1902.

486 Reyles, Carlos. "El nuevo sentido de la narración gauchesca," Reyles, *Historia sintética,* III.

487 Ríos-Ríos, Maximiano. *Javier de Viana, cuentista, y el medio gauchesco.* M.A. thesis, Columbia, 1925.

488 Rivarola, Enrique E. ("Santos Vega.") "El teatro nacional. Su carácter y sus obras," *Revista de la universidad de Buenos Aires,* III, 351-353.

489 Rojas, Ricardo. *La literatura argentina. Los gauchescos.* I-II, Buenos Aires, 1924-1925.

490 Rossi, Vicente. *Teatro nacional rioplatense.* Córdoba, 1910.

491 Sabat Pebet, Juan Carlos. "Teatro nacional," Reyles, *Historia sintética,* III.

492 Salaverría, José María. *Vida de Martín Fierro, el gaucho ejemplar.* Madrid, 1934.

493 Sánchez Loria, Dr. "La comedia argentina" (Conferencia, *Anuario teatral argentino,* III-IV, 236-242).

494 Segovia, Eladio. "El paisaje en el *Martín Fierro,*" *Nosotros,* LXXXI, 322-331.

495 Senet, Rodolfo. *La psycología gauchesca en el "Martín Fierro."* Buenos Aires, 1927.

496 Slutzkin, Herman Bernard. *The gaucho novel of Benito Lynch.* M.A. thesis, Columbia University, 1931.

497 Suárez Calimano, Emilio. "Directrices de la novela y el cuento argentinos (1920-1932)," *Nosotros, LXXX, 337-370.

498 Tiscornia, Eleuterio F. *La vida de Hernández y la elaboración del "Martín Fierro."* Buenos Aires, 1937.

499 Umphrey, George Wallace. "The gaucho poetry of Argentina," *Hispania,* I, 144-156.

500 Vega, Carlos. "Los bailes criollos en el teatro nacional," Argentine Republic, *Instituto nacional de estudios de teatro,* VI, 61-82.

501 Velasco y Arias, María. *Dramaturgia argentina.* Thesis. Buenos Aires, 1913.

502 ———— "La transformación del romance en la Argentina," *Revista de derecho, historia y letras,* LXXI, 73-91.

503 Warren, Vanetta Hosford. *The gauchos of Hilario Ascasubi.* M.A. thesis, Kansas, 1916.

504 Werner, Gustave Adolph. See item 116.

505 Wolfe, Mrs. Ella G. *Santos Vega o Los mellizos de La Flor.* M.A. thesis, Columbia University, 1931.

506 Wood, Sara Lillian. *Nature as reflected in the gaucho literature.* M.A. thesis, University of Southern California, 1932.

LITERATURE

This section on gaucho literature has five parts: Anthologies and Collections (General Collections, which also contain gaucho works and Gaucho Collections), Gaucho Prose Fiction, The Gaucho Theater, Gaucho Verse, Gaucho Periodical Literature. This does not mean, however, an inclusion of all works on gaucho literature. Many a suspicious gaucho title has been deliberately omitted. The attempt has been to attain the greatest possible completeness compatible with a reasonable certainty that the titles really referred to gaucho works. Again it must be remembered that in this bibliography single titles often represent many separate gaucho works. This is particularly true of the works of Lehmann-Nitsche, where hundreds of titles of poems and periodical materials are to be found only indirectly under that author's name. Naturally, this is also true of gaucho periodical titles.

There are other bibliographical omissions besides those of actual titles. Many of these works are unsigned and undated. There are many works of the same title by different authors, and the confusion is augmented by repeated editions of the several works. (For example, the poem of *Juan Cuello* was read in its ninth edition!) In the theater it is quite possible that gaucho works were played but never actually published; again, titles of the *género chico* and of gaucho plays were encountered in appalling confusion. And not the least of the difficulties has been due to a reckless use of pseudonyms, with several different authors discovered writing under the same nom de plume. Again, there was noted a quite general tendency of authors to write upon the topic of gaucho literature without first reading the literature whereof they wrote. Many a work solemnly noted as a piece of gaucho literature was found not to be gaucho at all.

In an attempt to reduce the number of errors, about 70 per cent of the works noted in this bibliography *have been read* and are thus known to contain gauchos. The other titles were included either because of a specific mention of gauchos or because they were definitely reported as gaucho by usually reliable writers.

Anthologies

General Anthologies of Prose and Verse

507 Lasplaces, Alberto. *Lecturas uruguayas.* Montevideo, 1933.

508 Martínez, Felipe. *Antología argentina.* 2 vols. Buenos Aires, 1891.

General Anthologies of Verse

509 Academia Española. *Antología de poetas hispano-americanos.* 4 vols. Madrid, 1895.

510 *Antología criolla.* Rosario, n.d.

511 Arreguine, Víctor. *Colección de poesías uruguayas.* Montevideo, 1895.

512 Artucio Ferreira, Antonia. *Parnaso uruguayo. 1905-1922.* Barcelona, 1922.

513 Barreda, Ernesto Mario. *Nuestro Parnaso.* 4 vols. Buenos Aires, 1914.

514 Bayo, Ciro. *Poesía popular hispano-americana.* Madrid, 1913.

515 "Biblioteca de escritores en verso nacidos en la América de habla española, antiguos y modernos, Primera serie," *Revista del Río de la Plata,* I-V.

516 Falcao Espalter, Mario. *Antología de poetas uruguayos, 1807-1921.* Montevideo, 1921.

517 Fernández y Medina, Benjamín. *Antología uruguaya.* Montevideo. 1894.

518 Gosson, Alfonso, ed. *Trozos selectos de poesía.* Buenos Aires, 1888.

519 Montero Bustamante, Raúl. *El Parnaso Oriental.* Montevideo, 1905.

520 Noé, Julio. *Antología de la poesía argentina moderna. 1900-1925.* Buenos Aires, 1926.

521 Onís, Federico de. *Antología de la poesía española e hispano-americana (1882-1932).* Madrid, 1934.

522 Oyuela, Calixto. *Antología poética hispano-americana.* 3 vols. Buenos Aires, 1919.

523 *El Parnaso argentino. Antología de poetas del Plata desde los tiempos coloniales hasta nuestros días.* Buenos Aires, 1914.

524 Pereda Valdés, Ildefonso. *Antología de la moderna poesía uruguaya.* Buenos Aires, 1927.

525 Puig, Juan de la Cruz. *Antología de poetas argentinos.* 10 vols. Buenos Aires, 1910.

526 Zeballos, Estanislao. "Cancionero," *Revista de derecho, historia y letras,* II, 321-331; VI, 459-468; IX, 117-130, 574-588; X, 125-136, 280-290.

Gaucho Anthologies—Verse

527 *Biblioteca criolla.* (Casa editora de Salvador Matera.)

Dos payadores de contrapunto	*El hijo de Pancho Bravo*
El gaucho de la frontera	*El hijo de Martín Fierro*
El gaucho Juan Acero	*El hijo del desierto*
El gaucho Juan Soldao	*Los méritos de un payador*
El gaucho Juan Valiente	*Mi guitarra*
El gaucho maldito	*La muerte de Mataco*
El gaucho pampa	*El payador porteño*
El gaucho Pancho Bravo	*Relaciones*
El gaucho Picardía	*Truco y retruco*
El gaucho Santa Fe	

528 *Biblioteca gauchesca.* (Casa editora de Salvador Matera.)

Agapito	*Canciones amorosas*
Los amores de Pastor Luna con la cordobesa Gumersinda	*Canciones del payador argentino*
	Cantos de contrapunto

El Chacho
Contrapunto entre Félix Hidalgo
    y Gabino Ezeiza
Estilos criollos para guitarra
El gaucho de Cañuelas
Los hermanos Barrientos
Higinio de Cazón
Hormiga negra
Juan Cuello
Juan Moreira
Juan sin patria
Juanita la provinciana
Julián Giménez

Martín Fierro
Milongas variadas
La muerte de un héroe
Nueva colección de cantares
Pastor Luna
Payadas entre Lucero y Amore
El payador oriental
El rastreador
Santos Vega
El tigre del Quequén
El tigrero
Los tres gauchos orientales
Vidalitas

529 *Colección: Poemas gauchescos en versos.* (Casa editora de Alfonso Longo, Rosario.)

Agapito
El Chacho
Contrapunto Ezeiza y Vázquez
Contrapunto nacional
Facundo Quiroga
El gaucho de Cañuelas
El gaucho de Santa Fe
El gaucho oriental
El gaucho Paja Brava
El gaucho Picaflor
El gaucho Picardía
El gaucho Tranquera
Hermanos Barrientos
El hijo de Martín Fierro
Hormiga Negra
Juan Cuello
Juan Manuel de Rosas

Juan Moreira
Juan sin patria
Juan Soldao
Julián Giménez
Martín Fierro
La mazorca
Los montoneros
La muerta de Carmona
La muerte de un héroe
Pastor Luna
El puñal del tirano
El rastreador
Santos Vega
El tigre de los llanos
El tigre del desierto
El tigre del Quequén
La venganza del Mataco

530 *Colección de payadores nacionales.* (Cited in Quesada, *Criollismo,* item 347.)

There were reported to be some fifty volumes in this collection, and Quesada mentions still another collection of *payadores nacionales* which is less known. Among the payadores named are: "Abuelo Carlo Lanza," "Bismarck Mosquito," Faustino Díaz, Gabino Ezeiza, Sebastián Berón, Félix Hidalgo, "Papino el 88," and R. Iturriaga y López.

531 Furt, Jorge M. *Antología gauchesca.* Buenos Aires, 1930.

532 ——— *Cancionero popular rioplatense. Lírica gauchesca.* 2 vols. Buenos Aires, 1923, 1925.

533 Morales, Ernesto. *Antología gaucha.* Buenos Aires, 1927.

534 ——— *Lírica popular rioplatense—Antología gaucha.* Buenos Aires, 1927.

535 Pi, Wifredo Francisco. *Antología gauchesca. Los clásicos.* Montevideo, 1917.

536 ——— *Antología gauchesca. Los modernos.* (En preparación.)

Gaucho Anthologies—Prose

537 *Antología criolla.* Buenos Aires, n.d.

538 *Cuentos criollos.* Buenos Aires, n.d.

539 *Cuentos criollos.* Rosario, n.d.

540 Fernández y Medina, Benjamín. *Cuentos y narraciones de autores uruguayos contemporáneos.* Montevideo, 1895.

541 ——— *Uruguay.* Montevideo, 1895.

542 Gálvez, Manuel. *Los mejores cuentos.* Buenos Aires, 1919.

543 Gosson, Alfonso. *Trozos selectos de prosa.* 2 vols. Buenos Aires, 1885.

544 Salaverri, Vicente A. *Florilegio de prosistas uruguayos.* Buenos Aires, 1918.

Gaucho Anthologies—Theater

545 *Colección teatral.* (Casa editora Andrés Pérez, Buenos Aires.)
    While according to Quesada (item 347) this collection contains many a gaucho play, only three are named: *El payador, Pobre gaucho,* and *En la güella.*

Gaucho Prose Fiction

546 Acevedo Díaz, Eduardo. *El combate de la tapera.* Montevideo, 1931.

547 ——— *Ismael.* Buenos Aires, 1888.

548 ——— *Lanza y sable.* Montevideo, 1914.

549 ——— *Nativa.* Montevideo, 1931.

550 ——— *Soledad.* Montevideo, 1894.

551 Acevedo Díaz, Eduardo, hijo. *Ramón Hazaña.* Buenos Aires, 1932.

552 Acosta y Lara, Manuel. *Juan Inés.* Montevideo, 1935.

553 Alencar, José Martiniano ("Senio"). *O gaúcho.* 2 vols. Rio de Janeiro, 1870.

554 Álvarez, José Sixto ("Fray Mocho"). *Cuentos de Fray Mocho.* Buenos Aires, 1920.

555 ——— *Salero criollo.* Buenos Aires, 1920.

556 ——— *Tierra de matreros.* La Plata, 1910. 1st ed., 1897.

557 Amorim, Enrique. *El paisano Aguilar.* Montevideo, 1934.

558 ——— *La plaza de las carretas.* Buenos Aires, 1937.

559 ——— *Tangarupá.* Buenos Aires, 1925.

560 Arena, Domingo. "La doma," Lasplaces (item 507).

561 Arreguine, Víctor. *Lanzas y potros.* Montevideo, 1913.

562 Astudillo Menéndez, Eulalio. "Gaucho malo." (Cuento.)

563 Aulino, Pedro. *Leña floja*. Buenos Aires, 1931.

564 Barros, Álvaro. "La mulita del teniente," *Revista del Río de la Plata*, X, 160-168, 277-290.

565 Bermúdez Acevedo, Pedro Wáshington. *Hojarasca*. Montevideo, 1902.

566 Bernárdez, Manuel P. *Claros de luna*. Buenos Aires, 1890.

567 ——— *De Buenos Aires al Iguazú*. Buenos Aires, 1901.

568 ——— "El desquite," Salaverri (item 544), pp. 121-140.

569 ——— "La fumada," Lasplaces (item 507).

570 ——— *Tumbos y rodeos*. Montevideo, 1894.

571 ——— *Veinticinco días de campo*. Montevideo, 1887.

572 Bernárdez Jacques, Elbio. *El gaucho del Tuyú*. Buenos Aires, 1936.

573 ——— *Muestrario gaucho*. Buenos Aires, 1936.

574 Blixen, Samuel. *Cobre viejo*. Montevideo, 1890.

575 ——— *Un cuento del tío Marcelo*. Montevideo, 1892.

576 ——— *Primavera, Verano, Otoño, Invierno*. Montevideo, 1899.

577 Blomberg, Héctor Pedro. *La pulpera de Santa Lucía*. Buenos Aires, 1929.

578 Bonet, Carmelo M. *Ensayos literarios*. Buenos Aires, 1920. Contains "El gaucho uruguayo."

579 Braida, Lisímaco. *El rincón de las Achiras; vidas de dolor y oscuridad*. Montevideo, 1939.

580 Bucich Escobar, Ismael. *Éste era un buey (narraciones del campo)*. Buenos Aires, 192—.

581 Caillava, Domingo A. *Sierras y llanuras*. Montevideo, 1918.

582 Calderón, A. "Courtesy is all," *The Manchester guardian weekly*, August 23, 1935.

583 Cambaceres, Eugenio. *Sin rumbo*. Buenos Aires, 1885.

584 Cané, Miguel. *Prosa ligera*. Buenos Aires, 1919.

585 Carranza, Adolfo P. *Leyendas nacionales*. Buenos Aires, 1894.

586 Carrizo, César. *El domador*. Buenos Aires, 1934.

587 Casá, Agustín Guillermo. *Alma nativa*. Buenos Aires, 1923.

588 ——— *Cuentos argentinos*. Buenos Aires, 1935.

589 Cavilla Sinclair, Arsenio. *Tierra bruta*. Buenos Aires, 1932.

590 Cione, Otto Miguel. *Caraguatá y otros cuentos cortos*. Montevideo, 1920.

591 —— *Chola se casa.* Montevideo, 1924.

592 —— *La eterna esfinge.* Buenos Aires, 1938.

593 —— *Lauracha.* Buenos Aires, 1906.

594 —— *Maula.* Montevideo, 1920.

595 Cordero, Clodomiro. *Spleen.* Buenos Aires, 1929.

596 Cotta, Juan Manuel. *Retazos de pampa.* Buenos Aires, 1931.

597 Cruz Ghio, Julio. *Cariños. Cuentos camperos.* Buenos Aires, 1912.

598 —— "Lechuza," *Cuentos criollos* (item 538).

599 —— "El regalo del patrón," *Antología criolla* (item 537).

600 —— "La vuelta al pago," *Antología criolla* (item 537).

601 Cuadra, José de la. "El desertor," *Revista americana de Buenos Aires,* XXXVIII, 56-65.

602 Daireaux, Geoffroy. "Contes de la pampa." *La petite illustration.* Série Roman A.

603 —— *Las dos patrias.* Buenos Aires, 1908.

604 —— *Tipos y paisajes criollos.* Buenos Aires, 1913.

605 —— *Las veladas de tropero. Cuentos pampeanos.* Buenos Aires, 1906.

606 Daireaux, Max. *El guacho.* Buenos Aires, 1925.

607 Dávalos, Juan Carlos. *Airampo.* Buenos Aires, 1925.

608 —— *Los buscadores de oro.* Buenos Aires, 1928.

609 —— *Relatos lugareños.* Buenos Aires, 1930.

610 —— *El viento blanco.* Buenos Aires and Córdoba, 1925.

611 Díaz, José Virginio. *Odio de aldea.* Montevideo, 1913.

612 Dipetta, David. *Cardos . . . y margaritas.* Montevideo, 1938.

613 Dorraine, Julio. *Locura gaucha.* Buenos Aires, 1930.

614 Dotti, Víctor M. *Los alambradores.* Montevideo, 1929.

615 Dozo Lebeaud, Raúl. *Fogón campero. Cuentos.* Buenos Aires, n.d.

616 Echagüe, Pedro. *Memorias y tradiciones.* Buenos Aires, 1922.

617 Echeverría, Esteban. *El matadero.* Buenos Aires, 1926.

618 Escurra y Pardo, M. ("Muérdago"). *Pequeñas novelas del país.* Buenos Aires, 1887.

619 Espínola, Francisco, hijo. "Raza ciega," Lasplaces (item 507).

620 Estrada, Santiago. *El hogar en la pampa.* Buenos Aires, 1866.

621 Fernández, Juan Rómulo. *Serranía. Descripciones y relatos cuyanos.* Buenos Aires, 1930.

622 ——— *El valle de Tulún.* Buenos Aires, n.d.

623 Fernández, Mario. *El hogar en el campo.* Buenos Aires, 1924.

624 Fernández y Medina, Benjamín. *Charamuscas.* Montevideo, 1891.

625 ——— *Cuentos del pago.* Montevideo, 1895.

626 ——— *La flor del pago.* Barcelona, 1923.

627 Filartigas, Juan M. "Motivos de criolledad," Lasplaces (item 507).

628 Fontanella, Agustín. *Narraciones gauchescas.* n.p., n.d.

629 Fontela, José A. "Narraciones ríoplatenses," *Catálogo general de la bótica central homeopática de Fontela y Compañía.* Montevideo, 1910.

630 Gálvez, Manuel. *El gaucho de "Los Cerrillos."* Buenos Aires, 1931.

631 ——— *El general Quiroga.* Buenos Aires, 1932.

632 ——— *La pampa y su pasión.* Buenos Aires, 1926.

633 García Sáiz, Valentín. *Salvaje (cuentos regionales).* Montevideo, 1927.

634 Gerchunoff, Alberto. *Cuentos de ayer.* Buenos Aires, 1919.

635 ——— *Los gauchos judíos.* Buenos Aires, 1909.

636 ——— *La jofaina maravillosa.* Buenos Aires, 1927.

637 ——— *Pequeñas prosas.* Buenos Aires, 1926.

638 Ghiraldo, Alberto. *Carne doliente.* 2d ed. Madrid, 1917.

639 ——— *Humano ardor.* Madrid, 1930.

640 ——— *La novela de la pampa.* Santiago de Chile, 1934.

641 González Arrili, Bernardo. *Los charcos rojos.* Buenos Aires, 1927.

642 ——— *Mangangá. Cuentos criollos.* Buenos Aires, 1927.

643 ——— *Protasio Lucero. Un porteño en provincias.* Salta, 1919.

644 González Barbé, T. M. *Campo verde (cuentos gauchos).* Montevideo, 1931.

645 ——— *Cuentos gauchos de T. M. González Barbé.* Montevideo, 1930.

646 Graham, Robert Bontine Cunninghame. *The Ipané.* New York, 1925.

647 ——— *Thirty tales and sketches.* London, 1929.

648 ——— *Writ in sand.* London, 1932.

649 Grandmontagne, Francisco. *La Maldonada. Costumbres criollas.* Buenos Aires, 1898.

650 Gras, Mario César. *Los gauchos colonos.* Buenos Aires, 1928.

651 Greca, Alcides. *La pampa gringa, novela del sud santafesino.* Santiago de Chile, 1936.

652 Groussac, Paul. "Calandria," *Viaje intelectual* (item 271), pp. 77-86.

653 —— *Fruto vedado.* Buenos Aires, 1884.

654 Guezúraga, Margot. *Tierra de centauros.* Buenos Aires, 1932.

655 Güiraldes, Ricardo. *El cencerro de cristal.* Buenos Aires, 1915.

656 —— *Cuentos de muerte y de sangre, seguidos de Aventuras grotescas y Una trilogía cristiana.* Madrid, 1933.

657 —— *Don Segundo Sombra.* Buenos Aires, 1926.

658 —— *Raucho.* Madrid and Barcelona, 1932.

659 —— *Seis relatos.* Buenos Aires, 1929.

660 Gutiérrez, Eduardo. *Una amistad hasta la muerte.* Buenos Aires, n.d.

661 —— *Carlos Lanza.* Buenos Aires, 1886.

662 —— *El Chacho.* Buenos Aires, 1887.

663 —— *Juan Cuello.* Buenos Aires, 1880.

664 —— *Don Juan Manuel de Rosas.* Buenos Aires, 1883.

665 —— *Los hermanos Barrientos.* Buenos Aires, n.d.

666 —— *Hormiga negra.* Buenos Aires, 1881.

667 —— *Juan Moreira.* Buenos Aires, 1880.

668 —— *Juan sin patria.* Buenos Aires, 1886.

669 —— *Lanza, gran baqueano.* Buenos Aires, n.d.

670 —— *El Mataco.* Buenos Aires, n.d.

671 —— *La mazhorca.* Buenos Aires, 1882.

672 —— *Los montoneros.* Buenos Aires, 1888.

673 —— *La muerte de un héroe.* Buenos Aires, 1890.

674 —— *Pastor Luna.* Buenos Aires, 1886.

675 —— *El puñal del tirano.* Buenos Aires, 1888.

676 —— *El rastreador.* Buenos Aires, 1889.

677 —— *Santos Vega.* Buenos Aires, 1881.

678 —— *El tigre del Quequén.* Buenos Aires, 1880.

679 —— *Una tragedia de doce años.* Buenos Aires, 1882.

680 Herrera, Ernesto. *Cuentos brutales.* Montevideo, 1931.

681 Hudson, William Henry. *The purple land.* New York, 1916.

682 —— *Tales of the pampas.* New York, 1916.

683 Ipuche, Pedro Leandro. *Isla Patrulla.* Buenos Aires and Montevideo, 1935.

684 Lagomarsino, Juan B. *Terrones de güeya (cuentos criollos).* Buenos Aires, 1935.

685 Langara, ———. *Los gauchos. Cuentos y costumbres de estos habitantes de las pampas de Buenos Aires.* n.p. (*ca.* 1881).

686 Lassaga, Ramón J. *Tradiciones y recuerdos históricos.* Buenos Aires, 1895.

687 Lavalle Cobo, Jorge. "Ciencia fatal," Gálvez, *Cuentos* (item 542), pp. 116-121.

688 Leguizamón, Martiniano. *Alma nativa.* Buenos Aires, 1906. 2d ed., 1912.

689 ——— *La cinta colorada.* Buenos Aires, 1916.

690 ——— *De cepa criolla.* La Plata, 1908.

691 ——— "El forastero," Gálvez, *Cuentos* (item 542).

692 ——— *Montaraz.* Buenos Aires, 1914.

693 ——— *Recuerdos de la tierra.* Buenos Aires, 1896.

694 ——— "Una revancha," Gálvez, *Cuentos* (item 542).

695 ——— *La selva de Montiel.* Buenos Aires, 1903.

696 ——— *Tradiciones del pago.* Buenos Aires, 1920.

697 Leumann, Carlos Alberto. *Los gauchos a pie, novela.* Buenos Aires, 1938.

698 Lugones, Leopoldo. "Al rastro," Gálvez, *Cuentos* (item 542).

699 ——— *Cuentos fatales.* Buenos Aires, 1924.

700 ——— *La guerra gaucha.* Buenos Aires. 1st ed., 1905; 2d ed., 1926.

701 Lynch, Benito. *El antojo de la patrona.* Buenos Aires, 1925.

702 ——— *Los caranchos de "La Florida."* Buenos Aires, 1916.

703 ——— *De los campos porteños.* Buenos Aires, 1931.

704 ——— *La evasión.* Barcelona, 1923.

705 ——— *El inglés de los güesos.* Madrid, 1924.

706 ——— *Palo verde.* Buenos Aires, 1925.

707 ——— *Plata dorada.* Buenos Aires, 1909.

708 ——— *Ranquela.* Buenos Aires, 1918.

709 ——— *El romance de un gaucho.* Buenos Aires, 1933.

710 Maciel, Santiago. *Campo afuera.* n.p., n.d.

711 ——— *Los cuentos del viejo Quilques.* Buenos Aires, 1928.

712 —— *La estirpe brava.* Buenos Aires, 1922.

713 —— *Nativos.* Buenos Aires, 1893.

714 —— "Peñascos arriba," *Cuentos criollos* (item 538).

715 Maeso Tognochi, Carlos. *La estirpe brava.* Buenos Aires, 1922.

716 Magallanes, Juan Mario. *La Mariscala.* Montevideo, 1931.

717 Magariños Cervantes, Alejandro. *Caramurú.* 4th ed. Buenos Aires, 1865.

718 Maldonado, Horacio. *En el pago.* n.p., 1905.

719 Martínez, Benjamín Demetrio. *Flor de Achira.* n.p., n.d.

720 Martínez Zuviría, Gustavo Adolfo ("Hugo Wast"). *Casa de los cuervos.* Buenos Aires, 1917.

721 —— *Desierto de piedra.* Buenos Aires, 1925.

722 —— *Fuente sellada.* Buenos Aires, 1923.

723 —— *Valle negro.* Buenos Aires, 1918.

724 Maya, Alcides. *Ruinas vivas.* n.p., n.d.

725 —— *Tapera.* n.p., n.d.

726 Montiel Ballesteros, Adolfo. *Alma nuestra.* Montevideo, 1922.

727 —— *Cuentos uruguayos.* Florence, Italy, 1920.

728 Netto, Coelho. "La tapera," *Revue de l'Amérique latine,* III, 67-78, 147-153, 244-252.

729 Olivera Lavié, Héctor. *Las montoneras.* Buenos Aires, 1935.

730 Payró, Roberto Jorge. *El casamiento de Laucha.* 3d ed. Buenos Aires and Madrid, 1906.

731 —— *Divertidas aventuras del nieto de Juan Moreira.* Buenos Aires, 1910.

732 —— *Nuevos cuentos de Pago Chico.* Buenos Aires, 1928.

733 —— *Pago Chico.* Barcelona and Buenos Aires, 1908.

734 —— "Poesía," Gálvez, *Cuentos* (item 542).

735 Pedrero, Julián. *Pampa, cuentos.* Buenos Aires, 1935.

736 Pollock, Katherine G. *The gaucho's daughter.* Boston, 1941.

737 Quintana, Julián. "La galopiadora," Roxlo, VII.

738 Rapoport, Nicolás. *La querencia (entre arroyos y cuchillas).* Buenos Aires, 1929.

739 Razori, Amilcar. *Campo arado.* Buenos Aires, 1935.

740 Regules, Elías. *Pasto de cuchilla.* Montevideo, 1904.

741 Reyles, Carlos. *Beba.* Montevideo, 1888.

742 —— *El gaucho Florido.* Montevideo, 1932.

743 ———— *Primitivo.* Montevideo, 1896.

744 ———— *El terruño.* Montevideo, 1916.

745 Riva, Francisco Manuel. *Tierra adentro.* Buenos Aires, 1931.

746 Rivarola, Enrique E. ("Santos Vega"). *Narraciones populares, recogidas por Santos Vega.* Buenos Aires, 1886.

747 ———— *Mandingá.* Buenos Aires, 1895.

748 ———— *Menudencias.* Buenos Aires, 1896.

749 Rodríguez, Leopoldo Z. *Tierra arada.* Montevideo, 1932.

750 Rodríguez, Yamandú. *Bichito de luz.* Buenos Aires, 1933.

751 ———— *Cimarrones.* Buenos Aires, 1933.

752 Rodríguez Burgueño, Último. *Boscaje virgen.* Montevideo, 1935.

753 Rojas, Ricardo. *El país de la selva.* Buenos Aires, 1925.

754 Rossi, Vicente. *Cardos.* Córdoba, 1905.

755 Sáenz, Justo P., hijo. *Baguales.* Buenos Aires, 1930. 2d ed., 1931.

756 ———— *Pasto puna.* Buenos Aires, 1928.

757 Salaverri, Vicente A. *Este era un país.* Buenos Aires, 1920.

758 ———— *Deformarse es vivir.* Barcelona, 1923.

759 ———— *El hijo del león.* Buenos Aires, 1922.

760 ———— *El manantial y otros cuentos del campo.* Buenos Aires, 1927.

761 Segastume, ————. *Ráfagas de la pampa.* La Plata, 1913.

762 Soldavini, Benedicto A. *Cuentos de Baliño.* Buenos Aires, 1932.

763 Suárez, Juan Carlos. *El gaucho y el caballo; su origen en la Argentina.* Buenos Aires, 1931.

764 Supervielle, Jules. *El hombre de la pampa.* Paris, 1923.

765 Suríguez y Acha, ————. *En la pampa. Narraciones gauchescas de la República Argentina.* Buenos Aires and Milan, 1908.

766 Ugarte, Manuel. *Cuentos argentinos.* Paris, 1910.

767 ———— *Cuentos de la pampa.* Madrid, 1920; Santiago de Chile, 1940.

768 Valdés, Carmelo B. *Tradición riojaria. La última tentativa del gaucho Leandro.* Buenos Aires, 1913.

769 Vera, Fortún de. *Cuentos de tropa.* n.p., n.d.

770 Viana, Javier de. *Abrojos.* Montevideo, 1919.

771 ———— *La Biblia gaucha.* Montevideo, 1919.

772 ———— *Campo. Escenas de la vida de los campos de América.* Madrid, 1896.

773 ———— *Cardos.* Montevideo, 1914.

774 ———— *Con divisa blanca.* 1st ed. Buenos Aires, 1904.

775 ———— *Cuentos camperos.* Montevideo, 1912.

776 ———— *De la misma hoja.* Montevideo, 1920.

777 ———— *Del campo y de la ciudad.* Montevideo, 1921.

778 ———— *Gaucha.* Montevideo, 1913. 1st ed., 1899.

779 ———— *Gurí y otras novelas.* Madrid, 1916.

780 ———— *Leña seca. Costumbres del pueblo.* Montevideo, 1911.

781 ———— *Macachines. Cuentos breves.* Montevideo, 1913.

782 ———— *Paisanas. Cuentos del campo.* Montevideo, 1920.

783 ———— *Potros, toros y aperiases.* Montevideo, 1922.

784 ———— *Ranchos. Costumbres del campo.* Montevideo, 1920.

785 ———— *Sobre el recado.* Montevideo, 1919.

786 ———— *Tardes del fogón.* Montevideo, 1925.

787 ———— *Yuyos.* Buenos Aires and Montevideo, 1912.

788 ———— See Barbagelata, *Una centuria* (item 388).

789 ———— See Salaverri, *Florilegio* (item 544).

790 ———— See *Antología criolla* (item 537).

791 ———— See *Cuentos criollos* (item 538).

792 Vigil, Constancio C. *Cuentos.* n.p., n.d.

793 Vignola Mansilla, Julio. *Los demonios de Calfucurá.* Buenos Aires, 1935.

794 ———— *Fantasmas del agua.* Buenos Aires, 1935.

795 ———— *La noche de robar.* Buenos Aires, 1935.

796 ———— *La sombra del mal hombre.* Buenos Aires, 1935.

797 Villar, Emilio Huguet del. *En las pampas: narración de costumbres sudamericanas.* Barcelona, 192—.

798 Závala Muñiz, Justino. *Crónica de la reja.* Montevideo, 1930.

799 ———— *Crónica de Muñiz.* Montevideo, 1921.

800 ———— *Crónica de un crimen.* Buenos Aires and Montevideo, 1926.

801 Zocchi, Juan. *Martín Vega, misterio gaucho.* Buenos Aires, 1937.

802 Zorrilla de San Martín, Juan. *La epopeya de Artigas.* Barcelona, 1916-1917.

The Gaucho Theater

803 Aguirre, Ramón. *El facón.* n.p., n.d.

804 *La acción de Maipú; sainete gauchesco.* Buenos Aires, 1924.

805 *El amor de la estanciera* (ca. 1792). Summary in Bosch (item 436).

806 Araquistain, Luis. *El rodeo.* November 22, 1925.

807 Arizaga, Vicente. *Ricos y pobres.* Buenos Aires, 1911.

808 ———— *Sangre que honra.* Buenos Aires, n.d.

809 Arozamena, ———— (with Mario Fernández). *Gauchos y charros.* October 2, 1925.

810 Aroztegui, Abdón. *Ensayos dramáticos.* Buenos Aires, 1896.

811 ———— *El gaucho.* n.p., n.d.

812 ———— *Julián Giménez.* December 24, 1891.

813 Bado, J. *El payador.* n.p., n.d.

814 Basaldúa, J. *En la yerra.* n.p., n.d.

815 Bayón Herrera, Luis. *Santos Vega.* See Bierstadt (item 430).

816 Bermúdez, Wáshington Pedro. *Artigas.* n.p., n.d.

817 Berutti, José J. *Teatro.* 2 vols. Buenos Aires, 1924, 1926.

818 *Las bodas de Chivicó (1826).* See Bosch, item 436.

819 Bracco, Alberto José. *El gaucho enlutao.* n.p., n.d.

820 Braña, José María. *Corazón criollo.* Rosario, n.d.

821 *El brasilero fanfarrón i la batalla de Ituzaingó.* n.p., 1828.

822 Cantú, Carlos M. *Las ánimas.* Montevideo, 1919.

823 Caraballo, Gustavo. *Juan Cuello.* Buenos Aires, 1922.

824 Caruso, Juan A. *Aquí me pongo a cantar.* n.p., n.d.

825 ———— *El tigre de los llanos.* n.p., n.d.

826 ———— *Vengan todos a oír esta milonga.* n.p., n.d.

827 Chacel, Mariano. *Los desamparados.* Rosario, n.d.

828 Chiarello, Florencio. *Los gauchos de Güemes.* n.p., n.d.

829 Cione, Otto Miguel. *El corazón de la selva.* n.p., n.d.

830 ———— *Gallo ciego.* n.p., n.d.

831 ———— *Paja brava.* n.p., n.d.

832 ———— *Partenza.* Montevideo, 1911.

833 ———— *Presente griego.* Rosario, n.d.

834 Coronado, Martín. *Obras completas.* 8 vols. Buenos Aires, 1926.

835 Curotto, Ángel ("Ludovic"). *El rancho de las chinas.* n.p., n.d.

836 Daireaux, Godofredo. *Comedias argentinas.* Buenos Aires, 1909.

837 Dávalos, Juan Carlos. *Don Juan de Viniegra Herze.* Salta, 1917.

838 ———— "Los puesteros," *Relatos lugareños* (item 609), pp. 93-162.

839 De María, Enrique. *El cabo Melitón.* n.p., 1898.

840 —— *Ensalada criolla.* n.p., 1898.

841 De Paoli, Carlos. "El gaucho." (Movie.)

842 —— "Santos Vega." (Movie, 1917.)

843 *Un día de fiesta en Barracas, con mucho gaucho, bailarín y cantos y no pocas alusiones políticas; bailábase en ella el minuet federal . . . y el cielito.* n.p., 1836.

844 Fernández y Medina, Benjamín. *El Fausto criollo.* April 13, 1894.

845 Flores, Aurelio J. *Un gaucho que pasa.* n.p., n.d.

846 Fontanella, Agustín. *Camila, o La tiranía de don Juan Manuel Rosas.* n.p., n.d.

847 —— *Cardos y flores.* Rosario, n.d.

848 —— *Comandante militar.* Buenos Aires, 1905.

849 —— *El desertor.* n.p., n.d.

850 —— *Don Gregorio, el capataz.* n.p., n.d.

851 —— *Fausto criollo.* n.p., n.d.

852 —— *Justicia.* n.p., 1900.

853 —— *Historia gaucha.* March 2, 1910.

854 —— *Los matreros.* n.p., n.d.

855 —— *Tranquera.* n.p., 1898.

856 —— *Venganza.* n.p., n.d.

857 Foppa, Tito Livio. *El último caudillo.* n.p., 1911.

858 Ganduglia, José Bressano. *El defensor del gaucho.* n.p., n.d.

859 —— *El capataz de "La Blanca."* n.p., n.d.

860 García Velloso, Enrique. *El chiripá roto.* May 20, 1900.

861 —— (with Folco Testena and José González Castillo). *Los conquistadores del desierto.* n.p., n.d.

862 —— *La gauchita.* n.p., n.d.

863 —— *Jesús Nazareno.* n.p., 1902.

864 —— *Mamá Culepina.* n.p., n.d.

865 Ghiraldo, Alberto. *Alma gaucha.* Madrid and Buenos Aires, 1907.

866 —— *Los salvajes.* Madrid, n.d.

867 Giménez Pastor, Arturo. *Ganador y placé.* Buenos Aires, 1921.

868 Godoy, Señora Rosario P. de. *En buena ley.* n.p., n.d.

869 Gómez Mayorza, Virgilio. *Un gaucho que pasa.* Rosario, n.d.

870 González Castillo, José. *Los conquistadores del desi. rto.* See item 861.

871 ——— *Martín Fierro*. Buenos Aires, 1918.

872 ——— *Los payadores*. n.p., n.d.

873 ——— *Vidalita*. n.p., n.d.

874 ——— *Yunta brava*. n.p., n.d.

875 González Pacheco, Rodolfo. *La inundación*. n.p., 1917.

876 Granada, Nicolás. *Al campo*. n.p., n.d.

877 Herrera, Ernesto. *El estanque*. Montevideo, 1911.

878 ——— *El león ciego*. Montevideo, 1912.

879 ——— *Mala laya*. Montevideo, 1917.

880 ——— *El teatro uruguayo de Ernesto Herrera*. Montevideo, 1917.

881 Imhof, Francisco. *Cantos rodados*. Montevideo, 1918.

882 ——— *Sangre de hermanos*. Montevideo, 1917.

883 *Lázaro*. October 12, 1903.

884 Leguizamón, Martiniano. *Calandria*. Buenos Aires, 1896.

885 Lenchantin, José A. *Moreira en ópera*. n.p., 1898.

886 ——— *Patria i honor*. n.p., n.d.

887 Lenzi, Carlos César. *El domador*. n.p., n.d.

888 Libonati, Vicente J. *Palenque*. n.p., n.d.

889 López, Enrique. *El viejo Bonifacio*. n.p., n.d.

890 López, Eugenio Gerardo. *El alcalde Rojas*. Buenos Aires, 1918.

891 ——— *En la güella*. Rosario, n.d.

892 ——— *Exhalación del bandolero*. n.p., n.d.

893 ——— *Hermanos Barrientos*. n.p., n.d.

894 ——— *Huérfano*. n.p., n.d.

895 ——— *Luna*. n.p., n.d.

896 ——— *El Mataco*. n.p., n.d.

897 ——— *El ocho de marzo*. n.p., n.d.

898 ——— *Pastor Luna*. n.p., n.d.

899 ——— *La revancha*. n.p., n.d.

900 ——— *Santos Vega*. n.p., n.d.

901 ——— *El tigre del Quequén*. n.p., n.d.

902 ——— *El último malevo*. n.p., n.d.

903 López de Gomara, Justo Sanjurjo y. *Culpas ajenas*. n.p., n.d.

904 ——— *Gauchos i gringos*. Rosario, 1884.

905 Manco, Silverio ("Gaucho viejo"). *Juan Moreira*. See Bierstadt, item 430.

906 Marino, Ángel. *La huella final.* Buenos Aires, 1914.

907 Martínez, Guillermo A. *El último gaucho.* n.p., 1896.

908 Martínez Cuitiño, Vicente. *El caudillo.* Buenos Aires, 1913.

909 Martínez Payva, Claudio. *Cuentos de pulpería.* September 2, 1925.

910 ———— *En una chacra.* n.p., n.d.

911 ———— *La estancia nueva.* n.p., n.d.

912 ———— *Gaucho.* March 18, 1925.

913 ———— *El gaucho Casco.* n.p., n.d.

914 ———— *El gaucho negro.* n.p., 1927.

915 ———— *La lanza rota.* n.p., n.d.

916 ———— *El rancho del hermano.* n.p., n.d.

917 Maturana, José de. *Canción de primavera. Poema rústico en tres actos y en verso.* Buenos Aires, 1912.

918 Mejías, Luis. *Juan Cuello.* April 16, 1890.

919 Moratorio, Orosmán. "El baile de ña Toribia," *Obras dramáticas,* 1895. See item 923.

920 ———— *Ensayos dramáticos.* Montevideo, 1883.

921 ———— *La flor del pago.* Montevideo, 1894.

922 ———— *Juan Soldao.* Montevideo, 1890.

923 ———— *Obras dramáticas.* Montevideo, 1895.

924 ———— *Patria y amor.* Montevideo, 1885.

925 ———— *Pollera y chiripá.* June 7, 1894.

926 Muñoz Seca, Pedro (with J. L. Nuñez). *El rayo.* Rosario, n.d.

927 Nicolau Roig, V. *La doma.* n.p., n.d.

928 "Nobleza gaucha." (Movie.)

929 Nosiglia, Juan C. *El desgraciado o Vega, el cantor.* n.p., n.d.

930 ———— *Santos Vega.* n.p., 1894.

931 Novión, Alberto. *La gaucha.* June 21, 1907.

932 ———— *Mandingá.* n.p., n.d.

933 ———— *Misia Pancha, la brava.* n.p., 1914.

934 ———— *La tapera.* n.p., 1906.

935 Onrubia, Emilio. *Lo que sobra y lo que falta.* n.p., 1889.

936 Onrubia, Emilio, hijo. *El payador.* n.p., n.d.

937 Pacheco, Carlos María. *Una juerga.* n.p., n.d.

938 ———— (with Antonio Reynoso). *Don Quijano de la pampa.* September 9, 1907.

939 Pagano, José León. *El domador.* n.p., n.d.

940 Paso y Abati. *Los perros de presa.* Rosario, n.d.

941 Payró, Roberto Jorge. *Sobre las ruinas.* Buenos Aires, 1902.

942 Pedro, Valentín de. *El caudillo.* n.p., 1924.

943 Pelay y Amadori. *De Cyrano a Martín Fierro. Revista caricaturesca.* n.p., 1927.

944 Pellerano, Juan José. *La criolla.* n.p., 1909.

945 Peña, David. *Dorrego.* n.p., 1909.

946 Peralta, Eleodoro. *La china.* n.p., n.d.

947 Pérez Petit, Víctor. *Cobarde.* November 3, 1894.

948 ——— *Entre los pastos.* Montevideo, 1920.

949 ——— *Teatro.* Montevideo, 1912.

950 ——— *Tribulaciones de un criollo.* November 6, 1894.

951 Picasso, Rafael. *Don Juan con levita.* n.p., n.d.

952 Pico, Pedro E. *Tierra virgen.* Buenos Aires, n.d.

953 Piño, Rosario. *La moral de Misia Paca.* n.p., n.d.

954 Pisano, Francisco. *Nobleza criolla.* July 29, 1894.

955 Podestá, José J. *Juan Moreira.* n.p., 1886.

956 ———*Otelo criollo.* n.p., n.d.

957 Poggi Céspedes, Ricardo Nicolás. *Aquí me pongo a cantar.* n.p., n.d.

958 ——— *La tierra de Santos Vega.* n.p., n.d.

959 Pracanico, Francisco. *La pampa tiene el ombú.* n.p., n.d.

960 Princivalle, Carlos María. *El higuerón.* Montevideo, 1924.

961 ——— *El toro.* Montevideo, 1929.

962 Regules, Elías, hijo. *El entenao.* March 18, 1892.

963 ——— *Los guachitos.* March 1, 1894.

964 ——— *Martín Fierro.* n.p., 1890.

965 Rodríguez, Yamandú. *Los cachorros.* n.p., 1926.

966 ——— *El matrero.* Buenos Aires, 1931.

967 Romeu, José. *Ño Cirilo.* n.p., n.d.

968 Ruiz Martínez, Francisco. *En tierra de gauchos.* n.p., n.d.

969 Sáenz, Félix. *Aventuras.* n.p., 1895.

970 ——— *Ramón.* n.p., n.d.

971 Saldías, José Antonio. *El gaucho Robles.* Buenos Aires, 1916.

972 ——— *La montonera.* Buenos Aires, n.d.

973 Sánchez, Florencio. *Barranca abajo.* Buenos Aires, 1905.

974 —— *Cédulas de San Juan.* Buenos Aires, 1903.

975 —— *La gringa.* Buenos Aires, 1904.

976 —— *M'hijo el dotor.* Buenos Aires, 1903.

977 Sargenti, Octavio P. *La pampa tiene el ombú.* n.p., n.d.

978 Schaefer Gallo, Carlos. *El gaucho judío.* n.p., n.d.

979 —— *Justicia criolla.* n.p., n.d.

980 —— *La ley gaucha.* n.p., n.d.

981 —— *Lucha.* n.p., 1908.

982 —— *Santos Vega.* n.p., n.d.

983 —— *El Sargento Martín.* n.p., 1894.

984 Soria, Ezequiel. *Justicia criolla.* n.p., n.d.

985 Spíndola, Domingo. *Santos Vega.* n.p., 1903.

986 Trejo, Nemesio. *La esquila.* n.p., 1899.

987 Trelles, José Alonso y ("Viejo Pancho"). *Crimen de amor.* n.p., n.d.

988 —— *Guacha.* Montevideo, 1913.

989 Vacarezza, Alberto B. *Los gauchos.* n.p., n.d.

990 —— *Los montaraces.* n.p., n.d.

991 —— *Para los guachos, querencia.* n.p., n.d.

992 —— *Teatro criollo.* n.p., n.d.

993 —— *El último gaucho.* n.p., 1917.

994 —— *Ya se acabaron los criollos.* n.p., 1926.

995 Viana, Javier de. *Al truco.* n.p., n.d.

996 —— *Pial de volcao.* n.p., n.d.

997 —— *Puro campo.* n.p., n.d.

998 Warnes, Alejandro. *Flor del aire.* n.p., n.d.

999 —— *Revelación.* n.p., n.d.

1000 Weisbach, Alberto T. *En tierra de gauchos.* n.p., n.d.

Gaucho Verse

1001 Abaca, Hilarión. *Agapito.* 3d ed. Rosario, n.d.

1002 —— *Facundo Quiroga.* 3d ed. Rosario, n.d.

1003 —— *Hormiga negra.* 3d ed. Rosario, n.d.

1004 —— *Juan Soldao.* Rosario, n.d.

1005 —— *Julián Giménez.* 3d ed. Rosario, n.d.

1006 —— *La Mazorca.* 2d ed. Rosario, n.d.

1007 —— *La muerte de Carmona*. 5th ed. Rosario, n.d.

1008 —— *Paja brava*. 3d ed. Rosario, n.d.

1009 —— *Pastor Luna*. 5th ed. Rosario, n.d.

1010 —— *El puñal del tirano*. 2d ed. Rosario, n.d.

1011 —— *Santos Vega*. 7th ed. Rosario, n.d.

1012 —— *El tigre de los llanos*. 3d ed. Rosario, n.d.

1013 —— *El tigre del Quequén*. Rosario, n.d.

1014 —— *La venganza del Mataco*. 4th ed. Rosario, n.d.

1015 Abellá, Rafael J. *Junto al fogón*. Montevideo-Buenos Aires, 1928.

1016 Acosta, Luis. *El gaucho argentino*. Buenos Aires, 1940.

1017 Aguirre, Ramón. *El gaucho de Cañuelas*. Rosario, n.d.

1018 —— *Juan Cuello*. 9th ed. Rosario, n.d.

1019 —— *El tigre del desierto*. 3d ed. Rosario, n.d.

1020 Albarracén, Policarpo. *Santos Vega*. Rosario, 1914.

1021 Aller, Ángel. *Romance del gaucho perdido*. Montevideo, 1930.

1022 Amante, Ángel. *Juan Moreira*. 8th ed. Rosario, n.d.

1023 —— *Los hermanos Barrientos*. 4th ed. Rosario, n.d.

1024 Añon, Francisco. *Poesías*. Buenos Aires, 1922.

1025 Aprile, Bartolomé Rodolfo. *El ahijao de don Segundo Sombra o Fabio Cáceres*. Buenos Aires, 1935.

1026 —— *El hijo de Martín Fierro*. Buenos Aires, 1933.

1027 —— *El libro de los criollos*. *Poesías*. Buenos Aires, n.d.

1028 —— *Martín Laguna*. Buenos Aires, 1936.

1029 Arán, Artemio. *¡Pampa!* Buenos Aires, 1938.

1030 Araucho, Manuel de. *Cancionero popular argentino*. n.p., n.d.

1031 —— *Un paso en el Pindo*. Montevideo, 1835.

1032 Arrarte, Victoria Leandro. *Clarindas*. Montevideo, 1906.

1033 Ascasubi, Hilario. *Aniceto el Gallo*. Paris, 1872.

1034 —— *Santos Vega o Los mellizos de "La Flor."* Paris, 1872.

1035 —— *Trobas de Paulino Lucero*. Paris, 1872.

1036 Barreda, Ernesto. *Talimanes*. Madrid, 1908.

1037 Barrios, Evaristo. *Gauchas*. Buenos Aires, 1924.

1038 —— *Ráfagos*. Buenos Aires, n.d.

1039 —— *Renglones cortos*. Buenos Aires, 1927.

1040 Bauzá, Francisco. *Poesías*. Montevideo, 1869.

1041 Bergalli, Víctor V. *El primer gaucho*. Montevideo, 1934.

1042 Bergara, Eugenio P. *Baladas de los campos y de los arroyos.* Paysandú, Uruguay, 1931.

1043 Berón, Sebastián Celestino. *Décimas variadas para cantar con guitarra.* Buenos Aires, 1887.

1044 ———— *El gaucho Pancho Bravo. Versos gauchescos.* Buenos Aires, 1887.

1045 ———— *El hijo de Pancho, el Bravo. Relación criolla.* Buenos Aires, 1887.

1046 ———— *Juan Trueno.* Buenos Aires, 1892.

1047 ———— *El payador Santos Vega.* Buenos Aires, 1900.

1048 ———— *El tigre del desierto.* Buenos Aires, 1887.

1049 ———— *Truco y retruco. Segunda payada de los célebres payadores León Robles y Pedro González.* Buenos Aires, 1887.

1050 Betinotti, José. *Mis primeras hojas.* Buenos Aires, 1903.

1051 ———— *Últimas composiciones.* n.p., n.d.

1052 Bischoff, Efraín U. *Ponchos rojos.* Córdoba, 1935.

1053 Blixen, Samuel. "El viento en la cuchilla." See Roxlo, item 399.

1054 Bosque, Horacio del. *Los cantos de Santos Vega y su amistad con Carmona.* Buenos Aires, 1898.

1055 ———— *Santos Vega.* Buenos Aires, 1898.

1056 Bossi, C. B. *Juan sin patria.* Rosario, n.d.

1057 Braña, José María. *Juan sin patria.* 4th ed. Rosario, n.d.

1058 Bravo, Manuel P. *Poemas del campo y de la montaña.* Buenos Aires, 1909.

1059 Caggiano, ————. *Modulaciones. Improvisaciones nacionales.* Buenos Aires, 1913.

1060 Campo, Estanislao del ("Anastasio el Pollo"). *Fausto. Impresiones del gaucho Anastasio el Pollo en la representación de esta ópera.* 1st ed. Buenos Aires, 1866.

1061 ———— "El gobierno gaucho," *Poesías.* Buenos Aires, 1870.

1062 ———— See Puig, VIII (item 525), pp. 166-265.

1063 *Cancionero argentino.* Buenos Aires, 1837-1838. Cuatro cuadernos.

1064 *Cancionero popular rioplatense.* Buenos Aires, 1923.

1065 Cantilo, José María. "El 25 de Mayo," Puig, V (item 525), pp. 393-415.

1066 Carriego, Evaristo. *Misas herejes.* Buenos Aires, 1908.

1067 ———— "Los perros del barrio."

1068 Castellanos, Joaquín. "La leyenda argentina," Puig, X (item 525), pp. 321-348.

1069 —— *Poemas, viejos y nuevos.* Buenos Aires, 1926.

1070 Cavestany, Juan Antonio. "Tras los mares," Leguizamón, *Páginas argentinas* (item 296), pp. 309-330.

1071 Chocano, José Santos. "El gaucho."

1072 Cibils, José. *Flores nativas.* Rosario, 1903.

1073 —— *Rimas y estrofas.* n.p., n.d.

1074 Cientofante, Manuel M. *El gaucho de Cañuelas, verdadero libro e historia del famoso gaucho argentino.* Buenos Aires, n.d.

1075 —— *Martín Fierro. Relación criolla en versos gauchescos.* Buenos Aires, *ca.* 1906.

1076 —— *La muerte del Mataco, en versos gauchescos.* Buenos Aires, n.d.

1077 Clulow, Alfredo S. (with Carlos Alberto Clulow). "La guitarra," *Las rutas de Ofir.* Montevideo, 1925.

1078 *Contrapunto entre los famosos payadores, Pablo Vázquez y Gabino Ezeiza, tomado taquigráficamente por un testigo presencial.* 6th ed. Rosario, n.d.

1079 Coronado, Martín. "Los hijos de la pampa," *Obras completas* (Buenos Aires, 1926), pp. 25-27.

1080 Cotta, Juan Manuel. *Cambiantes líricos.* La Plata, 1915.

1081 Courbet, Carlos Alberto. *El gaucho 'el sú.* Buenos Aires, 1935.

1082 D'Amato, Generoso. *Mi poncho tucumano.* Buenos Aires, 1940.

1083 Darío, Rubén. "El gaucho."

1084 Dávalos, Juan Carlos. *Cantos agrestes.* Buenos Aires, 1918.

1085 De María, Alcides ("Calixto el Ñato"). *Apólogos y cantos patrios.* Montevideo, 1894.

1086 —— *Cantos tradicionales.* Buenos Aires, 1920.

1087 —— *Poesías criollas.* Montevideo, 1909.

1088 *Décimas variadas.* Buenos Aires, 1909.

1089 *Décimas variadas para cantar con guitarra.* Buenos Aires, 1906.

1090 Dedeu, ——. *De dos fuentes. Colección de poesías.* Buenos Aires, 1908.

1091 Díaz, Faustino. *El payador porteño.* Buenos Aires, 1886.

1092 Domínguez, Luis L. "A Mayo," Puig, V (item 525), pp. 330-346.

1093 —— "El ombú," Barreda, *Nuestro Parnaso* (item 513), pp. 165-169.

1094 Echeverría, Esteban. *Obras completas* (Buenos Aires, 1870), I, 181.

1095 Ezeiza, Gabino ("Gaucho Viejo"). *Canciones del payador argentino.* Buenos Aires, 1896.

1096 ———— *El cantor argentino.* n.p., n.d.

1097 ———— *Cantores criollos.* n.p., n.d.

1098 ———— *Colección de canciones.* n.p., n.d.

1099 ———— *Mi guitarra.* n.p., n.d.

1100 ———— See *Contrapunto* (item 1078).

1101 Falso, Ángel. *El alma de la raza.* Montevideo, 1911.

1102 Fernández, Horacio. *El poema campesino.* Buenos Aires, 1918.

1103 Fernández Espero, Diego. "Martín Fierro," Barreda, *Nuestro Parnaso,* III (item 513), pp. 111-112.

1104 Fernández y Medina, Benjamín. *Camperas y serranas.* Montevideo, 1894.

1105 ———— *Poesías.* Montevideo, 1912.

1106 Firpo y Firpo, B. *Simarrón.* Montevideo, 1929.

1107 Flores de los Llanos, Manuel. *El gaucho oriental.* Rosario, n.d.

1108 Fontanarrosa, D., hijo. *Angustia.* Rosario, 1917.

1109 Fragueiro, Rafael. "El gaucho."

1110 Frugoni, Emilio. "A la plebe gaucha," *El rancho.* n.p., n.d.

1111 Fuentes, Calixto. *El gaucho oriental.* Montevideo, 1872.

1112 Galarza, Desiderio R. *El poema de los campos, motivos y cuadros criollos.* Buenos Aires, 1937.

1113 García, Luis. "Afición," *Primer ensayo,* Buenos Aires, 1903.

1114 Garrido Cuadri, Santos ("Guillermo Cuadri" and "Santos Garrido"). *El agregao.* 2d ed. Montevideo, 1928.

1115 Garzón, Tobías. *Poesías.* Córdoba, 1881.

1116 ———— *Charamuscas. Versos criollos.* Buenos Aires, 1930.

1117 Ghiraldo, Alberto. "Ocaso," Barreda, *Nuestra Parnaso* (item 513), III, 158-160.

1118 ———— *Triunfos nuevos.* Madrid, n.d.

1119 Godoy, Juan Gualberto. "Los dos caballitos," Rojas, *Historia de la literatura argentina,* II (item 352), p. 590.

1120 ———— "Las llanuras de mi patria," Barreda, *Nuestra Parnaso,* I (item 513), pp. 173-177.

1121 ———— *Poesías.* Buenos Aires, 1889.

1122 González, Fausto. *Colección de composiciones poéticas en estilo gauchesco.* Montevideo, 1885.

1123 González Gastellú, Pedro. *De la ciudad y del campo.* Buenos Aires, 1916.

1124 Granada, Nicolás. *Cartas gauchas.* Buenos Aires, 1910.

1125 Guarnieri Mundín, Juan Carlos. *Tierra y raza; versos del terruño.* Montevideo, 1932.

1126 Guerrero, León. *Colección de versos gauchescos.* Buenos Aires, 1907.

1127 Guido y Spano, Carlos. *Ráfagas,* I, 282.

1128 Güiraldes, Ricardo. "Al hombre que pasó," Onís, *Antología* (item 521).

1129 Gutiérrez, Juan María. "A mi caballo," Barreda, *Nuestro Parnaso,* I (item 513), pp. 149-152.

1130 ———— "Armonías de la tarde," Puig, VII (item 525), pp. 218-223.

1131 ———— *Composiciones nacionales. Los amores del payador.* Buenos Aires, 1838.

1132 ———— "Dos jinetes," Rojas, *Historia de la literatura argentina,* II (item 352), p. 934.

1133 ———— "La endecha del gaucho."

1134 Gutiérrez, Martín. "La gloria del payador," *Las nuevas y verdaderas vidalitas santiagüinas.* Buenos Aires, 1897.

1135 Gutiérrez, Ricardo. *Lázaro.* See *Poemas* (Buenos Aires, 1915), pp. 131-264.

1136 ———— *Poesías escogidas.* Buenos Aires, 1878.

1137 Hamilton, ————. *El gaucho.* Buenos Aires (*ca.* 1900). (Printed with A. Banegas, *Rimas del alma.*)

1138 Hernández, José. *Martín Fierro.* Buenos Aires, 1872.

1139 ———— *La vuelta de Martín Fierro.* Buenos Aires, 1878.

1140 Hidalgo, Bartolomé. *Cielitos.* Montevideo, 1816-1821.

1141 ———— *Diálogos patrióticos.* Montevideo, 1820-1822.

1142 ———— "Un gaucho de la Guardia del Monte . . . ," *Revista de derecho, historia y letras,* IX, 127-230. Other poems, IX, 575-576, 581-588; X, 125-135, 280-282.

1143 Hidalgo, César. *Alma gaucha.* Buenos Aires, 1911.

1144 ———— *Gaucho pobre.* Buenos Aires-Montevideo, 1907.

1145 Hidalgo, Félix. *Décimas amorosas para cantar en guitarra.* n.p., n.d.

1146 ———— *Juan Cuello.* n.p., n.d.

1147 ———— *Milongas provincianas.* n.p., n.d.

1148 ———— *Pastor Luna.* n.p., n.d.

1149 Ignesón, ———— ("Gaucho Talerito"). *Agapito.* n.p., n.d.

1150 ———— *Chacho.* n.p., n.d.

1151 ———— *Décimas amorosas.* n.p., n.d.

1152 ———— *Hermanos Barrientos.* n.p., n.d.

1153 ———— *Hormiga Negra, su historia en versos gauchescos.* Buenos Aires, 1897.

1154 ———— *Juan Moreira.* n.p., n.d.

1155 ———— *Juan sin patria.* n.p., n.d.

1156 ———— *Martín Fierro.* n.p., n.d.

1157 ———— *Milongas.* n.p., n.d.

1158 ———— *Tigre del Quequén.* n.p., n.d.

1159 Ipuche, Pedro Leandro. *Alas nuevas.* Montevideo, 1922.

1160 ———— See Morales, *Antología* (item 533).

1161 Iturriaga y López, R. *Juan Guardia.* n.p., n.d.

1162 ———— *Matías, el domador.* n.p., n.d.

1163 ———— *El rescate de la cautiva.* n.p., n.d.

1164 ———— *La venganza de un gaucho.* 4th ed. Buenos Aires, 1898.

1165 "Juan Moreira." *Truco y retruco.* Montevideo, 1892.

1166 La Madrid, F. A. *El gaucho de Cañuelas.* Buenos Aires, 1887.

1167 Lamrod, Julio. *Por la pampa, Por mi barrio, Por el barrio de Carriego, Ayer y hoy.* Buenos Aires, 1937.

1168 Landó, Juan. *Melodías del terruño.* Montevideo, 1908.

1169 Lira, Luciano, ed. *El Parnaso Oriental.* n.p., n.d.

1170 *Lira argentina.* Buenos Aires, 1889.

1171 Lugones, Leopoldo. "Coplas de payada," *Poemas solariegos* (Buenos Aires, 1928).

1172 Lussich, Antonio D. *El matrero Luciano Santos.* Buenos Aires, 1873.

1173 ———— *Los tres gauchos orientales.* Buenos Aires, 1872.

1174 Lynch, Ventura R. *Cancionero bonaerense.* Buenos Aires, 1925.

1175 Machali Cazón, ————. *Alegrías y pesares. Canciones nacionales.* Buenos Aires, ca. 1910.

1176 Maciel, Santiago. *Camperas y serranas.* Montevideo, 1894.

1177 ———— *Flor de trébol.* Montevideo, 1893.

1178 Magariños Cervantes, Alejandro. *Brisas del Plata*. Montevideo, 1864.

1179 —— *Celiar*. Montevideo, 1852.

1180 —— *Palmas y ombúes*. Montevideo, 1850.

1181 Manco, Silverio ("Gaucho Viejo," "Alma Nativa"). *Ayes del corazón*. Buenos Aires, 1907.

1182 —— *El Chacho*. 3d ed. Rosario, n.d.

1183 —— *Estilos criollos*. Buenos Aires, *ca.* 1908.

1184 —— *El gaucho de Santa Fe*. Rosario, n.d.

1185 —— *El gaucho Picaflor*. 2d ed. Rosario, n.d.

1186 —— *El gaucho Picardía*. 2d ed. Rosario, n.d.

1187 —— *El gaucho Tranquera*. 2d ed. Rosario, n.d.

1188 —— *El hijo de Martín Fierro*. 7th ed. Rosario, n.d.

1189 —— *Lamentaciones de un paisano y narraciones criollas*. Buenos Aires, 1908.

1190 —— *La muerte de un héroe*. Rosario, n.d.

1191 —— *Los montoneros*. Rosario, n.d.

1192 —— *Santos Vega*. Buenos Aires, *ca.* 1910.

1193 —— *El trovador de la pampa y la pasión de un gaucho*. Buenos Aires, *ca.* 1910.

1194 Manso, Severo. *La mujer de Martín Fierro*. Buenos Aires, 1916.

1195 Marcó, Sebastián L. "Canción de un gaucho viejo," *Revista de derecho, historia y letras*, LXIX, 217-220.

1196 "Marco Polo." *Nueva raza. Buenos Aires ilustrado. Arte, comercio, industria*. Buenos Aires, 1913.

1197 Mármol, José. *Cantos del peregrino*.

1198 Marino, Ángel. *Acordes de mi lira*. Buenos Aires, 1914.

1199 Matera, Salvador, ed. *Estilos criollos, para cantar con guitarra*. n.p., n.d.

1200 Maucci, ——. *El álbum gauchesco y poético*. Buenos Aires, 1912.

1201 —— *Parnaso argentino*. Buenos Aires, n.d.

1202 Maziel, Juan Baltasar. "Canta un guaso en estilo campestre los triunfos del exemo. Sr. Pedro de Cevallos." 1777. See Barreda, *Nuestro Parnaso* (item 513), pp. 21-22.

1203 Miranda, Manuel. *Contrapunto entre un oriental y un argentino*. Rosario, 1914.

1204 Mitre, Bartolomé. *Rimas*. 1st ed. Buenos Aires, 1854.

1205 Molins, Wenceslao Jaime. *La pampa.* Buenos Aires, 1918.

1206 Monroy, F. C. *El gaucho de las fronteras.* Buenos Aires-Montevideo, 1897.

1207 Moratorio, Orosmán ("Julián Perujo"). *El brujo José Escribanis.* Montevideo, 1892.

1208 ———— *Guitarra nacional.* Montevideo, 1906.

1209 Muñoz, ————. *En la pampa.* Buenos Aires, 1890.

1210 Nava, Juan de. "Buenos Aires," *Colección de canciones.* Buenos Aires, 1898.

1211 ———— *Nuevas inspiraciones del payador oriental.* Montevideo, 1896.

1212 Nebel, Fernando. *Estampas.* n.p., n.d.

1213 Obligado, Rafael. *Tradiciones argentinas.* Buenos Aires, 1906.

1214 Ocampo, Luis ("Salvador Mario"). *Las criollas.* Buenos Aires, 1878.

1215 ———— *Flores y espinas.* n.p., n.d.

1216 Oribe, Emilio. "Perfección de las pampas," Pereda Valdés (item 524).

1217 Orozco Zárate, Epifanio. See Morales, *Antología* (item 533).

1218 Ortega, Miguel. *El gaucho.* Buenos Aires, 1863.

1219 Ortega Sanz, Atilano. *Don Fabián, poesías criollas.* Buenos Aires, 1932.

1220 Owen, Walter. *The gaucho Martín Fierro.* Oxford, 1935.

1221 Oyhanarte, Horacio B. *El gaucho.* n.p., n.d.

1222 Panizza, Delio. *Flores de cardo.* Buenos Aires, 1924.

1223 ———— *Guitarras y lanzas.* Buenos Aires, 1928; another edition, Montiel, 1930.

1224 Papini y Zas, Guzmán. See Barbagelata, *Centuria literaria* (item 388), pp. 396-397.

1225 *El payador argentino.* Buenos Aires, 1910.

1226 Peña, Eustaquio de la. *Nuevas milongas para cantar con guitarra.* Buenos Aires, 1911.

1227 Peralta, Pablo. *Cardal.* n.p., n.d.

1228 Pereda Valdés, Ildefonso. "La guitarra," in his *Antología* (item 524).

1229 Piñeyro del Campo, Luis. *El último gaucho.* Montevideo, 1891.

1230 Podestá, José J. ("Pepino el 88"). *Canciones completas.* n.p., n.d.

1231 —— *Canciones populares del Gran Pepino 88.* n.p., n.d.

1232 Ponce de León, Pedro F. *Mis versos.* Buenos Aires, *ca.* 1912.

1233 Quiroga, Adán. *El cantar de las montañas. Almanaque de Fra Diávolo.* Catamarca, 1891.

1234 —— "El ejército de los Andes," Puig, IX (item 525), pp. 372-388.

1235 Regules, Elías. *Mi pago.* Montevideo, 1924.

1236 —— *Pasto de cuchilla.* Montevideo, 1904.

1237 —— *Renglones sobre postales.* Montevideo, 1908.

1238 —— *Versitos criollos.* Montevideo, 1894.

1239 —— *Versos criollos.* Montevideo, 1894.

1240 Regules, Tabaré. *Margaritas rojas, poesías nativas.* Montevideo, 1936.

1241 Risso, Romildo. *Aroma, poemas nativos.* Buenos Aires, 1934.

1242 —— *Ñandubay.* Buenos Aires, 1931.

1243 Rivera Indarte, José. "Una noche en el cementerio viejo," Puig, VI (item 525), pp. 5-20.

1244 Rodríguez, Fray Cayetano José. "Cuento al caso," *Revista de derecho, historia y letras,* VI, 466-468.

1245 Rodríguez, Yamandú. *Aires de campo.* Montevideo, 1913.

1246 Roldán, Belisario. *El gaucho.* Buenos Aires, 1910.

1247 —— *El puñal de los troveros.* Buenos Aires, 1922.

1248 Roldán, Mario. *Garras y achuras, versos criollos.* Salto, Uruguay, 1936.

1249 Roxlo, Carlos. *Cantos de la tierra.* n.p., n.d.

1250 —— *Flores de ceibo.* n.p., n.d.

1251 —— "Las hordas gauchas."

1252 —— *Juan Robles.* Montevideo, 1916.

1253 —— "Los redodomones," Barbagelata, *Centuria literaria* (item 388), pp. 352-355.

1254 Sáenz, María Teresa L. de. *Pitangas y sina sina, poemas camperos.* Montevideo, 1926.

1255 Sallot, J. Eugenio. *Nuevas canciones variadas y poesías.* Buenos Aires, 1911.

1256 —— *Santos Vega. Canciones nacionales.* Buenos Aires, 1913.

1257 Salvat, M. A. *Plein air.* Buenos Aires, 1928.

1258 Santiago, Ramón de. *La loca de Bequeló.* Montevideo, n.d.

1259 *Santos Vega.* Buenos Aires, 1900.

1260 Silva Valdés, Fernán. *Agua del tiempo.* Montevideo, 1924.

1261 ——— *Intemperie.* Montevideo-Buenos Aires, 1930.

1262 ——— *Poemas nativos.* n.p., n.d.

1263 Silveira, Ernesto. *Tientos.* Montevideo, 1928.

1264 Soto y Calvo, Francisco. *Genio de la raza.* n.p., 1900.

1265 ——— *Nastasio.* Chartres, 1899.

1266 ——— *El gaucho.* n.p., n.d.

1267 ——— *Por la pampa y los Andes.* n.p., n.d.

1268 Suárez, Juan Carlos. (See item 763.)

1269 Supervielle, Jules. "El gaucho," *Revue de l'Amérique Latine,* I, 9-10.

1270 Sux, Alejandro. *De mi yunque.* Montevideo, 1906.

1271 "A tale of Tucumán," *Revista de derecho, historia y letras,* II, 321-322.

1272 Torres, A. *El cantar de un payador.* Colón, Argentina, 1927.

1273 Trelles, José Alonso y. *Gaucha.* Montevideo, 1913.

——— *Paja brava.* Montevideo, 1916.

1275 ——— "Poesías," *Nosotros,* L, 62-63.

1276 Trellor, S. *El gaucho Maragato en las fiestas de los españoles, terminando con la maldición de un amante; los postizos de las mujeres; los atorrantes de levita; el polizón.* Montevideo, 1892.

1277 Vaillant, ——— ("Anastasio Culebra"). *El gaucho Juan Acero, émulo de Martín Fierro.* 3d ed. Montevideo, 1901.

1278 Valdenegro, Eusebio. *Canciones de desafío.* Montevideo, ca. 1811.

1279 Vázquez, Pablo. See *Contrapunto,* item 1078.

1280 ——— *Poesías.* Buenos Aires, 1912.

1281 *La venganza de Mataco.* Rosario, n.d.

1282 "El viejo Viscacha." *Abrojos.* Buenos Aires, 1932.

1283 Zuviría, José María. "A Güemes," Puig, VIII (item 525), p. 7.

Gaucho Periodical Literature

Bibliographical Articles

1284 Caillava, Domingo A. See item 379.

1285 Giusti, Roberto Fernando (with Alfredo Antonio Bianchi). See *Nosotros,* LXXXI, 258-259.

1286 Lehmann-Nitsche, Robert. See item 297.

1287 Rojas, Ricardo. See item 352.

Periodicals

1288 *Aniceto el Gallo.* Buenos Aires, 1853.

1289 *El arriero argentino.* December 2, 1830. Founder and director, Hilario Ascasubi. One issue only.

1290 *La aurora.* Buenos Aires, n.d.

1291 *El cimarrón.* May 25, 1905; September 24, 1905; May 25, 1906. Three issues.

1292 *El criollo.* Minas, Uruguay. 479 issues. January 23, 1898-July 29, 1906.

1293 *El domador.* 1832. 2 issues. Editors: Bernardo P. Berro, Juan F. Giró, Francisco I. Muñoz, Miguel Barreiro.

1294 *La enramada.* Buenos Aires, n.d.

1295 *La estancia.* December, 1913, to middle of 1914. Editor, Félix Sáenz.

1296 *La flor pampeana.* La Plata and Ensenada. n.d.

1297 *El fogón.* Buenos Aires, 1926.

1298 *El fogón.* Montevideo. September, 1895, to middle of 1896; November, 1896, to December, 1900; and 1911 to 1913.

1299 *El fogón argentino.* Lomas de Zamora, Provincia de Buenos Aires, n.d.

1300 *El fogón criollo.* Montevideo, n.d.

1301 *El fogón pampeano.* Rosario de Santa Fe, n.d.

1302 *Fray Mocho.* Buenos Aires, 1915.

1303 *El gaucho argentino.* Buenos Aires, n.d.

1304 *El gaucho en campaña.* 1839. 4 issues. Founded by Ascasubi.

1305 *El gaucho Jacinto Cielo.* 1843. 12 issues. Editor, Ascasubi.

1306 *El gaucho oriental.* 1839. 7 issues. Editor, Isidoro de María.

1307 *El gaucho Paulino.* 1843. At least 10 issues.

1308 *El gaucho Relámpago.* Buenos Aires, n.d.

1309 *El guerrillero.* March 8, 1843. One issue only. Editors, José Mármol and Fernando Quijano.

1310 *Hormiga Negra.* San Antonio de Areco, Province of Buenos Aires, n.d.

1311 *Ideas y figuras.* Buenos Aires, n.d.

1312 *Juan Moreira.* August 8, 1891—. 4 issues.

1313 *La juventud.* Buenos Aires, n.d.

1314 *Letras y colores.* Buenos Aires, n.d.

1315 *El mangangá*. Montevideo. March 11, 1855, to August 26, 1855. 24 issues.

1316 *Martín Fierro. Revista popular ilustrada, de crítica y arte. Suplemento semanal de "La Protesta."* Buenos Aires, 1904-1905.

1317 *Martín Fierro. Revista quincenal*. Buenos Aires, 1919.

1318 *Mate amargo*. Buenos Aires, n.d.

1319 *El negro Timoteo*. n.p., n.d.

1320 *El ombú*. Buenos Aires, n.d.

1321 *El ombú*. Montevideo. January 1, 1896, to November 29, 1896. Editor, Orosmán Moratorio. 48 issues.

1322 *El palenque*. Buenos Aires, n.d.

1323 *El palenque*. Rocha, Uruguay, n.d.

1324 *La pampa*. Buenos Aires, n.d.

1325 *La pampa argentina*. Buenos Aires, n.d.

1326 *Pampa florida*. Las Flores, n.d.

1327 *Pampa florida*. Lomos de Zamora, n.d.

1328 *El payador*. Buenos Aires, n.d.

1329 *El picaflor nacional*. Buenos Aires, n.d.

1330 *El picaflor porteño*. Buenos Aires, n.d.

1331 *La picana*. Montevideo, May 24, 1908, to December 24, 1908.

1332 *El prado*. Avellaneda, n.d.

1333 *El prado*. Buenos Aires, n.d.

1334 *Pulgarcito*. Buenos Aires, 1904-1908.

1335 *Pulguita*. Buenos Aires, n.d.

1336 *Raza pampa*. Buenos Aires, n.d.

1337 *Raza pampeana*. La Plata. (Later moved to Buenos Aires.)

1338 *Revista criolla*. Buenos Aires, n.d.

1339 *Santos Vega*. Buenos Aires. January 3, 1914, to August 8, 1914. 32 issues.

1340 *La tapera*. Buenos Aires, n.d.

1341 *La tenaza*. La Plata, n.d.

1342 *El terruño*. Montevideo. July, 1917. The review was still being published in 1921. Editor, Agustín Smith.

1343 *La tradición*. Buenos Aires, n.d.

1344 *El trovador*. Buenos Aires, 1879.

1345 *El trovador*. Junín, n.d.

1346 *TVO.* Buenos Aires, n.d.

1347 *Vida argentina.* Buenos Aires, n.d.

LANGUAGE

1348 Alonso, Amado. "Preferencias mentales en el habla del gaucho," *Nosotros,* LXXX, 113-132.

1349 Álvares Pereira Coruja, Antonio. *Collecção de vocabulos e frases usados na provincia de S. Pedro do Rio Grande do Sul no Brazil.* Londres, 1856.

1350 Barbará, Federico. *Manual o vocabulario de la lengua pampa y del estilo familiar.* Buenos Aires, 1879.

1351 Bayo, Ciro. *Manual del lenguaje criollo de Centro y Sud-América.* Madrid, 1931.

1352 —— *Vocabulario criollo-español sudamericano.* Madrid, 1910.

1353 —— "Vocabulario de provincialismos argentinos y bolivianos," *Revue hispanique,* XIV, 241-564.

1354 Carriegos, Ramón C. *El porvenir del idioma español en la República Argentina.* Buenos Aires, 1928.

1355 Caviglia, Buenaventura. "Varias docenas de nuevos probables orígines de la palabra *gaucho,*" according to Falcao Espalter, in Reyles, *Historia sintética,* item 397.

1356 Costa Álvarez, Arturo. *El castellano en la Argentina.* La Plata, 1928.

1357 —— "El castellano en la Argentina," *Nosotros,* LVII, 189-219.

1358 —— "Las etimologías de *gaucho,*" *Nosotros,* LIV, 183-209.

1359 —— *Nuestra lengua.* Buenos Aires, 1922.

1360 —— "Otra etimología de *gaucho,*" *Nosotros,* LV, 212-217.

1361 Febrés, Padre Andrés. *Diccionario araucano-español.* Buenos Aires, 1882. 1st ed., 1765.

1362 Figueroa G., Julio. *Vocabulario etimolójico de nombres chilenos.* Santiago, 1903.

1363 Granada, Daniel. *Vocabulario ríoplatense razonado.* Montevideo, 1890.

1364 Groussac, Paul. "A propósito de americanismos," *Viaje intelectual* (item 271), pp. 408-415.

1365 Lafone Quevedo, Samuel Alexander. "Tesoro de catamarqueñismos," Buenos Aires, Sociedad científica argentina, *Anales,* XLIII and XLIV.

1366 Laytano, Dante de. *Os africanismos do dialecto gaucho.* Porte Alegre, 1936.

1367 Lenz, Rudolfo. *Diccionario etimolójico de las voces chilenas derivadas de lenguas indígenas americanas.* Santiago, 1905-1910.

1368 Lizondo Borda, Manuel. "Expresiones del *Martín Fierro*," *Nosotros,* LIV, 79-87.

1369 Martínez, Benigno T. *Diccionario de argentinismos e indigenismos.* 1887.

1370 Monner Sans, Ricardo. *Discurso sobre el lenguaje gauchesco.* (Conferencia, *La Nación,* July 23, 1894.)

1371 —— *Minucias lexicográficas.* Buenos Aires, 1896.

1372 —— *Notas al castellano en la Argentina.* Madrid, 1924.

1373 Nichols, Madaline Wallis. *Bibliographical guide to materials on American Spanish.* Cambridge, 1941.

1374 Quesada, Ernesto. "La evolución del idioma nacional," *Nosotros,* XL, 175-207.

1375 Rodríguez, Padre. *Diccionario de chilenismos.* Santiago, 1875.

1376 Román, Manuel Antonio. *Diccionario de chilenismos.* Santiago, 1908-1911.

1377 Rosenblat, Ángel. "La lengua y la cultura de Hispanoamérica," *Nosotros,* LXXIX, 5-27.

1378 Rossi, Vicente. *Desagravio al lenguaje de Martín Fierro.* Córdoba, Argentina, 1935.

1379 —— *Etimolojiomanía sobre el vocablo "gaucho."* Córdoba, 1927.

1380 Segovia, Eladio. "El paisaje en el *Martín Fierro*," *Nosotros,* LXXXI, 322-331.

1381 Segovia, Lisandro. *Diccionario de argentinismos, neologismos y barbarismos.* Buenos Aires, 1911.

1382 Selva, Juan B. *El castellano en América.* La Plata, 1906.

1383 Teschauer, Carlos. *Porandúba Rio-Grandense. Investigacoes sobre o idioma fablado no Brazil e particularmente no Rio Grande do Sul.* Porto Alegre, 1903.

1384 Tiscornia, Eleuterio F. *"Martín Fierro," comentado y anotado.* Buenos Aires, 1925.

1385 —— *La lengua de "Martín Fierro."* Buenos Aires, 1930.

The Gaucho in Art

critical articles

1386 Bellocq, Adolfo. See Donnis, Cayetano, "Crónica del arte," *Nosotros,* LXVI, 268-273.

1387 Bermúdez, Jorge. See Muzio Sáenz Peña, Carlos, "Jorge Bermúdez y el verdadero arte argentino," *Nosotros,* LIII, 20-25.

1388-1399 Bernaldo de Quirós, Cesáreo.

Brinton, Christian. *Cesáreo Bernaldo de Quirós.* New York, 1932.
Contains bibliography of other studies.

Chiappori, Atilio. "Nuestro ambiente artístico y las modernas evoluciones técnicas," *Nosotros,* LVII, 220-243.

Dellepiane, Antonio. See item 1402.

Donnis, Cayetano. "Bellas artes," *Nosotros,* LXVIII, 380-387.

"Exposición Quirós," *Nosotros,* LXI, 309.

Hispanic Society of America. *Exhibition of paintings by Cesáreo Bernaldo de Quirós.* New York, 1932.
Contains bibliography.

"Primera exposición de arte argentino en Chile," *Nosotros,* XXVI, 227-228.

Rinaldini, Julio. "Las bellas artes en la Argentina," *Nosotros,* XLVI, 426-429.

———— "Crónica de arte. Cesáreo Bernaldo de Quirós," *Nosotros,* XIX, 90-92.

———— "El cuarto salón," *Nosotros,* XV, 290-295.

———— "El cuarto salón. La pintura," *Nosotros,* XVI, 73-91.

Simpich, Frederick. "Cesáreo Bernaldo de Quirós," *The national geographic magazine* (October, 1933), pp. 449-491.

1400 Chiappori, Atilio. "Nuestro ambiente artístico y las modernas evoluciones técnicas," *Nosotros,* LVII, 220-243.

1401 ———— "El gaucho en la pintura argentina," *Revista americana de Buenos Aires.*

1402 Dellepiane, Antonio. *Estudios de historia y arte argentinos.* Buenos Aires, 1929.

The author lists the following artists who have made use of the gaucho motif: Bacle, Ballerini, Beer, Juan Manuel Blanes, Nicanor Blanes, Branvilla, Camaña, Charton, Claireaux, D'Hastrel de Rivedoi, De la Torre, DeMaría, Durand, Grand, Grashof, Ibarra, Kratzenstein, Monvoisin, Morel, Housse, Pallière, Paris, Pelvilain, Pellegrini, Pueyrredón, Rezabal, Ripamonte, Sheridan, Vabois, Vela, Ysola, Zollinger.

1403 Díaz Leguizamón, Héctor. *El signo de Euforión.* Buenos Aires, 1927.

1404 Fader. See Díaz Leguizamón (item 1403).

1405 Fernández Saldaña, José M. "Pintores y escultores uruguayos," Uruguay, Archivo y museo histórico nacional, *Revista histórica,* VI, 710-731.

1406 Pagano, José León. "Carlos Morel en la transfiguración del mito," *La Nación,* December 22, 1935.

1407 Prilidiano Pueyrredón, Pedro. See Schiaffino, Eduardo, "Prilidiano P. Pueyrredón," *Nosotros,* LXXXI, 332-345.

1408 Ripamonte, Carlos P. See Rinaldini, Rinaldo, "Crónica de arte," *Nosotros,* XXIII, 213-221.

ARTISTS AND PICTURES

1409 Bermúdez, Jorge.
  El gaucho

1410 Bernaldo de Quirós, Cesáreo.

Amaneciendo	Los jefes
Aves de presa	El juez federado
El aviador	El lancero colorado
El baile	Lanzas y guitarras
Los bichadores	El limosnero
Los bomberos	La ofrenda
El cantor y los troperos	El opa
El carneador	Oros de la tarde
El carnicero	La pareja y el sandiero
El curandero	La partida
Degolladores	El patrón, Don Juan de Sandoval
La doma	Patroncito
Don Anacleto	El pialador
Empacho	Rastreadores
La fiesta	Tunas y lechiguanas
Fritos y pasteles	El velorio
Gavilán	Y vamos, vieja
El hombre de los arreos	Yerbiando

1411 Blanes, Juan Manuel.
  El gaucho

1412 Della Valle, Ángel.
  El indio
  El rodeo

1413 Donati.
  ¡No volverá!

1414 Monvoisin, R. Q.
  El gaucho argentino en 1842

1415 Peláez, Juan.
  Rastreador serrano

1416 Prilidiano Pueyrredón, Pedro.
Dos gauchos de la provincia de Buenos Aires, con indumentaria campera posterior a la época de Rosas. Grabado en *La Prensa*, October 9, 1932.

1417 Ripamonte, Carlos P.
El baquiano

1418 Zavattaro, Mario.
Santos Vega cruza el llano, in *Santos Vega* (Buenos Aires), January 3, 1914.

THE GAUCHO IN MUSIC

ARTICLES AND BOOKS ON MUSIC

1419 Álvarez, Juan. "Orígines de la música argentina," *Revista de derecho, historia y letras*, XXXII, 26-67.

1420 Furt, Jorge M. *Coreografía gauchesca*. Buenos Aires, 1927.
Music and dances.

MUSIC

1421 Berutti, Arturo. *Facundo,* 1920. (Opera.)

1422 ———— *Juan Moreira.* (Opera.)

1423 ———— *Pampa.* (Opera.)

1424 Boero, ————. *El matrero.* (Opera.)

1425 Canaro, Francisco. *Sentimiento gaucho.* (Song.)

1426 Córdoba, P. Numa. *El gaucho vencido.* (Song.)

1427 *La muerte de Santos Vega.* Colombia Graphaphone Co., New York.

1428 Podestá, Pablo. Music for song of Bayón Herrera's *Santos Vega*. Discos Atlanta, No. 815.

1429 Tesseire, Luis. *El fogón.* (Song.)

1430 Williams, Alberto. *Los aires de la pampa.*

1431 ———— *Poema de las campañas.*

Index